*f*P

DON'T SHOOT
the MESSENGER

How Our Growing Hatred of the Media

Threatens Free Speech for All of Us

BRUCE W. SANFORD

THE FREE PRESS

*f*P

THE FREE PRESS
A Division of Simon & Schuster Inc.
1230 Avenue of the Americas
New York, NY 10020

Designed by Carla Bolte

Manufactured in the United States of America

10   9   8   7   6   5   4   3   2   1

Library of Congress Cataloging-in-Publication Data
Sanford, Bruce W.
Don't shoot the messenger: how our growing hatred of the media
threatens free speech for all of us/Bruce W. Sanford.
p.   cm.
Includes bibliographical references and index.
1. Press—United States—Public opinion. 2. Public opinion—United States.
3. Journalism—Objectivity. 4. Freedom of speech.
I. Title.
PN4888.P82S26   1999
302.23'0973—dc21   98–52182
CIP

ISBN 0-684-82813-8

FOR MARILOU

AND

LISA, ASHLEY AND BARRETT

Contents

DON'T SHOOT
the MESSENGER

PROLOGUE

A DANGEROUS NEW SEASON

The mist that rises from the Ohio River on cold autumn mornings could not obscure the hard truth emerging in late 1998 from Cincinnati: America's news media, bloated with profit, obsessed with its customers and agonized with insecurities, faces a century ahead utterly unlike the glorious twentieth-century epoch behind it.

The Gannett Co., proud innovator of *USA Today* and publisher of scores of newspapers such as the *Cincinnati Enquirer*, had paid more than $10 million to Chiquita Brands International and "renounced" a lengthy *Enquirer* series about the banana giant. The deal had been cut by Gannett's senior management in Washington. It averted a morass of litigation threatened by Chiquita and its formidable owner, billionaire Cincinnati financier Carl Lindner. The size of the settlement shocked media executives everywhere. By any measurement, it was unprecedented. *The New York Times* played the announcement of the payoff on its front page above the fold. But beyond the breathtaking amount of the financial transaction came the horrible recognition that Gannett may have been squeezed to disavow a story, substantial parts of which may have been true.

The cold news from Cincinnati ushers in a dangerous new season for both the media and the public that relies on it for knowledge. Aggressive business interests and celebrities of every stripe are using their wealth and a new arsenal of legal tactics to attack enterprise reporting. Media companies, with some reason, are caving. They know that they will not find the receptive audiences they once experienced in court. Judges have grown as

1

deeply contemptuous of the news media as the public. Faced with the prospect of complex, expensive litigation with uncertain outcomes, the companies are choosing to settle, not fight. Most of the public will not complain—certainly not those citizens who own Gannett's high-octane stock in their pension or mutual funds. Ten million dollars is cheap compared to the cost of years of litigation with Chiquita. (A year earlier, Knight Ridder shelled out more than $20 million to compromise a long-running lawsuit from a former Philadelphia prosecutor after spending millions of dollars for a strenuous but unsuccessful defense effort.) Generally, the public would cheer the comeuppance and punishment of a reporter whose newsgathering had strayed across ethical and legal lines. Most people would not see that they were being denied information about the world around them.

Criticizing the decisions of the media companies is not a simple matter since, ironically, many of the relevant facts are not readily available. In Gannett's case, the *Enquirer*'s carefully crafted apology for "creating a false and misleading impression of Chiquita's business practices" seemed to be limited to information gathered through reporter Mike Gallagher's interception of company voice-mail messages. There was no explicit retraction of the factual underpinnings or all key allegations of the eighteen-page article. Two weeks after the apology, however, *The New York Times* reported that "some of the allegations [of Chiquita's chicanery] cannot be dismissed" as easily as the company might want. "Determining the validity of the newspaper's claims is difficult," the *Times* said in a lengthy assessment by Douglas Frantz headlined "Chiquita Still Under Cloud After Newspaper's Retreat." The Securities and Exchange Commission continued to investigate assertions in the article that the company covered up a bribery scheme by employees in Colombia. Chiquita was furious with the *Times* story, since it had been largely successful at neutralizing the impact of the *Enquirer* series by deflecting attention to the newspaper's reporting practices.

At least some Cincinnati readers were not happy with the lack of clarity. Commented one local man in the *Enquirer*:

It is the *Enquirer*'s responsibility . . . to now attempt to clarify which allegations are factual, which are not, and which others cannot be verified by legal means. If, as I fear, part of the settlement with Chiquita involved an agreement to no longer report on this matter in any way, then this would constitute an egregious violation of journalistic ethics, much worse than the actions of a few rogue *Enquirer* reporters. Why? Because this would represent an institutional decision to deny readers the truth, which we are relying on the *Enquirer* to report.

The *American Journalism Review* concluded: "There are no winners in this story. The public is left confused about what, if anything, Chiquita did wrong and doubts about the ethics of journalism have been reinforced."

Atop the Gannett corporate headquarters in Washington, Chairman John Curley and Vice-Chairman Douglas McCorkindale weren't explaining. They couldn't. A confidentiality agreement with Chiquita had silenced them. There would be no exculpatory spinning here. Chiquita's lawyer, Thomas Yannucci, had driven a hard bargain. Yannucci, a polished stone from the same law firm that housed Kenneth Starr, Kirkland & Ellis, has developed a thriving career in recent years representing the rich and powerful with gripes against the news media. He had first plowed this fertile but hitherto unbroken ground in 1993 when he had helped General Motors demolish NBC's *Dateline* story on exploding trucks. Since then, he has advised more than fifty clients angry about media coverage. The $10 million bounty on Gannett's humiliation promised many more.

It would not be right, however, to see Yannucci as taking advantage of simpering rubes. Gannett's Curley and McCorkindale command respect in the industry as tough-minded, unsentimental corporate managers. Wall Street investment bankers love them, or at least pretend to. From their office windows overlooking the Potomac River, the Gannett officers can see the national monuments, the National Archives, where the Constitution is kept, and beyond, all the way to Capitol Hill and the Supreme Court. But the long view did not pollute what they clearly felt was a prudent call for Gannett's shareholders. The courts would not have dealt kindly with the newspaper, they suspected. And, if the corporation was lucky, its insurance carrier would be forced to pick up the lion's share of the $10-million-plus settlement. The company's mortification over the *Enquirer*'s flawed journalism would be painful, but at least the financial damage had been contained. In the 1980s, Katharine Graham's Washington Post Company had spent approximately $2 million defending a front-page news article which had reported that the president of Mobil had "set his son up" in the oil shipping business. The investigative story of corporate nepotism and favoritism had eventually been vindicated on appeal after a trial jury had socked the newspaper with a verdict of $250,000 in compensatory damages and $1.8 million in punitive damages. The $2 million of defense costs had been "real" money; the *Post*'s libel insurance policy did not reimburse for legal fees or other court expenses. Gannett would not be sloshing through the chillier and unpredictable waters swirling in the court system now. Things had changed. Decidedly for the worse.

Two other factors augured in favor of Curley and McCorkindale making a quick settlement. One was their adversary, Carl Lindner. The other was the comforting knowledge that they were not alone. Other major news organizations had compromised claims brought by powerful complainants, rather than take the arduous road of fighting for stories with truthful elements.

Carl Lindner was well known to the Gannett executives. In the not-so-distant past, he had been a royal pain in the ass. There was considerable history here. Lindner had once owned the *Enquirer*, selling it in 1975 to Combined Communications, which, in turn, sold its newspapers and billboard business to Gannett for stock in 1979. With a resulting 4 percent stakehold in Gannett, Lindner began buying up Gannett stock until he owned more than 5 percent of the company, making him the second-largest stockholder. Nobody, however, was going to wrest control of Gannett from its then CEO, the indomitable Allen H. Neuharth. Neuharth was convinced that Lindner was trying to "steal" his company.[1] In his autobiography, *Confessions of an S.O.B.,* he called him a "shark in sheep's clothing." He accused him of "greenmail" when Linder "demanded $50 million more than market value for his stock holdings in the company." When Lindner eventually lost his bid for a big buyback bonus and a pitch for board representation, Neuharth bought advertisements in major national newspapers saluting Gannett shareholders for rebuffing "funny money financiers." The ads didn't mention Lindner's name, but they didn't have to. Lindner was irate and dumped his Gannett stock at market value.

Undaunted, Lindner continued on his lifelong path of buying and selling hundreds of businesses, constructing an empire estimated in 1998 at $13 billion. In Cincinnati, he is an unparalleled force. He glides around the city in one of his three Rolls-Royces, handing out cards that read: "Only in America. Gee, am I lucky." He is regarded as an eccentric genius—Marge Schott's largest shareholder in the Cincinnati Reds, a philanthropic giant ($100 million to charities over the past decade), and a political benefactor of every politician (Republican or Democrat) who might be in a position to help him. Clinton, Dole, Gingrich, Gephardt and some fifty members of Congress from 1991 to 1996 have received contributions. Cincinnati pols with any ambition whatsoever know the wisdom of seeking his support. In 1998, one such rising star in the Republican Party, county prosecutor Joe Deters, leapt to statewide office as treasurer of the state of Ohio. Deters had not been responsible for the criminal investigation into the illegal interception of Chiquita's voice mails. He had recused himself because of his closeness to Lindner. Instead, a special prosecutor had been appointed, who in the fall of 1998 obtained a guilty plea from reporter Mike Gallagher. Neither Deters nor others in the Cincinnati establishment were reluctant, however, to wonder out loud whether executives up the Gannett chain of command could be prosecuted for their knowledge of the voice-mail theft. This perception was a fundamental problem for the Gannett brass, especially since the *Enquirer* series about Chiquita had been read and approved all the way up to the top. Gallagher had lied to them, all the editors and executives said. Still, Deters wondered and the special prosecutor probed. Chiquita lawyer Tom Yannucci could paint an ugly picture of Gannett officers being besieged by career-ruining criminal prosecutions as well as civil lawsuits that sucked the life out of them.

Next to developing brain cancer or burying a child, about the worst thing that can happen to you at the end of the American century is to get caught and mired in the so-called justice system. It wrecked the hope of the Clinton presidency. It drains energies and resources, frustrates the hopeful and begs to be avoided. Business executives loathe the legal system, offensive as it is to cost-benefit analysis. Yet there are thought to be times—usually when First Amendment freedoms are at stake—that have traditionally called for media companies to absorb whatever pain and expense may accompany litigation in order to preserve the independence and vitality of journalism. Basically, it can be seen as a cost of doing business, like ink or transmission towers. The tricky decision is when to incur the cost. In deciding whether to defend against Carl Lindner's onslaught, the Gannett executives not only knew their enemy and their vulnerability from Gallagher's voice-mail interceptions; they also knew that other media companies were increasingly finding settlement the better part of valor. Other companies that had backed off rather than face the perils of a battle included:

ABC

In 1994, the network had broadcast a report suggesting that the tobacco industry was "spiking" the nicotine level of its products during manufacture. The story changed the nature of the public debate over the regulation of cigarettes. It also landed ABC in court in tobacco country. Philip Morris sued the network for $10 billion in Virginia, alleging that the segment was libelous. For over a year, ABC vigorously defended the case. But in the summer of 1995, its merger with the Walt Disney Co. looming ahead, the network settled the lawsuit, reimbursing Philip Morris for the cost of its legal fees (which amounted to roughly $15 million) and apologizing in prime time. While it is endlessly arguable whether "spiking" was an accurate characterization of the production process ABC had uncovered, subsequent reporting by *The Wall Street Journal* and others confirmed that tobacco companies can control and manage the level of nicotine during the manufacturing of cigarettes. In fact, ABC had filed a confidential summary judgment motion in the case, the contents of which were later leaked, that indicated that it had acquired considerable evidence during discovery to document that charge.

CBS

In another showdown between a cigarette giant and network news, Brown & Williamson successfully pressured CBS's *60 Minutes* to cancel plans to broadcast an interview with industry whistle-blower Jeffrey Wigand in November 1995. CBS officials did not fear a libel action; rather, Brown & Williamson threatened to lob a newsgathering tort in its direction—"tortious interference with business relations." According to this theory, CBS would have been liable for persuading Wigand to reveal internal company practices in violation of an agreement he had signed with Brown & Williamson promising not to do so. Several months later, *The Wall Street Journal* published its own version of Wigand's charges. *60 Minutes* then broadcast its interview. Brown & Williamson did not file a lawsuit against either news organization.

NBC and CNN

Richard Jewell, the security guard who for months was a leading suspect in the bombing at the Atlanta Olympics, secured handsome payments from NBC and CNN after the FBI cleared him of all wrongdoing in October 1996. Jewell did not have to sue either network, just threaten. The NBC settlement, the terms of which were not disclosed, was later reported by *The Wall Street Journal* to approximate $500,000. The network admitted no wrongdoing or editorial error. Indeed, Jewell's potential libel case against the two networks was not strong—they reported that he was a principal focus of the investigation, which was true. But, highlighting the attenuated protection for newsgathering, NBC stated that shielding "confidential sources was a major consideration" in its decision. Jewell has used the proceeds of these settlements in part to pursue his defamation suits against the *Atlanta Journal & Constitution,* among others.

More than any of these surrenders by the television networks, the Gannett transaction with Chiquita was a watershed moment for the American media. It heralded the arrival of a full-scale crisis of unprecedented and systematic proportions—one that undermines our ability to comprehend our lives and times. Throughout the second half of the twentieth century, America's communications companies had fought diligently—and with mostly stunning success—to expand First Amendment rights to gather and report the news. No more. Loathed and distrusted by the public they hunger to serve, the media are discovering that their crumbling credibility with the public is reflected in the courts. Judges, dismayed by the media's newsgathering practices, are cutting back on constitutional protections for the press. The "breathing space" which Justice William Brennan once saw as essential for the press to report on public affairs is evaporating. The U.S. Supreme Court maintains a stony silence.

The signs of this crisis are everywhere. First Amendment law is stagnating in a nation grown as cynical about the value of free expression as it is enraptured with the dream of becoming a software millionaire and retiring to Aspen. Libel verdicts of enormous size are mounting in every part of the country: $220 million in Houston, $13 million in Miami, $3 million in Wilmington, Delaware. Mistakes in the media, once thought deserving of only passing notice, now command center stage. CNN and *Time* retract an implausible story about Vietnam and its star reporters, Peter Arnett and Christiane Amanpour, publicly squabble over the extent of a television correspondent's responsibility for the authenticity of a story. Lost in the media's egocentricity is the horizon the public sees rather clearly: the economic imperatives of the communications media, the star system of celebrity journalism and the need to supply the public with constant reinforcement or shock therapy have combined to make fools, not truth-seekers, out of journalists. A golden age that for fifty years saw the creation and expansion of a First Amendment right of the public to receive information has concluded.

This book is about expectations, the hopelessly unrealistic expectations we have for our news media and the media's equally vain desire to be well regarded at the same time as it slips away from its own traditional notions of public service. It is a book about what each player contributes to a deteriorating, destructive relationship that is endangering our nation and growing more ugly and tendentious. It is about how the public's anger toward the media is being played out in the nation's courts, where judge after judge is limiting the public's right to receive information all in the name of controlling the "profiteering" news media, to use the adjective favored by federal judge Susan Webber Wright in a 1998 decision involving the Paula Jones sexual harassment case which seethed with contempt for the press.

Some of the finest journalists of our times, James Fallows, E. J. Dionne, Howard Kurtz, James Squires, have described during the last decade the wounds their profession has inflicted upon itself. Their work has documented the wretched excesses and foolish pride of a gigantic media institution that overwhelms our public life, just as it becomes more irrelevant and an object of ridicule in our personal lives. Their focus on the sins of the media inevitably tends to make it seem as if the media bears responsibility for the gulf that has developed between it and the public. But it's more complicated than that. The media alone cannot be blamed for its credibility problems with the public. As in a troubled marriage, the public itself contributes to the disintegrating relationship at the same time as it points the finger at a ubiquitous, annoying media. These contributions come from shadowy quarters of our lives—our endless prurient interest, our moral confusions, our lazy, unthinking and undifferentiating way of approaching prepackaged news, our tolerance of declining educational standards and our preference for clarity (and simple answers) in a world of nuance and complexity. At the outset, this book explores the root causes for the public's hostility toward the media. It sifts through the historical evidence, including polling surveys and media criticism, of recent decades. It addresses the most common complaints of the public about the media—sensationalism and bias. It looks at how we participate in the media's false branding and stereotyping of public people. It seeks to clarify the ambiguities and contradictions inherent in our relationship with the media. The second part of the book moves on to examine the unhappy consequences for a nation that has traditionally been strong and secure enough to tolerate (even encourage) its media to be bumptious and offensive.

Shooting the messenger may be a time-honored emotional response to unwelcome news, but it is not a very effective method of remaining well informed. The consequences of the growing canyon of distrust between the public and the media are already discernible and should worry us even more than the knowledge that we understand the situation poorly. For the result of the public's misplaced fury has been a palpable willingness to silence the media—to curtail its ability to gather and report the news, and to make us more dependent than ever on the government for our understanding of human events. There is no more certain road to the loss of freedom.

1

The Canyon of Distrust

A canyon of disbelief and distrust has developed between the public and the news media. Deep, complex and so contradictory as to be airless at times, this gorge has widened at an accelerating rate during the last decade. Its darkness frightens the media. It threatens not just the communication industry's enviable financial power but its special role in ordering American democracy. It is a canyon of terrifying proportions.

The growing distance between the sides of the canyon has been measured with increasing precision (and alarm) since the early 1980s. Those of us charged with defending the media's libel cases and other transgressions (real and imagined) had detected during the 1970s that a rising river of anger was beginning to cut through soft rock. We did not need the acute vision and sophisticated polling techniques of the new age of jury consultants to tell us that attitudes toward our news media clients were qualitatively different and more hostile than in the Vietnam/Watergate era. (It is, though, an indication of how fast the situation has deteriorated that no media defense lawyer would dare to present a case to a jury today without relying on mock trials, focus groups and polling to select jurors who will be halfway receptive to the media's message.) Posttrial interviews with jurors in one Kentucky case in the mid-1970s set a benchmark. The litigation had arisen when the *Kentucky Post* had misdescribed a schoolyard fight as a "savage beating." What had actually happened was that one boy had hit another boy who fell first onto the pavement and later into a fatal coma. The surviving child was not named, but, of course, almost everyone in the school and community (except, ironically, the reporter) knew his identity. At trial, the youngster hardly made an apple-cheeked impression; he was so disagreeable that he made you wish the dead boy had gotten in a few licks before eating concrete. Nevertheless, the jury awarded the lout $32,500 in compensatory damages and $100,000 in punitive damages. When one of the jurors was asked why, under these circumstances, the jury felt compelled to enrich such an unappealing litigant, he replied:

> Well, we didn't much like that little shithead, but we liked the newspaper even less.

And then he sneered. It was the sneer used by the newly empowered to indicate that revenge is eminently justified and that the aristocrats of the media better get ready for a ride to the guillotine.

There was plenty of anecdotal evidence from the libel wars of the 1970s and 1980s to suggest that libel lawsuits had become emblematic in America. They signified the public's rising anger and uneasiness toward the media. They had become something more than mere product liability claims.

Coverage of the more celebrated trials—like those brought by two generals, Ariel Sharon of Israel and William Westmoreland of South Carolina—unfolded as high dramas with disturbing messages. On two different floors of the federal courthouse at Foley Square in New York, the generals blasted away during 1984. Sharon aimed his howitzers and legendary lawyer Milton Gould against Time, Inc. Westmoreland took on CBS and its correspondent Mike Wallace. Both plaintiffs lost. Westmoreland withdrew from the fray in much the same way America had withdrawn from Vietnam. Sharon at least extracted from Time an admission of error, which he then carried back to Israel to rejuvenate his political career. Tenacity would not, the outcomes seemed to say, overcome the high obstacles that the U.S. Supreme Court had erected for public figures in libel cases. Constitutional law had given the media the "breathing space" to make mistakes so that Americans could reap the benefits of a "robust" and "uninhibited" debate on public affairs.[1] In effect, the Supreme Court had surrounded the media in the landmark *New York Times Co. v. Sullivan* decision with a margin for error in the search for truth. The press would be insulated from punishing libel verdicts so long as they made only honest, not deliberate mistakes. Thus, "the fairness of the broadcast is not in issue in a libel suit," as Judge Pierre Leval said bluntly in the Westmoreland case.[2] CBS could broadcast an "unfair one-sided attack" on the general loaded with "categorical accusations" and not "commit" libel.[3] The judge summarized the hard-to-swallow gristle of modern American libel law when he wrote:

> A publisher who honestly believes in the truth of his accusations (and can point to a non-reckless basis for his beliefs) is under no obligation under the libel law to treat the subject of his accusations fairly or even-handedly.[4]

This accurate statement of current law is simply hard to take. If justice in America could be encapsulated in a single word, it would be "fairness." Fundamental fairness is the divining rod most juries use to reach their conclusions. To some people, the results in the Sharon and Westmoreland cases seemed wrong because fairness wasn't the issue. Throughout the last decade, some observers have wondered whether the policy underlying the *Sullivan* doctrine wasn't self-defeating. If it has contributed to a general loss of confidence in the media, can it truly be a sound policy in the long run?

"I see your journalist friends have been released from the tyranny of accurate reporting," one sarcastic congressman told me. "So now they can be unfair to someone and get away with it. They have a legal license to lie."

"Not at all," I would respond. "Libel law doesn't permit lies or deliberate falsification. It's only honest or accidental mistakes that the law protects."

"Oh, I get it. They don't have a license to lie. Just a license to be stupid, nasty and superficial."

It is fair to say that as the media was winning virtually all libel cases during the 1980s (sometimes at trial, but more often on appeal), the public was not necessarily joining in the celebration. The litigation successes had certainly not come cheaply. More than $10 million was devoted just to the defense efforts in the Sharon and Westmoreland cases. But with the hindsight of another decade, it seems clear that any cost-benefit analysis of constitutional libel law needs to include in the cost accounting the delayed price that arrived when the public gradually discovered that it could no longer hold the media accountable in damages for "unfairly" injuring reputations.

The obvious anti-news media bias displayed by jury pools during the libel wars of the early 1980s prompted some leaders of the communications industry to look a little harder at the general subject of public attitudes toward the media. What they discovered was an unsatisfactory dearth of basic research material. Existing polling studies tended to raise more questions than they answered.[5] Responses to pollsters' questions seemed to elicit a superficial "cut" into the public's collective brain. It was clear that people harbored some negative feelings and beliefs about the media, but it was quite impossible to tell much about the depth or dimensions of the problem or whether there was really a problem at all. Frequently, studies purporting to show the press in low repute with the public were easily dismissed as nothing more than cumulative evidence that messengers who deliver bad news are, if not killed, at least rarely appreciated.

Robert Erburu, a lawyer who had risen to the chief executive's office in the Times Mirror Company and who was increasingly influential in industry circles, was particularly impatient with the speculation swirling around the limited body of data on the subject. To him, the stunning inconsistencies of various public opinion surveys simply meant that the pollsters hadn't probed thoroughly enough to ascertain the public's true perspectives toward the media. Let's dig deeper, he thought. Little did he know that the inconsistencies weren't just part of the topsoil. Nonetheless, in 1985, Times Mirror engaged the Gallup Organization, and specifically its president, Andrew Kohut, to design and pursue a new kind of survey—one that "moved beyond traditional polling practices and conducted a full-scale investigation."[6] Focus groups in three metropolitan areas and four waves of national surveys with more than 4,000 interviews led to what Times Mirror proclaimed upon the release of its report in 1986 as the "largest, most fully integrated analysis ever conducted into public thinking about the American news media."[7] The interviewing was distinguished by its expensive use of "doubling-back," a polling methodology of reinterviewing usually used to measure changes in opinion over time but used in this instance to "explain some of the enigmas" in earlier research.[8]

Explaining the enigmas would prove elusive, but the impressive research itself in the 1986 Times Mirror survey established a benchmark. The designers of the survey decided to define "credibility" more narrowly than some other polls taken in 1984, most notably a widely publicized undertaking by the American Society of Newspaper Editors (ASNE).[9] Thus, "credibility" was restricted to "believability" as in the question: "[P]lease rate how much you think you can believe [your daily newspaper or a television network or a specific news organization] on a scale of 4 to 1."[10] The results indicated that the public gave specific news organizations better marks for believability than "news organizations" generally.[11] (These results echoed the tendency of the public to give a specific congressman better marks than Congress generally.) To the direct question: "In general, do you think news organizations get the facts straight, or do you think that their stories and reports are often inaccurate?" a majority of 55 percent said "basically accurate," a minority of 34 percent said inaccurate.[12] A 1939 Roper poll for *Fortune* magazine had determined that 78 percent of people thought newspaper stories were either "almost always" or "usually" accurate.[13] In case anyone wanted to attribute the forty-five-year decline from 78 to 55 percent to the arrival of television, the one thing that was unmistakably clear in 1985 from the Times Mirror and ASNE polls was that the public found television news more believable than newspapers.[14] Pictures, it seemed, had their own unfiltered authenticity.

But, otherwise, the two 1985 polls could not have been more different in their outlook, one dour, the other upbeat. ASNE, with a broad concept of credibility that encompassed public attitudes toward journalistic practices and ethics, concluded:

> Three-fourths of all adults have some problem with the credibility of the media, and . . . one-fifth . . . deeply distrust their news media.

> The breadth of the credibility problem is demonstrated by the three-fourths who say reporters are only concerned about getting a good story and don't worry much about hurting people.[15]

On the other hand, Times Mirror saw the bottle half full. "If one defines credibility narrowly, as believability, then the public expresses something of a consensus: the public believes the press," it announced.[16] To this rosy viewpoint, it added its findings on "favorability." Gallup had long been measuring the public's "overall opinion" about a wide variety of people and institutions.[17] When it added various types of news media (e.g., local newspapers, radio news, national TV news) to its list of political figures and organizations (e.g., Ronald Reagan, the military, business corporations), it reported that "9 out of 10 Americans who express an opinion express a favorable opinion concerning the nation's press."[18]

"In short, the public *likes* the press," the Times Mirror report heralded cheerfully and boldly.[19] In the text, three substantial caveats undermined that truncated sentence. "Pollsters have always found," the report cautioned, "that the public [has] a penchant for positivity—a tendency to say it likes most things."[20] (This is especially true when questions seek a wide, diffused response like an "overall opinion" toward something.) Second, the report suggested ominously that the "more intriguing" pattern "is that those who know more about the press tend to be less happy with it."[21] Last, the report recognized that "one of the greatest challenges . . . [was] to reconcile the public's overall approval of the national news media with a list of complaints it so readily voices."[22]

In essence, the Times Mirror report sought to balance the media's

16

own anxiety over a situation that didn't feel good with some healthy perspective. Hey, it's not so bad out there, it tried to say. They like us more than Ronald Reagan or any other politician. And they appreciate our product—information—even if they don't always like how we perform.

Certainly, part of the optimism in this interpretation of the research data could be traced to Professor Michael J. Robinson of Georgetown University and the American Enterprise Institute, who served as an academic adviser to the project.

"The media are such crybabies," Robinson would hoot.[23] Colorful and provocative, the good professor added spice to the dry data collection at the Times Mirror operation. And spin. Robinson basically believed the media fretted too much over negative numbers and didn't pay sufficient attention to the fundamental regard that the public has for the institutional press's role in society. He delighted in describing the media's leaders as masochists. He'd portray them as whiners, compulsively obsessed with their "approval" ratings and flagellating themselves over the public's supposed hatred of them. The overarching theme of Times Mirror's first study in 1986—that public attitudes toward the press were essentially inconsistent and "two-minded"—clearly reflected Robinson's interpretations of the data. Later that year, when Times Mirror rolled out its second "People & the Press" survey, Robinson was backpedaling. "All of us," the second report summed up, "have probably understated how hard it is to interpret the public image of the press."[24] The "two-mindedness" theory had migrated to the "enigma" theory.

Robinson was hardly alone in resisting the troubling signals emanating from the polls in the mid-1980s. Throughout the communications industry, editors and reporters saw a badge of honor in the statistics. This was the tough-minded, "do I look like I want a date?" school that permeates journalism. No one expressed it any better than Angus McEachran, who as editor of *The Pittsburgh Press* had driven the Scripps-Howard newspaper to a winning streak of Pulitzer Prizes. "If I wanted to be loved," he would say, "I would have been a ski instructor."[25] Journalists weren't in the business to be liked or popular. Even if Nielsen ratings and the "Q" quotients, which measured "likability," determined career success in television news and even if the newly conceived *USA Today* had been founded on the notion that America needed a "reader-friendly" newspaper, the first principle of the profession called for the honest dissemination of information, regardless of the consequences. Respect, if not popularity, would surely follow. Just as Ruth followed her mother-in-law. Eternal verities would prevail.

But Ruth was not following. And the confusion over whether the media ought to be liked (as opposed to respected) contributed to a fog that made it feasible to dismiss the problem as impenetrable. It would become apparent during the ensuing decade that respect for the news media was eroding with every passing year. The canyon was forming. Or, more precisely, the formation was being detected. By 1990, Robinson and Norman J. Ornstein of the American Enterprise Institute were writing in the *Washington Journalism Review* that "the public may like the press—but in increasing numbers it does not believe it."[26] (Gone was the suggestion from Robinson and Kohut in a 1988 *Public Opinion Quarterly* article that "there is no believability crisis for the press."[27]

Many other voices were beginning to join the chorus, some of them somewhat unlikely sopranos. Richard Harwood, the longtime *Washington Post* editor who was as crusty as Ben Bradlee or any casting director could concoct, diagnosed a virus of negativism infecting the media. "The belief is widespread (if rarely voiced)," he would write as the *Post's* ombudsman, "that the media's search for conflict, human imperfection, scandal and sensation demeans, trivializes and often distorts far more than any political commercial the reputations of not only politicians but the democratic system itself."[28] And then there was, of all people, Kurt Luedtke, a certifiable prophet because he had morphed himself from Detroit newspaper editor to successful Hollywood screenwriter with the film *Absence of Malice* (starring Sally Field, of all people, as the seemingly fresh-faced and demure but deep down inside unscrupulous and blindly ambitious reporter). For insight, or perhaps just sadomasochistic entertainment, America's newspaper publishers invited Luedtke to address them at their annual convention. He let them have it:

> There are good men and women who will not stand for office, concerned that you will find their flaws or invent them. Many people who have dealt with you wish they had not. You are capricious and unpredictable, you are fearsome and you are feared because there is never any way to know whether this time you will be fair and accurate or whether you will not. And there is virtually nothing we can do about it.[29]

This shift in emphasis—not seismic but jarring enough to make microphones and Pan-Cake makeup fall off tables—was due principally to the declining numbers. They were headed south. As Times Mirror continued its polling in the late 1980s and into the 1990s, the results reflected degenerating attitudes toward the media—what Times Mirror itself termed in 1995 the "burgeoning public discontent with the news media."[30] No matter what the pollsters' question—and there were scores of different ones—the composite created a picture of rocks falling into a ravine in slow motion. It was not easy to sense, much less measure, just how far the rocks were falling because the surveys did not lend themselves to ready comparison. Questions were phrased with different vocabulary and posed with little symmetry. But no one was denying the existence of the rubble, and some results could be compared quickly. Very telling, for instance, were the results of the "overall favorability" question, which had been used in 1986 to suggest that things weren't quite so bad as paranoid media mavens dreaded. By 1993, the number of people who regarded network television news "mostly unfavorably" or "very unfavorably" had tripled since 1985 from 10 percent to 29 percent.[31] The public's preference for television news over newspapers seemed to have evaporated. Loyalty to daily newspapers also showed a decline, although not as steep, from 11 percent to 18 percent.[32] This was as good as the news got. A January 1995 NBC/*Wall Street Journal* poll found that 50 percent of 500 surveyed adults had either a "somewhat negative" or a "very negative" impression of the news media. Likewise, the answer to another question in the Times Mirror survey which called for an overall conclusory response was downright chilling:

> Which of the following two statements about the news media do you agree with more . . . ?

> 25%   The news media helps society to solve its problems.
>
>   OR . . .
>
> 71%   The news media gets in the way of society solving its problems.
>
>   4%   Don't know/Refused
>
> 100%[33]

In 1995, after a decade of polling and more or less muted anxiety within the industry, all hell broke loose. Every major journalism review, trade publication and press organization discovered the "problem" of an angry public and pounced like a mountain lion. "Can the Media Win Back the Public?" queried a major cover story in the *American Journalism Review* by Linda Fibich, which inside the magazine was entitled "Under Siege."[34] It described "the mood out there" (ugly) and, through the voices of the media's own, laid the blame (as journalism reviews have a tendency to do) squarely at the media's doormat. Howard Kurtz, acute media reporter for *The Washington Post,* was quoted: "In no other profession would top executives scratch their heads and wonder why it is that a substantial proportion of the customers think they're scum."[35] The question on the cover, unsurprisingly, was not answered.

The American Editor, the publication of the American Society of Newspaper Editors, announced as the headline of its cover story on the subject: "It's Official: Most People Don't Like Us Anymore."[36] The "running head" at the top of the magazine's pages blazed in block type "The Media as Monsters," and a cute little computer cousin of Godzilla walked across collapsing skyscrapers just to graphically make some point. There was more finger-pointing. A *U.S. News & World Report* quote from Harvard professor and former NBC reporter Marvin Kalb was used: "Why do

Americans hate the press? Because," Kalb replied, "you deserve it."[37] There was also extensive treatment of what editors could do to regain public trust. "Reconnect" had clearly become the new buzzword. "The press must relearn how to be dispassionate without being disconnected," urged one article by Christopher Peck, editor of the Spokane (Washington) *Spokesman Review*.[38] Peck was chairing ASNE's Ethics and New Values Committee and its giant new study, "Timeless Values: Staying True to Journalistic Principles in the Age of New Media," being undertaken with a million-dollar grant from the Robert R. McCormick Tribune Foundation.[39] The "Timeless Values" project, a reconnection spaceship if there ever was one, focused on how journalists could reflect in their work six "enduring" values that the public saw as missing: balance, accuracy, editorial judgment, leadership in the community, public access and credibility.[40] Two other articles in *The American Editor* addressed a couple of the most common and intense complaints about the media: negativity and bias. Washington (and California) personality Arianna Huffington adapted a gentle knuckle rap she had given the newspaper editors at their 1995 convention, appropriately entitled: "Holding Up a Mirror That Makes Everything Ugly: How the American Media Are Betraying the American Public."[41] Sample sentence: "Much more fundamental than a liberal bias . . . is a cynical bias, a debunking bias, a nihilistic bias, a bias to believe the worst about us . . . an attitude of casual disdain and even casual cruelty."[42] Sample advice: "Angels fly, my mother used to tell me, because they take themselves lightly. . . . A sense of humor would be of enormous help in achieving [a] new perspective."[43] L. Brent Bozell III, president of the Conservative Victory Committee (a PAC), preferred to see liberal devils, not angels, in his "Here's Why Conservatives Don't Trust the Press: Persistent Liberal Bias and Refusing to Admit It Have Alienated the Public."[44] One did not have to read beyond the headline. In case all of this introspection and criticism gave editors a headache, there was, finally, a cure-all dispensed by the Associated Press's Washington hand Walter R. Mears, also descriptively and exhaustively entitled: "Let's Stop Agonizing and Get Back to Doing Our Job: Objective, Accurate, Straight-ahead

Reporting Always Has Been the First, Best Reply to Critics and Cynics."[45] But Mears was not dismissing the problem. If anything, he stated it most bleakly:

> Too many people dislike us because they don't think they can rely on us for an honest product. The next step could be worse. Follow this track, and increasing numbers of the readers we want to serve are going to discount and ignore us.[46]

That, of course, represented the media's worst fear: no one will pay attention. Instead of having a position of honor, influence and wealth in American democracy, they will be disregarded. If behavioral change was required to preserve a special place in the palace, then journalists should learn new tricks (and manners). Two nasty habits seemed particularly endangered: cynicism and relentless aggressiveness. The former was bashed in "A Generation of Vipers: Journalists and the New Cynicism" by Paul Starobin of the *National Journal,* which the *Columbia Journalism Review* published in 1995 as its contribution to the pile-on.[47] Poor Maureen Dowd of *The New York Times* was crowned queen of malice just for having a tart tongue and writing leads "so delicious, yet so dismissive and reductive" as the famous one that captured a presidential visit to Oxford University: "President Clinton returned today for a sentimental journey to the university where he didn't inhale, didn't get drafted and didn't get a degree."[48] Closely related, critically, was Adam Gopnik's powerful essay in a *New Yorker* late 1994, which, in addressing a number of recent books about the media, developed another theme: the media has undergone a transformation in the past twenty years "from an access culture to an aggression culture. . . . The reporter used to gain status by dining with his subjects; now he gains status by dining on them."[49] The cost of having a caricature of Sam Donaldson as a stereotype is paralysis, Gopnik reasoned. "Having turned themselves into a forum for the sort of craziness that was previously kept to the margins of American life, the media have nothing left to do but watch the process, and act as though it were entertaining," he wrote.[50] Both articles, thoughtful and strong, seemed to seek a softer, redirected reportorial behavior.

In the end, these qualitative assessments help us much more than quantitative or statistical research in understanding what has gone wrong between the public and the media and what to do about it. Stephen Hess, senior fellow and media seer at the Brookings Institution in Washington, undertook a comprehensive look at the years of accumulated polling material to render yet another "report card" on the "Credibility Gap Revisited 1985–1995," for *Presstime*, the magazine of the National Newspaper Association.[51] Hess devised his own sensible, if complicated rating system in order to cross-tabulate the asymmetrical surveys over the years. He produced an overall "impressionistic" negative rating for the media of 60 percent, up from 51 percent in 1985.[52] Respect for all institutions, not just the media, declined during the period, he noted, although the rate of decline for the media was decidedly more pronounced and clearly the numbers had grown steadfastly more negative over the decade. After completing the article for *Presstime*, Hess agreed that when you pored through all the mounds of polling data, you emerged with an overwhelming sense that the amount pollsters can tell us about the situation is limited. For one thing, some of the quantitative analysis can seem counterintuitive. Times Mirror's study in 1995, for example, indicates that the poorest and least educated among us are the most supportive of the media.[53] Yet that result undoubtedly stems from the acquiescent or agreeable style in responding to polling questions that tends to typify lower-income people. Similarly, the apparent big winner in the Times Mirror 1995 survey and, again, in a 1997 Roper Center survey commissioned by the Newseum and the Freedom Forum, was local television news. In the Times Mirror survey, it drew the highest approval marks (i.e., A's and B's) from all demographic groups except college graduates and the 18–29 age group.[54] In the Newseum poll, a full 60 percent thought local television newscasts were "excellent" or "good." But what does that mean? Local television news is terrible. Or at least that is the nearly universal anecdotal response you draw, even from people in the business. Why don't the polls mirror the widespread complaint that local television news is vapid, violent and so repetitive as to be numbing? The answer points to a key truth about all polling on this subject—the public harbors some massive and fundamentally contradictory attitudes toward the media. People rate highly the news source they use the most, such as local television news, inadequate as it may be, and then lambaste the generic industry for behavior commonly found on the very outlets they watch or read. This unavoidable conclusion paralyzes people in the business. If solutions to the problem involve changing "News at Eleven" in ways that might attract fewer viewers or readers, only suicidal executives would forge ahead. For all the public moaning about excessive crime reporting on local television, in the Newseum poll of 1997 a robust 68 percent of Americans listed crime news as the subject in which they were "extremely" or "very" interested. Clearly, the public, or at least 68 percent of it, is responsible for news that bleeds. "The public is not an investigating creature," the late CBS anchor and commentator Eric Sevareid told me in 1990. "It loves the obvious. That's why anchors get rich and commentators don't."

Similarly, the most frustrating aspect of the statistical approach to the situation, dangerous as it is to say in this egalitarian age, is that the results also chronically understate the significance of what might be called the "leader" class in America (which is not coextensive with any identifiable demographic group, including the so-called college-educated). Everyone's opinion is not, of course, equal in this or any other society. Some carry more influence than others. Most of the media's opinion polling, and for that matter demographic marketing studies, do not measure the views of "opinion makers," those people whose word of mouth can shape public attitudes, sometimes powerfully. Carefully selected, a group of "opinion makers" can tell a company whether a BMW convertible will be "cool" or "cramped" or whether *The Truman Show* will be a summer blockbuster or is in need of more prerelease editing. Up to now, the media's polling has largely sought to measure what moves or offends its mass audience, rather than trying to identify how "opinion leaders" might be mobilized to foster a better understanding of the public's own contribution to the disintegrating relationship.

Hard as it may be to quantify or bottle our ethereal attitudes toward the media, there is no question, statistically or otherwise, that matters have grown worse during the last decade. Is this temporary? Cyclical? To grasp where we are and where we might be headed, we must first look further back to see how public attitudes toward the media have changed, qualitatively as well as quantitatively, as the media itself has changed. Then we consider the reasons that have created the canyon of distrust and distance between the public and the media. Finally, we look at the troubling consequences for a nation founded on the notion that a free press's chief value is bringing us information, sometimes about ourselves, which we may not want to know.

PART ONE

ORIGINS AND CAUSES

2

From Benchley to Brill, Luce to Levin

If you really want to dismay yourself with polling statistics, ask people who Robert Benchley is. At a cocktail party in the sweet, Cotswold-like village of Siasconset on Nantucket Island, I once conducted a wholly unprofessional, but unquestionably random survey among a group of sweet, rich summer residents who were as demographically homogeneous as a dry martini. Virtually all of these beach lovers had at one time or another scared themselves out of the water by devouring *Jaws,* the novel (and movie) by Robert Benchley's grandson Peter, about shark fins rippling through the ocean toward a human lunch. Unsurprisingly, some of the Nantucket crowd recognized the family's name (Peter has a house nearby; Robert himself was supposed to be buried in the local cemetery, but his ashes were somehow placed in an incorrect urn). So some wondered vaguely whether Robert was related to Peter. Only three out of forty-two, a depressing 7 percent, could correctly identify Robert as the accomplished writer, humorist and film actor of the 1920s and 1930s who lunched on Dorothy Parker, Alexander Woollcott and other members of the Algonquin Hotel's Roundtable. (Even more dismal survey results were obtained when the question was posed at locations less frequented by aging Ivy Leaguers in rose-colored trousers.)

It will also surprise no one that the 7 percenters were silver foxes who had lived through the 1920s and 1930s and who remembered Mr. Benchley from personal experience with his writings. Historical knowledge of the twentieth century is confined, it seems, to those who have lived it. (Try asking a twenty-five-year-old for a ten-minute explanation of the Vietnam War. You won't have to worry about the toast burning.) What accounts for this pervasive *ignoramus gigundus*? No doubt, the deplorable possibility exists that our culture ranks humorists less retentively vital than Ty Cobb or Herbert Hoover.

To be fair, there is a limited megabyte capacity to the brain. Bombarded by ever-expanding loads of information, pressured to stay au courant or face obsolescence, our minds jettison dispensable old programs in favor of the new. Context and perspective are lost. Understanding anything becomes as difficult as swimming in an aquarium. Before we lament the new distrust of the media, then, let's bring back some lost, dead white males for perspective.

MUTATIONS IN MEDIA SELF-CRITICISM

For twelve years, from 1927 to 1939, Robert Benchley, using the pseudonym Guy Fawkes, wrote press criticism for *The New Yorker*.[1] Both the tone and content of the seventy-three columns he authored during that period, especially when compared to recent media criticism, reveal how much more coldly furious we are toward the media today. Benchley excelled at poking fun at newsmaker and reporter alike. When the *New York World* reported that President Calvin Coolidge, on arriving at his summer home, "wise-cracked good-humoredly" and "chuckled with anticipation," Benchley felt compelled to "denounce" this "palpably false" newspaper story.[2] "It is," he wrote, "exaggerations and distorted writing like this which have brought journalism into ill-repute. Mr. Coolidge could sue the *World* if he were so minded."[3] This light touch meshed nicely, of course, with the magazine's studied sophistication. (A cartoon from an early issue depicted a newspaper boy holding up two newspapers for sale, one with the banner headline "MURDER" and the other screaming "EXPLOSION"; a customer on the street says, "I think I'll take the murder. . . ."[4])

For all the wry wit, there was no doubt why Benchley had been commissioned to critique the press. It was powerful. He began one of his first columns by observing: "[A]s so often happens in a world not yet under the complete control of the managing editors of newspapers . . ."[5] In 1930, he admitted that if he seemed "unduly attentive to the little foibles of *The New York Times*, . . . it is because *The New York Times* is the only newspaper we really give a hang about."[6] (Thus, in 1929, he could term the *Times* and its correspondent in Italy "strictly Fascist" because of an opening sentence in a dispatch from Rome which read: "Premier Mussolini, who assiduously kept himself in the background . . ."[7] "One need read no further," Benchley concluded, "to realize that whatever followed was dictated either by a strong personal love for Il Duce or by Il Duce himself."[8]) The Hearst newspapers and the Scripps-Howard–controlled *Telegram* were more easily discounted: "[O]ne is so accustomed to seeing half the front page of [these newspapers] given over to a big box promoting a Policy or Program that it soon becomes a simple matter to skip that section and just see who won the ball game."[9] His strongest views, laced with plenty of bite and precious little humor at all, were reserved for moments when the independence or credibility of the press was threatened by a self-inflicted wound. When the Hearst newspapers lavishly reviewed a new Ziegfeld musical appearing at a theater owned by Hearst and his editor Arthur Brisbane, Benchley railed against the newspapers for "making themselves free advertising mediums for a supposedly outside business in a manner which definitely tossed aside any pretense of respect for their readers."[10] It represented "about as blatant and insulting a piece of news-perversion as has ever been crammed down the throats of the public."[11] Undisclosed conflicts of interest were not to be tolerated.[12]

Media criticism today cannot be described as gently satirical or morally indignant. At its best, it tends to be reportorial. David Shaw of the *Los Angeles Times*, Howard Kurtz of *The Washington Post*, Jonathan Alter of *Newsweek*, Jonathan Katz of *Wired*, Jeff Greenfield of ABC and, later, CNN, ombudsmen too numerous to mention and others similarly situated have difficulty just reporting the information on their "beat" fully, much less commenting expansively. *The New Yorker*'s man on the media scene, prodigious reporter Ken Auletta, covers the financial prowess and machinations of the captains of the communications industry as high drama. And as terribly important. The business strategies of Rupert Murdoch or Michael Eisner are reported breathlessly, tirelessly. The most wicked satire remotely analogous to Benchley's dealt not with the media or its owners, but with Auletta himself. In 1995, *The New Republic* spoofed the tendency of Auletta's copy to dwell on the intimacy of his relationships with the rich and famous "info-barons."[13] In a make-believe *New Yorker* piece "by Ken Fellata," the author races awestruck from mogul to mogul, sleeping "on a small cot at the foot" of Michael Eisner's bed or big-game hunting with NBC's Robert Wright.[14] The billionaire "info-barons" are either "humble but . . . intensely proud," "legendary" or "visionary."[15]

Perhaps the most incisive and thoughtful observer of the news media in recent decades has been Lewis Lapham, editor-in-chief of *Harper's* magazine. His essays, often ironic or sarcastic, are rarely funny. They have an edge. Angry and ruthless, they reflect more than their author's impatience with fools. Lapham has seen a public with hopelessly high and unrealistic expectations of journalism. "Not only do they expect [the news] to be entertaining, they expect it to be true," he wrote in a prophetic piece entitled "Gilding the News" in 1981.[16] Lapham did not believe the public recognized the media's widespread propensity to report "formula" stories designed to reinforce conventional worldviews (e.g., "cities are dangerous"). Such structural constraints on news reporting inevitably lead to a journalism that distorts rather than reflects reality. When the public senses this distortion, and doesn't comprehend the mechanical reason for its existence, they accurately "suspect that the difference between fact and fiction [in journalism] may be as random as a number drawn in a lottery."[17] Their resulting "resentment will wreak an expensive vengeance," he predicted.[18] By 1991, Lapham detected another kind of distortion in media coverage of the Gulf War. In a *Harper's* column entitled "Trained Seals and Sitting Ducks," he castigated the "pitiably weak" journalists for acting like "prisoners of war."[19] CBS's Dan Rather earned a special commendation of contempt for an on-the-air salute to the soldiers in Saudi Arabia since it "established the tone of the media's grateful attendance at what everybody was pleased to call a war" (but which Lapham preferred to call the "Pentagon's trade show" or a "television miniseries . . . that borrowed elements of *Monday Night Football, The A Team,* and *Revenge of the Nerds*").[20] His scathing criticism of the "credulous and jingoistic press" concluded with the pointed reminder that "a servile press is a circus act, as loudly and laughingly cheered by a military dictatorship as by a democratic republic."[21]

Lapham's goading at the beginning of the decade foreshadowed the arrival by the end of the 1990s of a full-fledged, mass-market periodical devoted to media criticism. Steven Brill, father of Court TV and mastermind of *The American Lawyer*'s innovative approach to reporting on and evaluating lawyers, had turned his full attention to scrutinizing his fellow journalists. The squirming was noticeable. Brill loved to bear down on slipshod professional practices, be they performed by dopey lawyers or craven reporters. During the year before the debut of *Brill's Content,* the conventional "line" among journalists on the forthcoming magazine was odd, but telling. Invariably, people in the business would concede that more media criticism was healthy (a debatable proposition, but what else could they say?) and then dispense almost uniformly a judgment about Brill's commercial prospects. "He can't possibly make money," came the refrain. It was hard to know whether this assessment was wishful thinking that the intensely competitive and famously abrasive Brill had miscalculated his financial pro formas or simply a reflection of the quickened capitalistic fervor that now pervaded journalism. By 1998, journalists had become armchair entrepreneurs when it came to the media "biz." Apart from these investment banking predictions, what was most striking about *Brill's Content* when it was launched was that it was loaded with content. The fat book was brimming with information. It was overwhelming, even to media junkies. Many of the features, no doubt of some interest to someone someplace, seemed about as riveting as articles in other industry publications such as "Iron Ore Shipping Lanes" in *Iron Age*. The comprehensive coverage of every carrel of journalism left one wondering whether the magazine's survival might be mostly endangered by the unavoidable dullness that accompanies microscopic coverage of any industry, even the very rich and very important communications industry.

In an earlier time, when journalists were still supposedly ink-stained and financially retarded, Benchley (who was neither) had chided the press for toadying up to the needs of the central government when "there is any public reassurance to be done." As banks collapsed and the Depression deepened in 1931, he had written:

> The Press, as usual, has been quite willing to do all that it could to bolster up public confidence and has loaned its rewrite men, ink, and printing presses to the point of lavishness. The only trouble has come in not knowing exactly what to say. If the Head Masters want the Press to help out, they have got to give it better copy than Communist plots to work with.[22]

Next to Benchley's gentle elbow in the ribs, Lapham's prose and Brill's attitude resemble Patriot missiles with multiple warheads. The tone of media criticism has grown progressively more caustic and severe with each passing decade of the twentieth century. To some, it may seem unfair to compare Benchley to Lapham and Brill, although comparisons of successful social commentators—be they Lucille Ball and Roseanne or Walter Winchell and *Entertainment Tonight*—inevitably give us insightful glimpses at where the march of *Time* has taken us.

Even more significant than the alteration in the tone of the press critic's assessments has been the remarkable growth in the press's willingness to tolerate and encourage criticism of itself. Benchley stands out in his era partially because he had few competitors. Lapham and Brill stand out generations later not because there is a scarcity of media critics (there are hordes), but because of their trenchant perspicacity and authoritative command of the subject. Until the late 1950s, there was not much

34

appetite within the press for public self-examination. When the illustrious Hutchins Commission (set up by Time, Inc., founder Henry Luce and chaired by University of Chicago president Robert M. Hutchins to study the obligations of a free press) called in its 1947 report[23] for journalists to engage in more mutual criticism, there was little enthusiasm within the publishing industry, as Stephen Bates, senior fellow at the Annenberg Washington Program, has pointed out. The *Los Angeles Times* thought such criticism was "ineffective," Arthur Hays Sulzberger "saw no reason" for it and even Walter Lippmann likened it to "marital criticism—too hard for mortal men to take."[24]

Walter Lippmann meet Maggie Scarf. She and her fellow environmental engineers have made modern marriages a veritable wetlands of communications. And just as we now either share feelings or risk dysfunction, media companies now actually pay employees to dish out self-criticism in the name of health. The appetite for this self-examination would sometimes embarrass Plato.

When the actress Kathleen Turner made an "unglamorous entrance" into the Hotel du Pont in downtown Wilmington (Delaware), an observant, if earthbound reporter, Valerie Helmbreck, faithfully reported in the local *News-Journal*:

> Without make-up, Turner's skin is exceptionally pale and not as smooth as it appears in publicity photos.[25]

Wilmington readers howled.

> "It looks like it was revenge for not granting the reporter an interview," Barbara Faulkaber wrote the newspaper.

> "It was sexist and tasteless," Chris Larson complained.[26]

A "dispirited" manager of the hotel, who had been quoted in the newspaper as saying Turner "isn't nearly so good-looking in person," denied ever making such an inhospitable remark to the reporter, who, in turn, stuck by her story.[27]

All this—and much more—was refried, stir-fried and hashed over in a *News-Journal* column by its public editor, John Sweeney. He concluded:

> The arrival of a Hollywood star in town is news. The front page needs relief from the daily barrage of bad news.
>
> Where the article went wrong was in its execution. [Its] tone was nasty.[28]

Whatever else may have changed in the world of communications during the twentieth century, it is comforting to know that film actresses still provide relief and that their arrival in Wilmington is still news. (Bulletin to William Morris and ICM agents: All clients should wear full-dress makeup when entering Wilmington.)

Now, of course, this catty commentary on Mr. Sweeney's commentary is just as snotty as any unkind slash at Kathleen Turner. But this is the inevitable way station that the Road (paved with good intentions) of Heightened Self-Examination passes through: one cannot tolerate the humorless monotony of modern media criticism, however earnest, without lapsing now and then into giddiness or at least a little meowing. No work published in the 1990s better skewered the foibles and excesses of the media, especially the Washington media machine, than James Fallows' *Breaking the News: How the Media Undermines American Democracy* (Pantheon, 1995). Fallows ruthlessly examined a world of television stars and print journalists who wannabe television stars (most of whom stood accused of playing the role of journalist rather than performing the hard work that earns journalists' respect). The book seemed to offer evidence supporting Danish philosopher Søren Kierkegaard's view that

> [t]he race's deepest separation from God is epitomized by "the journalist." . . . If I were a father and had a daughter who was seduced, I would not despair of her. I would hope for salvation. But if I had a son who became a journalist and remained one for five years, I should give him up.[29]

Relentlessly, Fallows toted up the sins of the new breed of journalist millionaires: undisclosed conflicts of interest (greed), laziness among the

White House press corps (sloth), "know-it-all" punditry on television's yakety-yak shows, where you're dead if you don't have another pungent opinion (no facts, please) every forty-five seconds. His most scathing indictment aimed at the knee-jerk cynicism that permeates coverage of the gamesmanship of politics. Fallows' book was well received by fellow journalists, not very surprising now that the fragrance of self-criticism within the profession was in full flower. Richard Harwood of *The Washington Post* and other mandarins of the business generally found Fallows' criticisms right on the mark and timely.[30] Outside of the Harvard-to-Washington corridor, enthusiasm for Fallows' carping waned. Editorial-page columnist Ross Anderson scoffed in the *Seattle Times*:

> Fallows reveals himself as precisely what he critiques, a creature of the Beltway. . . .
>
> What this guy needs is a good local newspaper, one that understands that there is life and politics beyond Pennsylvania Avenue. . . .
>
> Journalism out here in the provinces is alive and well, struggling to provide an alternative to TV news.[31]

You didn't have to live in Seattle to detect the irony of Fallows, Walter Isaacson of *Time* magazine and other guests on *The Charlie Rose Show* pontificating about "what was wrong with the media," all the while pumping Fallows' book.[32] After fifteen minutes of opinions delivered with all the "I am seldom in doubt and never wrong" certainty of the very pundits the book deplored, viewers could see that the rapid-fire ("Don't be dull!") format of such television shows ("Quick, people are reaching for the remote control") virtually shoehorns the participants into seeming arrogant and overbearing. Someone (probably a family member) would have long ago muzzled Messrs. Rose, Fallows and Isaacson if they were actually as blabby as they seemed on this program.

This tendency of new age media criticism to fall into grim sanctimony and smug condemnations has been spotted by David Remnick, an industrious reporter whose skill earned him the editor's position at *The New Yorker* in 1998. In a review of *Breaking the News* for that magazine, he found the tone of Fallows' treatment of journalistic misdeeds "prig-gish."[33] "At times," he wrote, Fallows "seems like Carry Nation sent out to review a tavern: he disapproves."[34] Nor was Remnick persuaded by Fallows' analysis. "The top papers are packed to the gunwales with earnest" coverage of major national issues, not just stories clocking the political chase or portraying conflict.[35] And Remnick had no use for Fallows' concluding endorsement of the so-called public journalism movement, a trendy and mystifying cult of some academics and newspaper editors determined to revitalize communities by reconnecting with them.

"Excuse me while I run screaming from the room," wrote Remnick. "[W]hy abandon the entire enterprise of informed aggressive skepticism . . . in the hope of pleasing an imagined public? When journalists begin acting like waiters and taking orders from the public and pollsters, the results are not pretty. . . . Like it or not, part of the job of a great editor is to listen to public desires and then, if necessary, act against them."[36]

What seemed eminently debatable to Remnick seemed like "well-worn observations" to Ellen Hume, the former *Wall Street Journal* political writer turned PBS and think-tank guru, who reviewed *Breaking the News* for the *Columbia Journalism Review*.[37] "Fallows writes as if he's just returned from Mars to write a book from the clips, and he's shocked! shocked! to find that American journalism has gone to hell," she wrote.[38] Grateful for the "blast" of publicity that Fallows' book directed to these "important issues," Hume nonetheless faulted him for ignoring the earlier research and work of such academics as Thomas Patterson, Kathleen Hall Jamieson and Michael Schudson.[39] "The fact that so many journalists are trumpeting Fallows' ideas as if they were new shows just how cut off the media are from their own critics," wrote the newly minted academic with a gracious bow to her colleagues.[40] Her insistence that Fallows was merely "restat[ing] the obvious" reflected the hard-held conviction among practitioners turned professors that the profession is accelerating, not preventing, the decline of public life.[41] While this attitude is doubtlessly more "obvious" amid the ivy of the academy than around the philodendron of the newsroom, it is an idea no longer in need of either oxygen or fertilizer to flourish, particularly when promoted by a veteran of the presidential campaign bus. Ellen Hume, it will be remembered, is no stranger to the deconstruction of political coverage. She is not popular in Huntington, Indiana. It was there on August 19, 1988, at a press conference before some 12,000 people gathered in front of the local courthouse in the hometown of the Republican candidate for Vice President of the United States, that Ellen asked Dan Quayle, or "screamed at me," to use his words, how it had felt when "people were dying in Vietnam" to be "writing press releases" with his National Guard unit. The angry crowd erupted with boos, calling her names that could not be published in *The Wall Street Journal.*[42]

Like the increasingly fragmented communications industry itself, the media's introspection has mutated during the twentieth century from the drollness of Robert Benchley to the ubiquity, bite and diversity of Lapham, Brill, Fallows, Remnick, Hume, and scores of other critics. They are anything but monolithic. And if, thankfully, a sense of humor has not been entirely discarded, there is also a deadly seriousness. In earlier decades, the media knew that it was useful. Now it senses, and dreads, an awful truth: that for all the "news that can be used," for all the power it plays in ordering our daily lives, the public constantly wonders: what in the world is the media really about besides money?

THE TRADITION OF SENSATIONALISM

No one can sift through a century's worth of public complaints about the media without realizing that some are endemic—they go with the territory. Take sensationalism, for instance.

It is the most durable of the public's complaints about the media. In 1995, the Times Mirror survey asked:

What's your biggest complaint about the way the news is generally covered these days?

The largest percentage (22 percent) answered "fluff/sensationalism/

tabloidization."[43] A Newseum/Freedom Forum poll in 1997 similarly identified "sensationalism" as the chief bane of the public, with 65 percent saying it is a "major problem."

Sixty years earlier, the first polling on attitudes toward the media revealed that 56 percent of the public thought the press published "too much sensational news."[44] Over the years, while percentages have fluctuated depending on the pollster's question and the general tenor of the times, you can find one marvelous consistency in the data: people find the media's product too sensational. Thus, in a 1949 study, 36 percent agreed with the statement that newspapers in general devote too much space to "trivialities, scandals and sensations."[45] Even during the Eisenhower era of good feeling, a rosy survey that gave the press as hearty a pat on the back as one could ask counted approximately 35 to 43 percent of people who felt there were kinds of news that the press "gave too much attention."[46] Analysis of twentieth-century polling clearly indicates a deterioration in the public's assessment of whether the press is "fair," but a reasonably constant view about sensationalism. In 1938, the first Gallup survey found 73 percent of people characterizing the press as "fair," a figure that *Fortune* refined in 1939 by slicing up attitudes into categories to find that 59 percent thought reporting on "religion" was "fair," with somewhat less commanding majorities for other subject matters.[47] By the 1980s, polling essentially showed a "flip-flop" on the fairness issue. The 1997 Newseum/Freedom Forum survey indicated that 63 percent thought that news was too manipulated by special interests, while about half thought it was too biased or negative in tone. Thus, the public's distaste for "sensationalism" has been largely unrelated to its growing disenchantment with the media's "unfairness."

Where does the chronic dislike of sensationalism come from? Probably from the good old-fashioned roots of successful American journalism. Sensationalism was the single most important ingredient to the wildly popular "yellow journalism" that was invented by the newspaper barons of the late nineteenth century. Joseph Pulitzer, generally credited with creating the brazen journalistic style, used it to win readership and build the largest newspaper chain of his time. Starting in St. Louis, Pulitzer migrated East in 1883 when he learned that the *New York World* was available for sale and bought it on a whim.[48] He immediately began a battle for circulation on the East Coast by applying the formula that he had developed in St. Louis: front-page exposés, banner headlines and inflammatory stories about sex and crime. "A BROTHER ON THE WARPATH—HE ATTACKS HIS SISTER'S DENTIST AND THEN TRIES TO SHOOT HIM," Pulitzer's *World* screamed on the front page. "DID SHE STEAL THE DIAMONDS?: A HOTEL MAID ACCUSED OF STEALING JEWELS," the paper would blast.

While Pulitzer has been recognized for fathering yellow journalism, Charles Dana of the *New York Sun* had actually begun to use a similar scheme more than a decade earlier, dealing out ample quantities of cynicism toward all politicians, unions, foreigners, farmers and reformers.[49] The new yellow papers discovered they could cultivate brand-new readers or, to a lesser extent, steal readers away from the old-money conservative papers by a combination of lurid tales and lower prices. Dana instigated price competition when he lowered the price of the *Sun* to two cents. He also recognized the need for "condensation, clearness and point" and limited the paper to four pages. The *Sun*'s prospectus proudly claimed "[i]t will not take as long to read the *Sun* as to read the *London Times* or Webster's dictionary; but when you have read it, you will know about all that has happened in both hemispheres."[50] While abbreviating length, Dana expanded the types of events that were considered "news" by the press. His city editor, John Bogart, is cited as coining the phrase "When a dog bites a man, that is not news, because it happens so often. But if a man bites a dog, that is news."[51] Dana also insisted on a change in writing style. "Besides using colorful detail, the *Sun*'s reporters applied the storyteller's art—the fiction form—to journalism. Instead of summarizing the facts in the lead, the reporter started from the beginning of the current happenings, sometimes going back twenty years or more."[52]

In the 1890s, the success of sensationalism beckoned a young William Randolph Hearst, who believed that Pulitzer was getting old and ripe for competitive attack. In pursuit of his goal to create the largest newspaper group in the country, Hearst surpassed Pulitzer's readership, building an influential empire that stretched from coast to coast. Hearst's model for launching a paper was anything but timid. He would pour in large amounts of money up front and take a city by storm. In New York, for example, he bought the *Morning Journal,* founded by Pulitzer, for $180,000 and then hired noted reporter Arthur Brisbane away from Pulitzer.

Hearst believed that he had to give the public something that they would want to read. He recognized that the country was experiencing a large influx of immigration and saw his duty as helping these new Americans. His son has explained, "[My father] was going to help make them Americans—teach them to read and write, and understand the city and nation in which they were strangers. He had to publish a newspaper that they could read and comprehend. [He] saw this as a great adventure— and, if he himself were to survive, it could be profitable as well."[53]

Hearst had a knack for doing what was necessary to compete with Pulitzer. He advised his editors: "Please bear in mind that we are not making short stories to save money. We are making them to save readers . . . Nobody likes a long article any more than they like a long speech."[54] When it came to headlines, Hearst proved that he could excel. Who could keep a penny in his pocket while a newsboy was holding up "SNAKES ARE THEIR GODS: CUBAN DISCIPLES OF THE DEVIL HAVE HIDEOUS MIDNIGHT ORGIES," or "FIGHTING A BULL TER-RIER: AN EX–FOOTBALL PLAYER SHOWS HOW TO TACKLE THE VICIOUS BRUTE." Respectability was sacrificed. Mark Twain referred to Hearst's *New York Journal* as "the calamity of calamities."[55] Editor Arthur Brisbane would tear up the publication before letting the newspaper in his house and within the view of his daughter.[56]

Pulitzer also faced competition from E. W. Scripps, the determined Illinois farm boy who had tutored in newspapering with his brother James at the *Detroit News* and then launched his own blazing career with the *Penny Press* in Cleveland in 1878. Scripps's formula for success was also market-driven: his newspapers were *cheap* (one or two cents versus the five cents of the stuffier traditional papers), *terse* (four pages or fewer) and *published in the afternoon* when blue-collar workers had time to read a newspaper that promised "not one line of uninteresting matter." As his biographer Vance Trimble has explained, Scripps mastered the art of editing a story to deliver both pithiness and punch.[57] His favorite admonition to a reporter was "Boil that down!" A story about a water-pipe burst was reduced to four lines and the barest essentials:

> In repairing it today, the ground caved in, partially burying an Irishman under the wet clay. With his head just out from under the mud, he shouted, "I'm drowning. Be Jesus, sin for the Pope!"[58]

The longest pieces in the Scripps newspapers were committed to the sensational. The inaugural issue of the *Penny Press* featured an 800-word account of a squabble between a General Slayton and his French-Spanish wife. It told of a punching-and-shoving match in their Cleveland home and included intimate details with a question-and-answer interview between the reporter and the bruised wife. Jerry Springer would have been hard-pressed to do better. In 1879, the *Penny Press* filled two whole pages with the horrible specifics of the public hanging of one McGill for killing his sweetheart Mary Kelly. And when nonfiction was too dull, Scripps editors would opt for fiction—publishing short stories (usually about rich lads and their beautiful but ungrateful wives) that tended to be serialized and break at the breathless pinnacle of suspense. By the time circulation of the *Penny Press* hit 14,000 it was the largest in the city and its rivals no longer scoffed. Scripps embarked on his aggressive plan to establish similar newspapers in cities throughout the nation, including Pulitzer's home turf of St. Louis.

Competition spawned even greater heights of sensationalism—by everyone. It was not just the front page of Hearst's *New York American* that splashed stories about "MILLIONAIRE FACES TWO TRAGEDIES:

W. G. NEWMAN AT DAUGHTER'S FUNERAL; SITTING BY CAS-
KET, HE IS SUMMONED TO BEDSIDE OF SECOND WIFE" (Oc-
tober 1, 1900). Both *The New York Times* and *The Washington Post* carried
front-page accounts on January 1, 1910, of a freakish New Year's Eve accident at the swanky Cafe Martin when "a tongue of flame" enveloped a
wealthy patron. "Woman Set Ablaze; Revelers in Panic," headlined the
Times. "Ablaze in Gay Crowd," teased the *Post*. The tradition of relying on
sensationalism to attract readers was so commonly used and so commonly
deplored by the 1930s that entire academic studies undertook to identify
who the "bad boys" of journalism were, with the implicit understanding
that, of course, boys will be boys. One such study, for instance, was conducted by Susan M. Kingsbury and Hornell Hart of Bryn Mawr College
in 1933.[59] The study, entitled "Measuring the Ethics of American Newspapers," set out to accomplish this feat via a "comprehensive scientific
investigation" analyzing headline size and frequency devoted to various subjects. Obviously in need of objective criteria to compare various newspapers,
the study relied on an old favorite, the "Socialization-Sensationalism
Index" as derived from the "Spectrum of News Interest" analysis— showing
a continuum (in cut-and-paste graphics) of newspaper morality by com-
paring the number of headline square inches a paper devoted to subject
areas of varying degrees of social worthiness.

The study demonstrated, with a certain starchiness, that the Hearst
papers, Pulitzer's *New York World*, among others, devoted a significant
amount of headline space to stories about money, sex and crime. Papers
such as *The New York Times* and the *Christian Science Monitor*, on the other
hand, tended to use attention-grabbing headline space for stories about
business, foreign news and citizenship. Having successfully quantified what
everyone already knew, the study added a slightly more interesting dimension: a calculation of the circulation of each story genre. The study sepa-
rated the circulation of each New York paper by the percentage of headline
space devoted to the six main subject categories. The circulation of each
category was as follows: foreign problems—484,000; U.S.-international—

437,000; citizenship—292,000; money-sensational—815,000; sex—1,072,000; and money-sex—1,000,000. The study's calculations for other cities were similar. For instance, the *Boston Transcript* received a "Socialization Index" of 19.8 (on a par with *The New York Times,* near the top of the list) while distributing 35,000 copies per day. The *Boston Post,* conversely, sold 397,000 of its papers boasting a "Socialization Index" of 9.0 (below Hearst's *New York American,* but above several other tabloids and Hearst's *New York Journal,* which received negative ratings).

Academics could measure and rail against sensationalism, but there is no doubt it worked. And still does. Much maligned Geraldo Rivera opens Al Capone's vault just as the *New York Herald* used sensational stunts like Stanley's journey to Africa to find Dr. Livingstone. When the yellows ran out of stories about beleaguered heiresses or gory murders, they turned to stunts like breaking around-the-world records or starting the Spanish-American War. Readers were drawn like flies to cupcakes. Viewed realistically, sensationalism may be a bit like rich desserts—most people talk about how terrible the Chocolate Praline Decadence is just as they devour it.[60] One thing seems certain—sensationalism has always tested the outer caloric boundaries of good taste, but however sincere the public's objections to the excesses may be, we have had a century-old love affair with it.[61]

"It is ironic," journalism historian Hazel Dicken-Garcia has written, "that while critics lambasted sensationalism, journalists countered that it 'sold' papers; hence, 'offensiveness' sold but controversial ideas were treated as unsalable commodities."[62] Indeed, from the 1890s onward, the press has preferred "the business model" of pleasing everyone and maximizing readership instead of promoting a single strong viewpoint which would lead people to purchase other news material to find another point of view. The yellow roots of American journalism developed both a mass market orientation and a sort of Victorian morality about standards and practices. William David Sloan traces the rise of "professional" journalism to the influence of the straightforward, neutral, fact-laden style of the

Associated Press after 1900 and to public criticism of yellow journalism, which while compelling was seen as crass, irresponsible and vulgar.[63]

The chief lesson from history is that journalism's attachment to sensationalism (and our own) is as deep as it is conflicted. One thing is certain. "Sensationalism" cannot account for our new hatred of the media. Ricki Lake and Geraldo are eternal. The reasons lie elsewhere.

THE TRADITION OF PUBLIC SERVICE

Pulitzer, Scripps, Hearst and their fellow entrepreneurs shared another characteristic beyond their understanding of the public's appetite for sensationalism. They merged their ambitions for profit with core convictions about serving the people of America. Looking back at them through the prism of today's emphasis on quarterly earnings, it is easy to attribute their commercial successes to business acumen and relegate their philosophies about journalism to noble window dressing. Yet it is undeniable that the financial prowess of these men was inextricably connected to their sense of duty to their countrymen. They possessed an astute grasp the marketplace, but their enterprises were grounded on the power of public service. E. W. Scripps wrote:

> The first of my [editorial] principles is that I have constituted myself the advocate of that large majority of the people who are not so rich in worldly goods and native intelligence as to make them equal, man for man, in the struggle with individuals of the wealthier and more intellectual class.
>
> The press of this country is now, and always has been, so thoroughly dominated by the wealthy few of the country that it cannot be depended upon to give the great mass of people . . . correct information. . . .
>
> In fact, I have not a whole series of editorial principles. I have only one principle . . . to make it harder for the rich to grow richer and easier for the poor to keep from growing poorer.[64]

Pulitzer also embraced the blue-collar cause, promising that his

St. Louis Post-Dispatch "will serve no party but the people—will oppose all frauds and shams whatever and wherever they are."[65] Shortly before his death in 1911, he wrote with feeling about the "care" of the journalist: "He promotes every hopeful plan of progress. Without him public opinion would be shapeless and dumb."[66] In words that could encircle the awards that bear his name, Pulitzer continued:

> Our Republic and its press will rise or fall together. An able, disinterested, public-spirited press, with trained intelligence to know the right and courage to do it, can preserve that public virtue without which popular government is a sham and a mockery.[67]

Out of this public-spiritedness, and out of the need for sensational stories, arose the muckrakers. With only so many natural opportunities to report dazzling stories about sex and crime, the press had to turn to investigation. Tellingly, they gave these ventures a term with a religious connotation: a crusade. Instead of merely reporting the occurrence of events, enterprising reporters would ferret out corruption in business and government. This reckless disturbance of the status quo had been made possible by the commercial success of yellow journalism; profit had given the newspapers financial independence and freedom from special-interest pressures and advertisers. No one captured the amalgamation of profit and public service better than the crusty H. L. Mencken, editor of the *Baltimore Sun,* who said in *The Atlantic Monthly,* "The primary purpose of a newspaper crusade is to 'give a good show' by first selecting a deserving victim and then putting him magnificently to the torture."[68]

Besides the traditional muckraking which turned over dirt on public officials and business, papers increasingly invested in other types of investigative journalism. Hearst's *Journal* put thirty reporters on a murder investigation which had befuddled the police. When one of the reporters had success, the *Journal* gloated on the front page: "HOW THE GREAT MURDER MYSTERY WAS UNRAVELED, A GLIMPSE BEHIND THE SCENES AT THE TIRELESS NEWSGATHERING-MACHINERY OF A POWERFUL NEWSPAPER; JUST HOW THE

JOURNAL FOLLOWED OUT THE SLENDER THREAD OF SE-
CRET CLUES AND SOLVED THE REAL TRAGEDY."[69] Hearst did
his best to live up to the motto While Others Talk, the Journal Acts by
uncovering the sugar trusts in 1897.[70] He especially relished attacking the
trusts because his rival Dana was decidedly pro–big business in the *New
York Sun*. Hearst proclaimed on the front page of the *Journal*: "TRUSTS
ARE CANCERS—INDUSTRIAL CANCERS: Their Causes and Pernicious Effects on the Social and Industrial Body Politic Vividly Portrayed
by U.S. Senator Butler in an article to be presented in the [muckraking
magazine] *Arena* tomorrow."[71] (Headlines were about as long as the
teasers or promos used today on *Dateline* or *20/20*.)

The muckraking reporters often worked for periodical magazines,
where their investigative efforts would be an issue's main feature. Newspapers were also in on the game. Perhaps the most famous of the crusad-
ing journalists was Lincoln Steffens, who frequently wrote for *McClure's*
after getting his start uncovering police bribes for the *Evening Post*. In one
of E. W. Scripps's more daring moves, he allied with Steffens in taking on
Cincinnati boss George Cox. Steffens had been interested in the difference in the political systems of Ohio's two largest cities, Cleveland under
the reformer mayor Tom Johnson and Cincinnati under Boss Cox. Cox
owned the town and was making millions off patronage kickbacks and
other schemes. Steffens published his article, "Ohio: A Tale of Two
Cities," in July 1904 in *McClure's*, calling the city of Cincinnati "corrupt"
and its citizens "craven cowards." Scripps had his *Cincinnati Post* give the
article extensive coverage, running a front-page editorial that employed
some reverse psychology: "We have the absolute conviction that the people of Cincinnati are as patriotic and liberty loving as other Americans.
We resent with indignation the charge that the people of this city are cowards."[72] A couple of days later, the *Post* ran copies of a telegram it had sent
to Steffens demanding a public apology if the citizens turned out not to be
cowards, and Steffens' response: "If Cincinnati will, with votes, prove me
wrong, I will admit the injustice." Steffens and Scripps raised such an up-

roar that the Republican nominee for President, William Howard Taft, made a trip out to Ohio to denounce municipal GOP leaders. (Embarrassingly, Taft's brother Charles owned the Cox-supporting rival of Scripps's *Post,* the *Cincinnati Times-Star.*) Cox was crushed in the next election. Scripps tried not to let this victory go to his head: "I am not a damn bit holy or good, and I don't pretend to be," he said, "but once in a while I indulge myself in a decent action."[73] The Scripps effort to defeat Cox mirrored Hearst's national effort to all but take over the William Jennings Bryan campaign against William McKinley in 1896. Each used his paper in a fiercely partisan manner. Hearst, of course, later manipulated his newspapers to advance his own political ambitions.[74] But he also opposed the Tammany Hall political machine in New York and pursued various "rackets," including labor union skulduggery and public officials' affiliations with liquor, gambling and "vice rings." In San Francisco, he posed a reporter as an accident victim and nabbed doctors faking an X-ray. Doctors, orderlies and ambulance drivers were fired or suspended.

The muckrakers and their imitators and offspring exposed a generation of corruption but they did not enhance the press's credibility. Their stories, though true, were so fantastic that the public's natural instinct was to be skeptical.[75] A prior Republican, Abraham Lincoln, had wisely observed that one can only do as much good as the public will bear. A current one, Teddy Roosevelt, echoed the thoughts of many when he called Lincoln Steffens, Upton Sinclair and others "the lunatic fringe" and labeled them in a 1906 speech:

> There are times and places where . . . there is filth on the floor and it must be scraped up with the muckrake. . . . But the man who never does anything else, who never thinks or speaks or writes save of his feats with the muckrake, speedily becomes, not a help to society, not an incitement to good, but one of the most potent forces of evil.[76]

Walter Lippmann later wrote in 1913 that Steffens was "too whimsical for a permanent diet" and that his articles exposing the banking monopoly never "got down to grips with anything." According to Justin Kaplan, Steffens' biographer, "Lippmann concluded . . . the work of the muckrakers had been a waste."[77] Willa Cather described her friend, magazine editor S. S. McClure, and his staff this way:

> He found he could take an average reporter from the daily press, give him a "line to follow, a trust to fight, a vice to expose—this was all in the good time when people were eager to read about their own wickedness—and in two years the reporter would be recognized as an authority . . .[78]

By 1912, muckraking was on the way out.[79] The primary cause was simply reader apathy; the novelty factor had worn off. But it is also the case that pure muckraking can be as degrading as the muck itself. And as prosperity headed toward the Roaring Twenties, people did not want to concern themselves with reports that life might not be as grand as they expected. Yet one thing the public understood even if it didn't want to pay attention: the owners of the press, as egocentric and rich as they might be, were deeply committed to improving the lives of ordinary Americans. No less an observer than the former president of Harvard University, Charles William Eliot, pronounced a grateful and measured judgment in 1923. The newspapers, he wrote, may be "as yet very imperfect instruments, much of their work being done so hastily and so cheaply as to preclude accuracy; but as a means of publicity they visibly improve from decade to decade and, taken together with the magazines and the controversial pamphlet, they shed more light on the social, industrial, and political life of the people of the United States than was ever shed before on the doings and ways of any people. This force is distinctly new within the century, and it affords a new and strong guarantee for the American Republic."[80]

By the 1920s, the tradition of public service in journalism, of which the muckrakers had been only the most flamboyant expression, found its twentieth-century embodiment in a new generation of owner-editors, and especially Henry Luce, the son of a Presbyterian missionary. Other men, like Roy Howard, of United Press International and the Scripps-

Howard organization, Eugene Pulliam of Indiana and Colonel Mc-
Cormick in Chicago and independent newspaper owner-operators all
over the nation, were combining capitalistic pride and accomplishment
with a sense of national duty and honor. Luce, however, personified the
culture. For almost fifty years, he dominated not just American but global
journalism. At his death in 1967, *Newsweek,* his most ardent competitor,
said he had "infused all of U.S. journalism with a new sense of drive, . . .
[and] transformed the art and practice of news writing—not only in
America, but in just about every other nation on the globe as well." West
Germany's *Der Spiegel,* France's *Express,* even *The New York Times*'s Sunday "Week in Review," could trace their origins to Luce's influence. His
legendary intellectual restlessness and furnacelike energy launched not
just *Time* but brilliant new coverage of business (*Fortune*), picture journalism (*Life*) and after World War II sophisticated sports coverage (*Sports
Illustrated*). In 1923 his newsmagazine proclaimed at the outset its conviction that "complete neutrality on public questions and important news
is probably as undesirable as it is impossible." Bias was acknowledged.
Journalism should bear the personal stamp of its creators. Shamelessly.
Openly. Happily. Luce's initial credo for *Time* included:

- A prejudice against the rising cost of government.
- Faith in the things which money cannot buy.
- A respect for the old, particularly in manners.
- An interest in the new, particularly in ideas.
- "To keep men well-informed"—that, first and last, is the only axe this
  magazine has to grind.[81]

To some extent, Luce's candor about his biases reflected what everyone already knew (or suspected) about his predecessors in publishing.[82]
Newspaper owners of the nineteenth and early twentieth century had had
no reluctance to fill their news columns with personal viewpoint, even
caprice or pique. Hearst once became so angry at Stanford University that
he banned the use of its name in the *San Francisco Examiner.* Instead, the

newspaper reported on football games by referring to "the boys from Palo Alto." Similarly, Colonel McCormick once ordered his *Chicago Tribune* staff to remove Rhode Island from maps because it had passed horse-racing legislation.[83] The public sensed this vanity. It also sensed that men of the caliber of Colonel McCormick and Mr. Hearst were leaving a lot on the table for others.

Luce's forthrightness about his passions was nearly endearing. "I am a Protestant, a Republican and a free-enterpriser," he said in Paris in the 1950s, "which means I am biased in favor of God, Eisenhower, and the stockholders of Time, Inc., and if anyone who objects doesn't know this by now, why the hell are they still spending 35 cents for the magazine." One of his close associates for twelve years at Time, Inc., Emmet John Hughes, described him as "a fiercely American zealot, a truly American intellectual" who was charged [by liberal critics] "with behavior unbecoming a disinterested journalist."[84] His causes, "governed by a reigning reliance on intuition,"[85] spanned the ideological spectrum from the Marshall Plan and the United Nations to the fight against McCarthyism and the struggle for civil rights. His biographer termed him, somewhat deprecatingly, "the world's most powerful unacknowledged political propagandist."[86] But his influence on American journalism can hardly be overstated. Even the acidic Gore Vidal, who as recently as 1997 declared that he had been "fictionalized" in *Time*'s "giggly pages," concluded reluctantly: "*Time* set, alas, the tone for most journalism since [the 1920s]. The malice was unremitting, the humor merry as an open grave."[87]

So much was made of the inventive writing style that Luce brought to journalism that his impact upon the public's awareness of journalism has been overshadowed. Envious critics likened *Time* sentences to "railway accidents." Luce's ongoing testy rivalry with Harold Ross of *The New Yorker* contributed to the myopia. A devastating parody of *Time*-style in 1936 by Wolcott Gibbs spoofed Luce's use of the Homeric inversion: "Backward ran sentences until reeled the mind," giggled Ross and Gibbs. "Where it all will end, knows God." When Luce angrily complained to Ross about a proof of the parody he had been permitted to see, Ross told him with sly reference to a *Time* phrase he most despised, "that is what you get for being a *baby tycoon.*"

In retrospect, Luce symbolized the acme of public confidence in the media. Eventually, the man of ideas lost. The tycoon won. Three decades after his death, Luce would recognize only the publishing segment of the media conglomerate Time Warner. With cable systems, movie studios, and a huge music recording business, the successor to Luce's print operations now competes for the title of "world's largest media-entertainment company." (It rivals Disney, depending on which corporate acquisition shareholders and the federal government are approving most currently.)

Luce's successor as chief executive officer of the sprawling corporation would probably be glad to be called a "baby tycoon." He has been called far worse. Despite having devoted a lifetime career to developing a twenty-first-century destiny for Time, Inc., despite a track record of stunning accomplishments that include designing HBO's success, the merger with Warner Communications itself, and an enormously complicated deal integrating irrepressible Ted Turner and CNN into his company, Gerald Levin has had a hard time gaining respect. Time, Inc.'s longtime editor-in-chief in the 1970s and 1980s, Henry Grunwald, describes him as "thoughtful" but "ostentatiously calm, with a sense of humor so understated that it was apt to be invisible and a mustache that gave him the air of wearing a disguise."[88] And that's a comment from a colleague. Outside the Time-Life building, journalists and media analysts have watched and reported his every move as if he were the ruler of a country far more important than Pakistan or Austria, and have been incessantly critical. Until the bull market of 1997 and 1998 carried Time Warner's stock price into new heights, Wall Street mavens had not been happy with him; he had not made Time Warner stock sizzle during the seven years following the Warner merger when the Dow Jones average was rising more than 50 percent. The reviews he drew from business writers were harsh. An uncomplimentary fourteen-page dissection of him by Connie Bruck published in *The New Yorker* in 1996 described him as making "moves worthy of the most ruthless corporate infighter, seemingly designed to bolster his position, and . . . preserve his job, at any cost." He has "presided over the rank destabilization of Warner Music" (a music industry consultant is quoted as saying, "What happened in Music was a clear example of Jerry's lack of vision, weak people skills and unwillingness to make hard choices"). He trades on an "image of impotence," an investment banker "who knows him well" adds. (Who *are* these investment bankers? They prosper from deals and then anonymously bash their benefactors.) He is guilty of "gracelessness." And since, "for all his intelligence," he is not "charismatic and larger-than-life" like the late Steve Ross, the founder of Warner and former CEO of Time Warner (about whom Bruck has written an admiring biography), the company has "suffered from a great absence at its core."[89]

Whew! Aren't we glad he makes the big bucks? He deserves them. In his day, Henry Luce was no stranger to caustic criticism. Literary critic Edmund Wilson wrote in 1943 that "the competence of presentation [in *Time*] tends to mask the ineptitude and the cynicism of the mentality behind the report."[90] Winston Churchill's son, Randolph, wrote to Luce, "What is the point of being rich and powerful if you can't tell the truth?"[91] Yet, even when Luce or his handiwork (it was usually the latter) was being attacked most severely, there was nothing like the regular public (and usually personal) thrashing delivered to Jerry Levin. His chief offense, it seems, is that portfolio managers were displeased with Time Warner's stock performance.

What does the public see and think about all this? What else can they think except to know quite confidently that however Jerry Levin might want to continue the tradition of public service epitomized by Henry Luce, our pension fund managers couldn't care less. Wall Street won't give Levin or his company high marks and higher multiples unless they can perceive a commercial benefit (rather than just cost) flowing from public service journalism. But the most compelling business reason for Time Warner and other communications companies to nurture their public service traditions is that the public believes, quite firmly and not irrationally, that today's news media has abandoned that which it once held dear. This is the most basic cause for the rising tide of anger rushing over the media's breakwalls. The public believes that too few owners of communications companies—be they public or private—are devoting enough time, talent and money to the task of improving America. The gulf between the public and the media is not caused by mere sensationalism or overzealous muckraking. The true causes are more disturbing and curable only by the owners of the media, which, to a large extent, is us.

3

Dan Quayle Meet Hillary Clinton

Right after sensationalism, "bias" is the most widespread complaint leveled at the media. Conservatives attack the media as liberal elitists; liberals find the news timid, statist and too easy on Ronald Reagan and Rush Limbaugh. In recent years, there is no public figure whose treatment better reflects the real "bias" that pervades the media than the former Vice President of the United States of America, Dan Quayle.

Quayle is signing copies of the second book he has written since leaving Washington this sunny June morning in a middle-class neighborhood of Charlotte. The line out the door of the Little Professor bookstore stretches down the sidewalk of the old Park Road shopping center.

"It's hard writing a book," he tells me, echoing a familiar author's complaint but noting analytically (and modestly) that his second work, *The American Family* (co-authored by Diane Medved), is mostly "just reporting." His first book, *Standing Firm,* a personal assessment of the pain and politics of his vice presidency, was tougher to write. Playfully, he has teased George Bush about his 2 to 0 advantage over the former President in the competition for published books. Poor Bush. Surrounded by authors—his wife, his Vice President. Even Marilyn Quayle has written two novels. He'll catch up. After the publication of his foreign policy book (written with his national security adviser, General Brent Scowcroft), he plans (with Jean Becker) an evocative book of his letters to friends over the years.

If you wanted to have some fun at Quayle's expense, or if you wanted to reinforce a worldview of Dan Quayle, you could seize on the name of the Little Professor bookstore or his installation behind a table at the rear of the store under a huge sign denominating the "Children's Books" section. But to be fair, the children's section is the only open location in the bookstore that can accommodate celebrity-author signings. And there is a nice feeling to this event—something more than the usual polite bookstore decorum.

These people like Dan Quayle. You can feel it in their warmth, see it in patient smiles as they wait in line, hear it in their conversations with him. They are a wildly diverse bunch, yet unified by friendliness. The faithful, of course, are here. But so are the curious, mothers with children, and the ever-hopeful ("I'm seventy-four years old, ride a motorcycle and hope you'll run for President in 2000"). Many encourage him. "You're adored in our community," says a thirty-something man who asks Quayle to sign five copies of *The American Family.* "I saw you on a morning show last week, when they tried to get you to criticize Madonna. You held the line beautifully. I was very proud of you," says an attractive fortyish woman, beaming. (During a promotional appearance on CBS's *This Morning* arranged by his book publisher, Quayle had artfully refrained from dumping on the pop star for having a child out of wedlock, even though Peter Van Sandt had pressed him to do so. "Madonna should read my book," he had said, grinning.)

"I'll knock on doors for you, Dan," a businessman exclaims.

"Give him five, Evan," a mother urges the African-American five-year-old in her arms, and Evan and the Vice President enthusiastically smack hands.

"We've got a one-fifty tee time and are looking for a fourth," a man with an impish smile in a dark gray suit suggests.

"Where are you playing?" Quayle banters while he inscribes, as requested, "To Bill: Keep the backswing low and slow."

"Raintree."

Quayle nods approvingly and then groans, "I *may* get to play later this week . . . *maybe*." Busy schedule. Book tour. Jay Leno next week. A trip to China in the autumn. Campaign America, the Republican policy and fund-raising organization he heads for the candidate, Bob Dole, that he might have been. Political speeches, paid speeches, graduation speeches. He and Marilyn have just given a joint speech at their eldest son's commencement from Lehigh University. He told the graduates, "Success is measured, not by what you get, but by what you give." Marilyn set the stage for this thought by referring to the perception of Washington as "an alien place, full of tall monuments and taller egos—a city of hot air, pointing fingers, and manufactured controversies. If that feeling is allowed to grow," she says with the poignancy that flows from their personal experience in the federal city, "it becomes all too easy to turn inward, to take refuge in the storm cellar of self-absorption, or to measure life in purely material terms. You know—a pool in the backyard—a Ferrari."

"Lehigh has prepared you for something better," says the father. "Society's highest values are not calculated in dollars and cents."

Near the end of the long line at the bookstore, a handsome young man in a blue shirt, gray slacks and quiet tie offers Quayle a book to sign and says unabashedly, "Thanks for being public about your faith in God and Christ." Other than one other college-age man who asks Quayle to sign his Bible (as well as his copy of Quayle's book), there is little evidence here of Quayle's following among devout Christians. It is obvious, however, that most of the ordinary, good people who have come out to the Little Professor simply like Dan Quayle because they sense that he is decent and hardworking. He is one of them. "We appreciate your moral standards, Dan," a man tells him.

Quayle's response to all these proffered compliments and loyalty is interesting. Certainly, he is a grizzled veteran of the receiving line, the autograph line and the photo opportunity line. ("Get your picture taken with the Vice President" seems to have become the centerpiece of choice for most public events involving our second-in-command, be it Quayle or Gore, although most grin-and-grippers forget to remove their convention badges when their Kodak moment with the big guy arrives.) So Quayle knows how to move these assembly lines along with maximum efficiency and minimum wear and tear on the machine (him). While there is gracefulness, there is precious little graciousness. Quayle uses the situational requirements (300 more people in line—only ninety minutes left) to reasonable advantage. But he doesn't seem to either bask in the steady adoration of these people or ooze false charm. There's no Nelson Rockefeller wink or arm squeeze, no Nixonian palaver and feigned bonhomie, no Reaganesque amiability and aw-shucks, "don't embarrass me" gratitude. Mostly, he is a bit brusque. He has long been somewhat abrupt conversationally, but what is noteworthy is that he does not especially "milk" or exploit the people who have come to touch him. Perhaps, it is his Scottish heritage that accounts for what might be neutrally termed a professional reserve, a coolness more effective on television than in person. Or it could be that he is determined to shed the boyish effusiveness that generated excesses like his first public appearance at the Republican National Convention in New Orleans after his selection as Bush's running mate. On that occasion, in his own words, he "looked like the guy on the game show who'd just won the Oldsmobile."[1] Whatever the reason, Quayle chooses not to engage in the forced intimacy that robs politicians of their dignity just as it also makes devotees out of those laser-beamed by a magic moment.

In fact, you could watch Dan Quayle interact with people all morning at the Little Professor and detect virtually no basis for the caricature that has been drawn about him by the American media. Instinctively, the public knows this: Dan Quayle is so much better than the dumb stick figure manufactured for popular consumption and ridicule. Nothing has been more destructive of the bonds of faith between the press and the public during the last quarter century than our unspoken understanding that the media create myths about public figures in order to improve the drama of our public life. Thus, Dan Quayle became a shallow cipher—a self-described "wealthy, lucky, good-looking WASP, an avid golfer, who'd never done any harder work than cashing his trust fund checks at the bank."[2] If you dislike the things he or the Republicans stand for, you can believe in the myth. It has been conveniently created for your viewing and political pleasure. But just because some of us wanted to typecast Dan Quayle doesn't mean he actually is like that.

The origin of his caricature actually predates the 1988 presidential campaign. Quayle had already served two years in the House of Representatives when a *Washington Post* "Style" section writer, Elisabeth Bumiller, delivered his real "Welcome to Washington" in January 1981. In a lengthy profile entitled "The Charmed Life of Indiana's Golden Boy; Dan Quayle's Easy Passage to the Senate," Bumiller established the typecasting that would shadow him for eight years in the Senate and emerge into full sunshine on a stage in New Orleans in 1988. A clever wordsmith, Bumiller portrayed the new thirty-three-year-old senator as too good-looking ("Strawberry-blond hair. Blue eyes. Cute"), a Robert Redford look-alike who defeated Birch Bayh, the powerful and popular (especially in Washington) liberal on the basis of his "rosy cheeks" and "charm" even though critics called him a "lazy and ineffectual congressman" and "beyond a doubt the shallowest person ever to come out of Indiana." Perhaps the most devastating aspect of the piece was its organizational use of Quayle's athletic interests—jogging, tennis, golf—to provide a progression toward an inevitable conclusion: he is "part of the 'wet hair' crowd—one of those who spend a good deal of time in the House showers." Bumiller's penknife carved an indelible impression that Washingtonians could sneer at and scorn: the handsome, empty-headed, rich jock who had had everything easy. "Life has been very good to me," he is quoted as saying. "I never had to worry about where I was going to go. But I do say, 'Dan, you know, sometime in life there's going to be a tragedy.'" Years later, you cannot read that line and the "Style" section profile without feeling that at least one tragedy was opening the door to Ms. Bumiller. Another one was looming ahead.

Quayle himself does not trace the manufacturing of the myth to the "Style" section article or the resentment that can naturally attach to golden boys. Instead, he attributes the problem to his "surprise" selection for the Republican ticket in 1988. "The media doesn't like surprises," he says and, worse, "they didn't know me." Media leaders, he believes, couldn't accept the fact that someone who had not been to their houses for dinner could be the vice presidential nominee. Logistically, he also blames the Bush campaign organization for not being prepared to define him to the national media in the critical few days following Bush's announcement. ("They had no national campaign experience," he spits in disgust even today. "They were so unprepared they were handing out to the media the description of me in Michael Barone's *Almanac of American Politics* which, while accurate, is not the full story the campaign should have been telling.") Once the void was filled by the media—with the National Guard story used as just another example of a privileged, pampered life, "there was no interest" in changing a theme that the media was firmly invested in and committed to. Quayle is adamant that there was "just no way" he could have done anything to change the image or debunk the myth while he was Vice President.[3] That may be an overstatement, but there is no doubt that his role as loyal lieutenant to President Bush restricted opportunities to redefine himself. And there is overwhelming evidence that the myth, once established in the popular culture and reinforced with regular Carson/Letterman/Leno jokes and periodic tidbits of "news," was powerfully ensconced.

The myth was so resistant to change that when two of Washington's most respected reporters, Bob Woodward and David Broder, wrote a 37,000-word, seven-part series on Quayle, "The President's Understudy,"[4] all hell broke loose. Interviews with more than "200-plus people" and six months of reporting "revealed," the article said, "a more complex and resourceful politician than the comic-strip caricature." The idea for the series had grown out of Woodward's research for *The Commanders,* his book on the Gulf War. He had learned from countless conversations with White House insiders that Quayle had been in most of the critical meetings during the war and that his judgment and advice had been influential. Woodward and Broder's new, unprecedented scrutiny of Quayle found him, factually, to be so much better than the conventional wisdom that it jolted official Washington, including the journalism community. The series described him as fundamentally decent, even-tempered, optimistic, tolerant, hardworking, steady under pressure, a conscientious parent, a valued Vice President and an employer of talented aides of "exceptional academic credentials." David Rockefeller praised him for his skills on a Latin American trip. A pol termed him "a young Ronald Reagan." William T. Esrey, chairman of US Sprint, and Donald B. Marron, chairman of PaineWebber, Inc., bestowed the bottom line of the tough-minded corporate community: "We've talked among ourselves," said Marron, "and I think everyone [is] really impressed. All these things you hear about him don't match up to the reality."

Quayle himself remembers the series being "not all that great," in part because one article cast Marilyn as the "hard half" of the Quayle partnership and because of its backhanded remark that "six months of reporting . . . did not dispel the impression that this former C- student is a man of average gifts." But if Quayle didn't like the series because it wasn't favorable enough, journalists hated it because it was too favorable. Woodward's reputation as a prodigious reporter of fact and Broder's trademark for fairness and insightfulness made the series virtually impossible to dismiss. One lengthy sidebar examined "Quayle's Reputation v. The Record" and concluded that "some serious charges made against [him]—including allegations of academic failure, manipulation of National Guard rules and descriptions of vast wealth, appear to be false." What had to be particularly galling to the media was Woodward and Broder's blunt statement that the lasting damage to Quayle's reputation essentially grew out of the "sloppiness of some of the early reporting" as well as "attempts by political opponents to discredit him" and his own "failure to be forthright" early on. Faced with the facts, much of the journalistic community—in Washington and elsewhere—nonetheless entered a high state of denial. Woodward and Broder were just trying to "suck up" to the Bush administration, it was said. Why these two heroes of journalism needed or wanted to go "into the tank" was not explained. The pervasive criticism of the series—

Washington Post chairman Katharine Graham was said to have told David Broder, "My friends don't like these stories"—only proved the immutable power of the myth. By the time he was running for President in 1999, the *Post* was reporting that Quayle "doesn't see himself as others see him." In a front-page, April 14, 1999, "curtain-raiser" on the kickoff of his campaign, the newspaper reiterated the myth (in case anyone had forgotten): "Dan Quayle, the human punch line . . . shoo-in for the late night talk show Hall of Fame—enshrined somewhere between Joey Buttafucco and Kato Kaelin." He "no longer has the air of a fading frat boy," having "aged into an almost unbelievably handsome man." Veteran *Post* reporter David Von Drehle concluded, "[I]f passing fifty were like this for all men, there would be no more market for red convertibles."

It is ironic, of course, that the public official clobbered most completely by media mythmaking is himself a son of journalism. To be sure, there have been other victims. Gerald Ford, probably our most athletically gifted President of the twentieth century, was stereotyped on the basis of a few mishaps as a "klutz," a clod who fell down stairs and endangered lives with his golf shots. Similarly, some reporters liked to depict Ronald Reagan—in Clark Clifford's words—as an "amiable dunce," when it was clear that he was smart and shrewd enough to become one of the most successful—and well-liked—political figures of his times. Yet it has been the grandson of Eugene C. Pulliam, newspaper baron and founder of what is today the largest and oldest organization of journalists in the country, who has suffered most at the hands of the mythmaking machine. While his family's company, Central Newspapers, Inc., publishers of the dominant newspapers in Arizona and Indiana, generously and quietly endowed the Sigma Delta Chi Foundation, Quayle has unobtrusively fought for First Amendment values and the public's right to an open government. As a junior senator in the early 1980s, he bucked his party's leadership to oppose efforts of the Reagan administration and the Republican-controlled Senate to gut the Freedom of Information Act (FOIA), the law that guarantees public access to government records except those shielded by specific exemptions such as national security or privacy interests. On one occasion, when liberals like senators Kennedy and Dodd were unwilling to assist press groups and the American Civil Liberties Union, which were opposing the amendments to FOIA, Quayle stood up on the Senate floor and put a personal "hold" on a bill that was greased for bipartisan passage. As supporters of the bill—from the White House to FBI Director William Webster, the U.S. Chamber of Commerce and the powerful chairman of the Senate Labor and Human Resources Committee on which Quayle sat, Senator Orrin Hatch—rained a firestorm of protest on his head, Quayle coolly met with the press groups to plot strategy. With the time provided by Quayle's "hold" on the bill, the amendments were killed.

This is the famous Quayle scrappiness. Dan the dogged competitor. When Barry Goldwater once termed him as stubborn as his grandfather, he "took it as a compliment." He personifies the adage "When the going gets tough, the tough get going."[5] In *Standing Firm,* he wrote, "Throughout my life, I've loved beating the odds." Small and late to develop, he found it difficult to play sports as a youth, "but most of the time I'd work my way from the bench to the starting team."[6]

It is probably his scrappy nature, especially as applied to politics, that accounts for his lack of sympathy for another White House victim of media mythmaking—Hillary Clinton. "I really don't know her," he says with a shrug. He should. They have so much in common.

Hillary Clinton. The shrew. The arrogant, manipulative, socialist Lady Macbeth. The dirty-mouthed lamp thrower. The cold, hard business partner of the philanderer. She's left other negative stereotypes of First Ladies in the rearview mirror. However steely the magnolias framing Rosalynn Carter, there was a soft Southern fragrance. Whatever the cost of the new White House china or the de la Rentas, Nancy Reagan was simply standing by her man. But despite the indisputable reality that Hillary Rodham Clinton is a dutiful mother, a bright, disciplined politician, the family executive and generally a lovely woman whose kindness and strength radiate from an open face, she is treated as the Bitch on Wheels.

There is, in fact, no basis for the myth at all. The two most penetrating books about the Clintons contain no support for the caricature and only a few clues about its origin. David Maraniss' biography of Bill Clinton, *First in His Class,* describes a woman "evenly matched" with her mate. "From the opening round of courtship," he writes, as if romance among baby boomers were a boxing event (and for many it has been), there was a "fair fight" between "two strong-willed personalities."[7] Their partnership was "intellectually invigorating," but "their personal relationship stormy."[8] Arkansas aides and drivers talk about heated arguments between a man who could be hot-tempered and impulsive and a woman who handed it back rather than just taking it. What does all this realistically tell us about a bright, purposeful Wellesley graduate who grew to middle age at a time when gender roles were in flux and the divorce rates among her classmates were heading skyward faster than a flying teapot? (At reunion dinners of one class of Yale Law graduates, a bit older than the Clintons, they ask the first wives to stand up; they can now be counted on one hand.) The Clintons argue. Big deal. They argued more vehemently when they were in their twenties or when he was philandering. How surprising. Is this much different than any other marriage confronted with similar strains and stresses? Isn't it self-evident that the arguments have kept them together and the angry words inevitably deepened a loving relationship? Friends who have known them for decades, and who observe them today quietly holding hands while reading, believe they have reached a comfortable equilibrium. They have overcome the competitiveness and self-absorption that have afflicted their generation's relationships. In private, Hillary Clinton is warm, funny, self-deprecating. "I've never heard her curse, never seen a temper tantrum," says one intimate friend. "If she's mad at you, she'll just give you a cold look." Another friend who has kept company with political figures and celebrities for several decades says, with a baffled tone, "There is a greater disparity between what she is actually like and her public image than any other public person I have ever known." When James Stewart, the author of *Blood Sport: The President and His Adversaries,* visited the White House to see her for the first time, he found, "as many people had told me," a woman "much more attractive in person than on television or in pictures. She had a vitality, a liveliness that I hadn't anticipated."[9] No doubt partisan distortion and a multimillion-dollar negative advertising campaign during the health care debate contributed to the formation of a false image, but so has the limitation of the camera lens. It does not capture the fullness of Hillary Clinton in the way that it presents, quite accurately, and rather completely, the many dimensions of her husband. The camera not only does not adore her, it bathes her in unsympathetic lights. We see her edges, her drive, hear her intelligence as lawyerlike and brittle. Her self-confidence becomes irritating, not inspiring. A definitional article in *The New Yorker* on May 30, 1994, entitled "Hillary the Pol," by Connie Bruck concluded that her "cardinal trait" was probably "her sureness about her own judgment—at its extreme, a sense that she alone is wise." What some might perceive as admirable incisiveness is instead seen as "intensely insular and unbending." It had to generate a "strain" on Bill Clinton "of living with such absolutism."[10]

With the publication in 1996 of *Primary Colors* by Anonymous (Joe Klein), the fictionalization of Mrs. Clinton entered a new dimension. Now, in addition to political adversaries, antifeminists and accomplices in the media painting an ugly portrait of her, we have a best-selling book and later a Mike Nichols film that purports to be drawn from real-life experiences in the Clinton campaign of 1992. Except, of course, the book is a novel and, for dramatic effect, it fictionalizes situations and characters. Joe Klein is no admirer of Mrs. Clinton. She is depicted as a cussing, scheming witch. Many people who have either read or heard of the novel now accept, as a truism, that Mrs. Clinton is actually exactly like Mrs. Jack Stanton, a garbage-mouth harpy. Emma Thompson's lines were somewhat more flattering, but at last, fiction has been used to define the character of our public leaders.

Like the Quayle myth, the power behind the Hillary myth defies easy explanation. "It is a fundamental mystery," says Ruth Marcus, who covered the White House for *The Washington Post* during the first Clinton administration. The durability of the myth is certainly tied in some ways to our complicated attitudes toward changing gender roles. There is another element, however, an unwillingness to accept her at face value, a deeply cynical suspiciousness that blocks us from knowing her. "She's so warm, so engaged especially with children and women's groups when she's out on the road," says Ann McFeatters, the longtime White House correspondent for Scripps-Howard. "It's peculiar" that people don't accept the simple fact that she obviously loves children. It goes beyond political necessity. She worked with the Children's Defense Fund and other groups which help children long before she arrived on the national scene. Friends believe that it is a source of some personal sorrow that she was able to conceive and give birth to only one child. "It doesn't rip her apart, or anything like that," says a woman who has an only child herself and has known Hillary well for two decades. She's not built like that. But is it one of life's greater disappointments for her? Of course."

In 1996, with Chelsea turning sixteen and leaving for college soon after the reelection campaign, Hillary began, rather naturally, to grow wistful on the subject. In an unguarded moment during an interview with *Time* managing editor Walter Isaacson, some vulnerability showed. She spoke candidly and, for a political wife, perhaps too offhandedly about wanting another child. The full text of the interview, published in the June 3, 1996, edition as the uneventful and predictable presidential reelection campaign snored along as it had all year, makes it apparent that she and the President were not seriously considering adoption, just "talking about it" as any similarly situated couple might.

TIME: You've had trouble having kids. Have you ever considered adoption?

Mrs. Clinton: Well, we have talked about it. I must say we're hoping that we have another child.

TIME: Are you still hoping you'll have a second child?

Mrs. Clinton: (Laughing) I have to tell you I would be surprised but not disappointed. My friends would be appalled, I'm sure. But I think it would be terrific.

TIME: So are you considering adoption?

Mrs. Clinton: We continue to talk about it. Because we really believe in adoption, and I have worked hard to promote adoption, particularly for older kids and across racial lines and kids with special needs. We'd have to think hard, especially if it were an older child, about the pressures of the White House on a child like that. We've thought about it.

TIME: What has been your involvement with adoption legislation?

Mrs. Clinton: [answer]

TIME: When did the two of you start considering adopting?

Mrs. Clinton: Well, "considering" may be too strong. I think "talking about" it . . . We have, off and on, for a long time.

TIME: Are you talking about it more now?

Mrs. Clinton: Yeah, I think we're talking about it more now. We'd obviously wait to get serious about it until after the election. There's just too much going on in our lives right now. I just think that giving a child a chance and sharing what you have with a child is one of the greatest gifts you can give yourself, as well as a child. So I hope that something will come of our thinking about it.

TIME: Might you do a cross-racial adoption?

Mrs. Clinton: We haven't gone into that kind of detail.[11]

The ridicule came fast. A column by Mona Charen published in many newspapers, including the *St. Louis Post-Dispatch,* was ruthless but typical: "Here we go again. Mrs. Clinton is playing the femininity card. Whenever she thinks it may be politically useful, this tough, combative woman drapes herself in the mantle of femininity—or at least the kind of femininity she imagines the great unwashed prefer."[12] Larry Sabato, the University of Virginia political scientist often called the "walking sound bite" for his quick draw in the quote-slinging business, summed up the conventional political take on the *Time* interview. "Bill and Hillary Clinton are quintessential politicians. No decision is made without considering the political implications of it. . . . Just talking about [adoption] is a political plus."[13] Mrs. Clinton and her staff were stung. She couldn't win.

Reveal a few honest thoughts and you're painted a calculating schemer just trying to "drape" yourself in kids for political advantage. "She goes bland on you pretty fast," a writer for *Esquire* once told me after an interview with Hillary Clinton. Is it any wonder? Either you stay within your shell, "on message" and disciplined, or you get hurt. They may be our public figures and we may read and listen to millions of words about them, but we don't know them at all.

How can we be certain that the portraits of Hillary the Shrew or Dan the Dumb are myths? Common sense. Facts. Both have given us lives of dedicated public service and substantial achievement not possible from human beings consumed by rage or devoid of wits. But even if one is not disposed to give Hillary or Dan the benefit of the doubt, there is so little evidence actually supporting the basis for either myth that one should be (but we are not) embarrassed to repeat it. We embrace and protect our entrenched stereotypes so fervently, is it any wonder that the media finds opportunities to explain public life to us in terms we not only understand but treasure.

Where does the mythmaking come from? What sustains it? Conservatives like Quayle have long attributed their problems to ideological bias among reporters. "The media do not lean our way," said Bob Dole in departing the Senate to run for the presidency. "Name one major White House correspondent that happens to be pro-life," challenges Quayle. "None are. There's no ideological diversity in the national news media. I don't know what you can do about it. How do you encourage bright young conservatives to enter journalism when they see the deck will be stacked against them? They believe that editors, given a choice, will promote people who think like they do." In 1996, conservatives howled with "we told you so" glee when the prestigious, nonpartisan Freedom Forum released a survey indicating that almost 90 percent of Washington-based bureau chiefs and congressional correspondents had voted for Clinton-Gore and 87 percent classified themselves as either Democrat (50 percent) or independent (37 percent). Asked to characterize their political orientation, 61 percent chose "liberal" or "liberal to moderate," with another 30 percent selecting "moderate." Only 9 percent chose "conserv-ative" or "moderate to conservative." People could quibble with the sur-vey methodology—it was a self-administered mailed questionnaire returned by 139 journalists (out of a total population of 323).[14]

Yet the results according to the Roper Center, which helped design the survey, had a "maximum sampling error of +2.8% at the 95% level of confidence." No one can seriously doubt that journalism draws from a pool that is more receptive to change, less tradition-bound and more tem-peramentally sympathetic to progressive causes and candidates. And to some degree—obviously variable depending on the reporter—personal agenda or orientation slips into news stories. If it were not so, newsrooms would not be aggressively recruiting minorities in order to bring a di-versity of viewpoint to their product. Admitting that the search for objec-tivity is aspirational, rather than consistently achievable, however, does not mean, as many believe, that there is rampant unprofessionalism and hopeless liberal bias infecting American journalism. The opposite is actually true, particularly in an era of unprecedented media self-criticism and self-examination. Journalism conferences are regularly filled with intense ses-sions on ethics and professional standards, and the major journalism organizations have virtual standing committees constantly reexamining their codes of ethics. Meetings of these committees can sometimes look like Cotton Mather collaborating with Church Lady, the Dana Carvey character from *Saturday Night Live,* as one sanctimonious defender of rec-titude one-ups another. Faces are permanently fixed in scowls. A profes-sional misstep earns a rebuke in *Brill's Content* or a journalism review.

Bias alone cannot account for the power behind the media's role in mythmaking. It is deeper than that, and more symbiotic. The public plays a part as well. When he is philosophical, Dan Quayle sees this: "Maybe it is just part of the coarseness of American society and culture nowadays. More and more there are haters out there. And they're loud. It comes through on television news: 'We're going to get him; we can't stand him.' It comes from our loss of civility."

This theme Quayle also shares with Mrs. Clinton. To her, the bias comes from the other end of the ideological spectrum—a cabal of right-wing zealots who conspire to infiltrate and poison the coverage of both her and her husband. The haters—the ones who relish Rush Limbaugh—they're responsible. In January 1997, the White House released a 332-page report describing the "conspiracy commerce" that conservative organizations use to place "fringe" stories about the Clintons into the mainstream media. On C-Span, just before the second inaugural, Hillary bemoaned "the character assassination and personal destruction aimed at her and others in public life." Overall, she felt the media was not biased, but from her perspective "you've got a conservative or right-wing press presence with really nothing on the other end of the political spectrum."[15] A year later, when she orchestrated the White House's tactical response to the Monica Lewinsky scandal by attributing the mess, on *Today*, to a "vast right-wing conspiracy," including independent counsel Kenneth Starr, she drew criticism for resorting to a familiar campaign-style attack mode rather than counseling full disclosure. What her critics may have missed was that her strategy was not simply tried, true and pragmatic (it successfully deflected the mounting focus on the "crisis" in her husband's presidency), it was genuinely and deeply believed. There must be *some* explanation, you could see her thinking, for this horrible treatment of us.

Whatever the vespertine sources of the hate in our American psyche, they are not a rap that can be blamed on the media. David Broder was not surprised by the public rejection of his and Bob Woodward's reporting on Dan Quayle, and Hillary Clinton shouldn't believe that the false stereotype of her would vanish if her right-wing scapegoats evaporated. Broder was not surprised by the public reaction because he had seen the skepticism among his editors in the *Post* newsroom. Broder still thinks Quayle would be a serious presidential contender, substantively. And this is a view shared by many of the most knowledgeable and savvy Republican political operatives. "We always thought he had the best political judgment of anyone in the Bush administration," says Tony Blankley, former Speaker

Newt Gingrich's longtime aide and press secretary. Broder does not, how-ever, harbor any illusions about the ability of any article—even a powerful series of articles in *The Washington Post*—to change public perceptions of Quayle. "This is the limitation of journalism," he says. An interesting phrase—realistic, but not one used often. The media usually acts as if there are no limitations on its capability to influence public opinion. Of course, this is hubris. The media's stereotyping of public figures feeds im-ages, fears and desires that are deeply ingrained in the popular culture. When we blame the media for being "biased," we forget that the report-ing is designed to appeal to us. The dramatis personae that we ask the media to dress up and trot out for our entertainment must not change or we will be forced to admit that they were fictions in the first place, in-vented mostly to confirm our daydreams.

4

The Girl from Yesterday

This the public also knows about the media: it is unfair, cruelly so at times. What the public is more reluctant to recognize is that it contributes to the unfairness. Just as we ask to be served up stereotypical myths about our political leaders, we demand that our dramas about public morality fit into familiar plots with standard characters.

Donna Rice knows the pain that comes from the public's voyeurism. She is, in the words of the song title from the Eagles' Glenn Frey, "The Girl from Yesterday." She has waited more than a decade now for the world to see her as something other than a scandal kitten whose friendship with Senator Gary Hart ended his presidential bid in 1988. She knows about the power and durability of media mythmaking, and also about being the object of the public's incessant sexual impulse. There is an interesting story here that reminds us of the cost to one woman of our careless prurient fantasies.

It is 1988 and we are headed, Donna and me, to the heartland—Cincinnati to be precise. The passengers on the late-afternoon Delta Air Lines flight from Washington National are so crowded, distracted and tired that they miss, moments before takeoff, Donna's spectacular walk down the aisle to her seat at the rear of the plane.

Too bad. If peonies came to life, one could bear her name. Lush, fragrant, silky and strong, Donna Rice is as beautiful a perennial as nature gives us.

"I have fake buckteeth to wear when I want to disguise myself," she confides once we are seated. Skeptically, I wonder why she has not used them for her glide down the aisle. Actresses, even would-be actresses like Donna, I conclude, love entrances.

"Wanna see?" she teases. Bending over and fishing in her purse, she pops back up with new teeth inserted, grinning like a mischievous eight-year-old who has just put toothpaste on the airplane's toilet seat. She has indeed transformed herself into a weed. Lord, I think, I'll never complain about the cost of orthodontic work for my daughters.

We are flying to Cincinnati to attend the annual convention of the largest and oldest organization of journalists in the nation. Other than two interviews with Barbara Walters and one with *Life* magazine, it will be Donna's first public appearance since her dates with Senator Gary Hart occasioned his withdrawal from the 1988 race for the presidency. (She does not count an ill-fated press conference for No Excuses jeans, a momentary lapse into commercial exploitation of her sudden fame which she now sees as a mistake.) Donna has decided, some seven months after the affair—er, I mean Hart's withdrawal—well, let's just say the scandal—to talk about the media coverage of the event.

"I was thinking about writing a book about the experience," she says. "I even talked to an agent, Sterling Lord. I had the title for the book already picked out: *Branded*. That's what I feel happened. I was branded." Branded a bimbo, an easy, good-time girl. To men, a real piece of ass. To women, a slut.

There is considerable evidence that she accurately perceives the mark now placed, if not on her rump, then certainly on her persona.

The week prior to this trip to Cincinnati, I have taken her to lunch at one of Washington's most glittering, power-packed restaurants. The lunch is meant to reassure her. She does not want to talk about Gary Hart or her water-slide rush to the sewer. But she is interested, earnestly, in explaining to journalists the pain, the rough treatment, the unfairness of saturation media coverage. Still timid and unsure about whether she should speak, she nevertheless wants journalists to understand how their reporting can wound. There is nobility in her willingness to take the risk. And, of course, naiveté.

As the Washington lawyer for the journalists' organization, I tell Donna, quite truthfully, that she will give journalism a generous gift if she tells her story. My colleague Henry Hoberman oozes equal amounts of sauce over the complicated cuisine. Henry is more handsome than the William Morris Agency could design, smoother than any lotion known to botany and smarter than the De Beers diamond cartel. In time, he will progress to the executive corridors of ABC. Women like Henry, I have noticed, for his intelligence, although being handsome and smooth do not hurt. Donna seems persuaded, although fully aware that the two hungry bears she is dining with want a piece of her soul for a client.

Suddenly, Bob Kincaid appears at our table. Bob is part owner and renowned chef of this destination-spot. His usual venue is the kitchen, but here he is, all sparkling, starched white, instead of sweaty and stained, ready to meet Donna. She smiles sweetly, graciously and compliments his food. Somewhere in Columbia, South Carolina, a mother aches with pride, for there has been bred, as Barbara Walters pronounced to ABC television viewers with the full voice Madame Walters reserves for her most profound and certain judgments, a "lady."

To her face, Chef Bob does not leer. But as cultivated an Irish wit and talent as he is, I harbor no doubt that his reaction in private would be about the same as the uniform reaction I get from all men when I mention that I am working with Donna Rice: shit-eating grins and elbows into the ribs. Women react differently; they scowl and move away. No one seems curious about her. They all know her, even though, factually, mystery surrounds her.

In Cincinnati, herds of journalists defy easy stereotyping by arising early for a 7:30 A.M. program, "The Right to Privacy: The Exploitation of the Human Condition," with Donna, me, Tim Gallagher, the editor of the *Albuquerque Tribune,* Paul McMasters, an editor of *USA Today,* and John Seigenthaler, a genuine journalism icon. The editors have been included on the panel to lend certifiable dignity to what might otherwise be seen as a shameless celebrity gawk. Gallagher, a rising young buck in the Scripps organization, will later write that Rice is a "strikingly attractive woman with a disarming knowledge of the media and its sins."[1] Seigenthaler is the former senior aide to Robert Kennedy and current political godfather to Al Gore (who once worked in his newsroom). He is also president of the American Society of Newspaper Editors; his jobs as editor and publisher of the *Nashville Tennessean* and editorial director of *USA Today* only hint at the pervasive influence he exercises in the American media. If things work out as planned, Donna will tell how a competitive, ubiquitous media has shattered her life, the editors will provide soft, wise voices of media reason and I'll clarify the legal perimeters of invasion of privacy. The legal rules of the road, of course, basically empower the media to report even the most intimate aspects of her life ("Come on, she toppled a presidential candidate!"), so long as in ferreting out the details reporters don't trespass, eavesdrop electronically or commit other felonies or misdemeanors.

Against the back wall of the convention center hall, lens to lens, await the camera eyes—maybe a dozen videocams and two dozen more Nikons. Their sheer volume spooks Donna. Everyone has thought that there would only be a few cameras from local media. Now she is told by an ebullient staffer for the journalists' organization: "Even *Entertainment Tonight* is here!"

After glancing at the room, Donna balks. With cameramen in hot pursuit, she retreats, racing through the convention center's hallways to her suite in the adjoining hotel. Henry Hoberman accompanies her. He will be identified in a newspaper caption the next day as her bodyguard.

In the convention center hall, I announce Donna's change of heart to the audience and read a handwritten statement she has composed hastily.

She had hoped for a thoughtful discussion, an "opportunity to quietly and candidly share with you some of my experiences and observations." When the symposium looked as if it had turned into a carnival, the main attraction quit. On the midway, after all, it is hard to hear, much less think.

The journalists are snarly. Clearly, this catastrophe could not have happened at a worse hour of the day. Bring on the Danish and sweet rolls, I signal the convention planners. But no amount of sugar and starch is likely to ameliorate the mob. "What did she expect?" some of them ask. "How naive." Not all the anger is directed at the absent speaker. Among the academics attending the convention and a few others, there is sympathy for her and condemnation of the working media. The cameramen were "rude," "too aggressive," "jackals."

"We terrify people," one reporter tells me. "They sense that given half a chance, we'll eat them alive."

"We're totally out of touch with reality," Guy Bachr, a reporter from Perth Amboy, New Jersey, will tell his fellow convention attendees. "This woman was trying to come here, after being beat up by the press for a long time because she happened to get mixed up in something that was newsworthy. . . . She was trying to approach us like a human being."

Donna Rice's flight from the speaking engagement becomes a bigger story in the next twenty-four-hour news cycle than had she spoken. (Inevitably, speculation starts that she intended to stage the drama all along. She knows, it is said, the first rule of the Jacqueline Onassis School of Media Relations: Acquiesce to the photographs but don't talk; mystery ensures coverage.) Television news is particularly ruthless. Anchors and "stand-ups" sneer, giggle and express amazement that someone could agree to address a journalists' convention and then tuck tail and run when too many cameras appear. "If you're allergic to animals, don't go to the zoo," sniffs Cincinnati broadcaster Beverly White. The judgment is confirmed: bimbo.

Eighteen months earlier, on May 5, 1987, as morning had first broken, the front page of *The New York Times* portrayed her differently.[2] Under a photograph from her modeling days that captured the tint of Southern femininity, the lead of the news article began: "Beauty, brains, talent, she had it all." Written by veteran reporter Jon Nordheimer, the article recited her Phi Beta Kappa achievements as a science major and varsity cheerleader at the University of South Carolina and her "all-American good looks." The principal of her high school was quoted: "Even if I tried to cook up something bad about her, I couldn't think of where to begin."

The barbecue came fast. Donna Rice jokes proliferated. She even had friends tell her the jokes. It served to connect her to her strange new world. By late summer, a coup de grâce was delivered by writer Gail Sheehy in a major sixteen-page article for the September issue of *Vanity Fair* entitled "The Road to Bimini."[3] Even though the "wreckage" of Hart's presidential campaign and life had stopped smoldering, the full-blown psychological study of a "pathological deficit in Hart's character" was justified because "many people fail to grasp what is really at issue here." Full-page photographs of Hart with Hollywood playboys Warren Beatty and Jack Nicholson and of Hart with Rice in his lap aboard the *Monkey Business* pleasure yacht introduced the piece. The headline announced that what Sheehy had "found" was "startling: the world of Donna Rice is much darker than it seemed, and Hart was on a collision course with it all along."

Even today, the Sheehy article seems breathtaking in its savagery. The world of Donna Rice is a "black hole," a "demimonde that thrives on the illusion that beautiful young women and drugs are effortlessly available as party favors." Sheehy is a skillful writer who weaves insinuations, fact, metaphor and quotations into stories with a powerful point of view. Thus, Donna is variously described in the piece as a "lowlife . . . a tramp," a character with no center, no concrete goal, the kind known to "knockabout guys as an 'action girl,' just drifting from party to party in a perpetual state of expectation." She was reported to have lived with a cocaine dealer, partied aboard the $70 million yacht of billionaire arms dealer Adnan Khashoggi (she was a friend of Khashoggi's daughter) and flown at Khashoggi's expense to Vegas where "the girls . . . were showered with bracelets and dresses and could always have a sniff of cocaine if they so desired."

For those who think it is dangerous to talk to journalists, Sheehy's modus operandi proves the opposite can be just as true. Donna was "not forthcoming and clearly had a manufactured story to tell." "So," without a trace of guilt, Sheehy proudly announces, "I sought out her father, who admitted his own doubts about his daughter's dubious lifestyle." This apparent scoop turns out, however, to consist of a telephone call in which the hapless Mr. Rice, badgered by the prosecutorial Ms. Sheehy regarding how his daughter supported herself in New York, wonders what information Ms. Sheehy may have had on this point. What *was* she doing in New York to make a living? "Have you got some information indicating she was a hooker?" The quotation is used in the article thusly: "All at once, Donna's father revealed his own worst fears."

But for a Christian faith that has taught her the power of forgiveness, Donna Rice would probably despise Gail Sheehy.

It is a three-hour drive from Washington, D.C., to Lexington, Virginia, the home of Washington and Lee University, and four months later, in March 1989, Donna and I are making a trip together—again. This time Dr. Louis Hodges, an ethics professor at the university where Robert E. Lee started the country's first journalism program when he retired from the military, has invited us to participate in his annual Journalism Ethics Institute. Even as we speed through the damp, brown countryside, we know the setting will be more comfortable than Cincinnati. There'll be, at most, a hundred students and faculty and a smattering of professional journalists. Ground rules have been, again, arduously negotiated. Dr. Hodges has explained to Donna that the session must be on the record since one of the institute's goals encourages the professionals in attendance to write about the sticky issues raised. No advance publicity has been trumpeted.

On campus, Donna has other ideas. She wants to read a statement

and "convey my desire that our discussion remain within the classroom."
Her statement is charming and delivered winsomely:

> It's a privilege to come before you today to share some of my experiences
> with the media. This setting is particularly attractive for me since it is an
> environment that encourages a mutual exchange of thought and discus-
> sion. It is my hope that we will learn from one another.
>
> I trust that as I speak you will understand the spirit in which I do so.
> I'm not here to change my image or justify my choices. Nor am I here to
> lecture you about the rules of journalism, of which I am no expert. I
> chose to come here in the hope that my input can add another dimen-
> sion to this discussion of privacy. Experience has been my teacher. As one
> who has been on the receiving end of negative reporting and comment,
> I think I have an unusual, though unfortunately not unique, vantage
> point. . . .
>
> I'd like to . . . lay some groundwork. First, let me emphasize that I did
> not and have not sought the attention of the press. I have only partici-
> pated in six interviews and only in those after a great deal of thought and
> painstaking deliberation.
>
> I have had lucrative offers to exploit my notoriety and be a pawn in a
> high-stakes chess game. I chose not to. I did not authorize the release of
> any photographs, much less sell them. The photographs that were sold
> reportedly brought in hundreds of thousands of dollars. My silence and
> refusal to sell my story meant that gossip and baseless charges circulated
> without rebuttal.
>
> I believe in a free press. I believe the public has a right to know. But I
> also believe the media have a measure of responsibility to use their free-
> dom with care. The press has extraordinary power to shape public opin-
> ion. When that power is used carelessly, public opinion can shatter
> private lives.
>
> The dilemma that often occurs between an individual's right to pri-
> vacy and the public's right to know is too often impacted by the press's
> demand for profit and competition within the industry. I am sure we all

recognize this as a difficult problem with no easy solutions. I simply hope that my input will point to the excesses that can and do occur.

It's hard for me just to concentrate on the issue of privacy because of the devastating pain that was caused by libel. . . . It's like being burned in two places with varying degrees of severity. I liken it to having a third-degree burn on your finger and first-degree burns on your entire leg. They both hurt, but the pain in your leg sort of keeps your attention off of the pain in your finger. However, I'll do my best to keep my focus within the realm of our topic of discussion, privacy, which I equate [with the burn] that is on my finger. . . .

Let me wrap up these opening remarks with just a few more thoughts. When tragedy strikes, there is a choice—to let it destroy a life or build character. I have chosen to respond to my personal challenges and allow my experience to count—for myself and for the benefit of others.

On a personal note:

- Family relationships have been strengthened and quality friendships savored.
- I have experienced tremendous emotional, intellectual and spiritual growth.
- I clearly understand the price of integrity and compromise.
- And forgiveness has become a way of life.

This past year I have had the opportunity to work on a voluntary basis with a nonprofit organization in McLean, Virginia, and use my skills and abilities to help others. I've found that the healing process is accelerated when you can reach out beyond yourself to help another.

This summer, I came across a poster I had on my wall as a young teenager. It was a beautiful picture of a clear mountain stream. At the bottom of the scene were the words: "If you don't understand my silence, you'll never understand my words."

That pretty well sums it up for me.

The colloquy with the audience stimulates the kind of provocative exchange that teachers fantasize about. Slowly, gently, almost effortlessly, Donna persuades the room that she simply isn't the person depicted by the media. She blames no one for covering the original story, but feels utterly exploited by the constant rehashing. What is happening, of course, is that the audience begins detecting a fuller figure than the cardboard character flashed forward by one media outlet after another to enliven a dull day or stoke a little lust. The mood of the room moves from expectation to friendliness, and a playful Donna rewards the group's warmth by showing off the buckteeth disguise—to everyone's delight. This woman could make millions on the college lecture circuit.

Someone asks a question about the controversy du jour, the brewing Senate confirmation battle over President Bush's nominee for Secretary of Defense, Senator John Tower of Texas. Now amid friends, she is no longer on guard. Donna responds with what is obviously a personal opinion that senators are focusing on some considerations that should be off-limits. Although the comment is a bit cryptic, it seems directed at reports of Tower's womanizing while he was a single man. The comment is less remarkable and certainly murkier than almost everything else she has to say.

But it is news. At a reception following the classroom discussion, we are handed a copy of an Associated Press wire story that has just been transmitted out of Richmond to the AP's New York headquarters and will be relayed to its thousands of subscribers around the globe. A dutiful AP bureau chief has called in a story that leads with her comment about the Senate's inquiry of Tower's personal life and concludes with the buckteeth episode. Sandwiched in between is a truncated condensation of a three-hour session that captures none of the tone, flavor, texture or reality of the afternoon:

> Rice said she has suffered at the hands of reporters. She said she lost everything she worked for all her life—her job, her reputation and her credibility.
>
> But she said her problems could be blamed on just a few reporters. She said most did their jobs in a professional manner.

It will not be the first or last time that the merchants of hard news have missed the real news of the day. The ride back to Washington is nonetheless happy; the day has been successful and Donna has benefited from being able to talk. She has been heard, understood, respected, accepted. The confusion over whether the session was on the record or off the record seems extraneous. (When asked explicitly during the session whether the discussion was public record or not, Dr. Hodges had said, clearly enough for an ethics professor but not unambiguously, that things were on the record but that honorable people should consider Ms. Rice's request not to be directly quoted. Associated Press president Lou Boccardi will later tell him: "Leaving the ground rules ambiguous . . . is a formula for recrimination, if not disaster. It is simply not realistic to put a group of newspeople in a room with the leading lady in something like the Hart/Rice drama and just tell those assembled that you prefer no reporting. That's not ever going to work.")

Yet this will be Donna Rice's last foray into public explanation and execution. As we barrel up the highway to a celebratory supper with her friends at Charley's in McLean, rewrite editors all over the country are devising their own versions of the Associated Press story. None will be any crueler the next morning than this item in the "Personalities" column of *The Washington Post*:

> If you see a small, slender, attractive blond with buck teeth and sunglasses, it may be none other than Donna Rice, famed shipmate of Gary Hart aboard the *Monkey Business*. Out on the speaking circuit—where she not surprisingly blames her loss of credibility, reputation and livelihood on "irresponsible reporters" and not on her famous friendship with a married man trying to be president—she said she often must wear disguises so people won't harass her. Speaking at an "Ethics of Journalism" seminar at Washington and Lee University recently, she said she has tried to stay out of the public spotlight after being "basically a fugitive for months . . . a prisoner of perception." So she won't be recognized, she pulls back her fluffy blond hair and says "I have buck teeth that I put on.

They cost me 80 bucks." She modeled her teeth along with a pair of glasses, and her audience agreed she did look different.

The judgment is confirmed: bimbo.[4]

The prominent Georgetown surgeon listens to my story about the trip to Lexington, Virginia, with feigned interest.

"Oh yes, Donna Rice. I saw her dancing with Dickie Stephens—I think it was—at a club last weekend. You know he really gets around town. But, you know, she's really just—a *girl*. She's not, em, significant."

She is married now. Donna Rice Hughes. She did not avail herself of the opportunity to ditch a name that made her a "prisoner of perception." Silly, really, quite pointless, to imagine you could hide. But she does not blame the media. At least, not principally. Intuitively, she realizes it is not just the long leer of the news that "boxes her in." It's not just the periodic dredging-up returning the silt to the surface. It's more complicated than that. People approach her today—and really always have, even before Gary Hart—with a whole set of attitudes, prejudices, fantasies and dreams. It's our baggage—the way we approach a pretty woman on any subject. The media, of course, know this luggage. They have long studied it, measured it, assayed it. They monitor it with weekly focus groups and polish their understanding of it with marketing strategies. We cannot keep it locked away inside. Nor do we really want to. How else can the media tempt us? And enchant us, seize us and convey us on to a commercial advertiser. Donna knows. It's nothing personal. She was just the fuchsia balloon of the month.

Steadily, over the last ten years, she has built credibility and a different kind of reputation, especially among anti-child-pornography advocates, by working for Enough Is Enough, a Washington-based organization that fights to protect minors from hard-core trash. "It is so hard to break out of the box people put you in," she says without whining. She doesn't let it get her down. "It's all about making choices along the way, and not fitting into people's expectations." She understands how the media will pander to people's biases and preconceived ideas about her. It's weird really how the media can work so consistently to be politically correct about minorities and careful about avoiding ethnic stereotyping, while still typecasting players in any national news drama. Newt Gingrich is "The Loser," asserts the cover of *Newsweek,* even though his resignation as Speaker of the House could be seen in a society less obsessed with winners and losers as both timely and gracious, even honorable.

The poignancy of Donna Rice's story tells us that the root causes underlying the public's deepened anger with the media have more to do with our own foibles and dissatisfactions as a people than with platitudes about media "sensationalism" or "bias." True, there are journalists with agendas, and wire services need to reduce nuance to hardened headlines. But that has always been so. There is no more "sensationalism" or "bias" in the media today than there ever was, and, indeed, the professionalization of journalism since World War II has brought greater awareness of both of these occupational hazards and enough hand-wringing to have actually produced some demonstrable moments of self-restraint. "I do not think that bias is a big problem in America's newspapers. I think there are biased reporters; I think there are crooked lawyers," says David Hall, former editor of the Cleveland *Plain Dealer* and other newspapers.[5] The media's need to feed our appetites, reflect our biases and fabricate easily understandable myths has intensified but not changed much either. What has changed, and the public clearly detects this even if it cannot properly label it, is the fading perception that the media have a higher role to play in American life than simply "business." In earlier decades of the twentieth century, the missionary zeal of media leaders could not be mistaken. Nowadays, the public suspects that they are only driven by capitalistic ardor. What else could account for the superficiality of the news? "Readers in city after city consider it 'biased' when a reporter approaches a subject without a deep and comprehensive knowledge of the topic," says Robert H. Giles of the Media Studies Center in New York, who runs the Free Press/Fair Press initiative of the Freedom Forum. Clearly, more dollars devoted to depth could help. "My station could be called WEPS—Earnings Per Share," moans a television news director in Dallas. He is confident the public senses the truth. "All we brag about is ratings and our EBITDA" (earnings before interest, taxes, depreciation, amortization). It is time to boast about something else—public service. And for CEOs of media companies to spend at least as much time talking about the value of journalism's work as they spend talking to investment analysts and portfolio managers. Unless they do so, there is no reason to believe the public will be inclined to grant them protections and encouragement for newsgathering.

5

The Public Service Quotient

Philip F. Lader, U.S. Ambassador to the Court of St. James, has not forgotten the kindness of his hometown newspaper.

Long before he was Bill Clinton's close friend, a presidential adviser and in Clinton's second term our Ambassador to England, Phil Lader was a bright and promising son of St. Petersburg, Florida, a Phi Beta Kappa graduate of Duke and the University of Michigan. Two weeks prior to Christmas, 1967, his father, the manager of the Royal Castle Restaurant at Ninth Street and Central Avenue in St. Petersburg, Florida, died of heart failure. Phil was not at home. He was reading history, theology and jurisprudence at Pembroke College, Oxford, under a Rotary Foundation graduate study grant and traveling throughout England and Europe speaking to Rotary Clubs. Before he had left Florida for Oxford, he had told the Clearwater Rotary Club that "if we can ever restore the family of man, the world will be a better place for the community of nations."

The global village was not quite as wired in those days. Three days after his father's death, Phil Lader had not been notified, or even located. He was traveling somewhere in Western Europe during a winter break.

Nelson Poynter knew what to do. Working the phones, the owner and publisher of the *St. Petersburg Times* enlisted the services of the International Red Cross and the U.S. State Department to locate the son. Then he anticipated another need. When the State Department found

Phil Lader in Vienna, Austria, the American consulate there had an airline ticket waiting for him. It had been purchased by the newspaper. Phil arrived home in time for the celebration of a requiem mass at Holy Name Catholic Church and the burial in Royal Palm Cemetery.

Stories like these can be told nostalgically, as if they were relics from a different world, one where people watched Lawrence Welk and *Bonanza* and the word "media" meant crayons or poster paint. They can be seen as schmaltzy or noblesse oblige or simply quaint. Phil Lader does not remember or tell the story that way. He is as grateful today for Nelson Poynter's generosity as he was in 1967. He knows he could not have afforded to fly home without that ticket waiting for him at the American consulate in Vienna.

Newspaper owners used to perform such random acts of "community service" regularly. When Jack Howard and a merry band of Scripps-Howard executives flew around the nation in a converted B-23 bomber on budget trips to various newspapers and broadcast stations during the 1950s and 1960s, he often took along Hamilton Bissell, the Director of Scholarship Students at Phillips Exeter, to talk with promising newspaper carriers or other local boys who might be lured to Exeter with financial aid. There were hundreds of similar stories. And there are thousands of them still today, for journalism breeds and attracts idealists. In Billings, Montana, for instance, the CBS affiliate, station KTVQ, has produced a campaign called "A Waiting Child" that typifies the public service work of local stations throughout the country. Beginning on Father's Day and continuing every Sunday thereafter for fourteen weeks, the station's 10 P.M. newscast devotes a two-minute segment to an interview with a foster child who needs a home. The campaign has helped Montana officials triple the pool of families willing to adopt a foster child.

Strangely, though, the public doesn't perceive these acts of kindness as personal or altruistic any longer. They're seen as institutional. Somehow the public senses (correctly) that the idea for KTVQ's noble work was dreamed up by the sales department or that the segments serve many needs, including the news department's. The interviews with the children "tug at your heartstrings," says weekend anchor Julie Koerber. And, unsurprisingly, local broadcasters use their public service initiatives to ward off additional government regulation. In 1998, as Congress considered granting free airtime to political candidates, the National Association of Broadcasters released what its president, Eddie Fritts, called the "most massive study undertaken during his tenure," a compilation that put dollar figures on the airtime donated annually by broadcasters to public service announcements ($4.6 billion), political debate ($148.4 million) and the amount raised by stations for charities ($2.1 billion). The grand total of $6.8 billion represented the NAB's "conservative estimate" of radio and television's contributions to community service. If off-air campaigns for various and sundry projects such as child abuse hotlines or local health fairs were added along with news coverage of local emergencies or crises, Fritts thinks the total number could be tripled to $19 billion, almost the amount of yearly U.S. expenditures on books.

"Not enough," insist the guardians of the public interest. "If there were enough public service, they wouldn't have to do studies to prove there was," Peggy Charren, founder of Action for Children's Television, told *Broadcasting & Cable* magazine somewhat harshly. "Broadcaster studies always make it look as if the stations have nothing on their mind besides serving the public. The bottom line can go to hell as long as we are serving the community. You don't have to be a genius to know that this is not how this world works."[1]

The trouble with this agenda-driven cynicism is that it simply ignores the reality that, by any kind of comparative measurement, you could hardly ask for better local citizens than the heads of local newspapers or television stations. In the Washington metropolitan area, for example, Donald Graham and Alan Spoon of the Washington Post Company have sought out the new "techno-millionaires," baby boomers whose successful computer companies surrounding the Beltway have made them quickly and fabulously wealthy. The Post executives try to weave these new rich kids on the block into the hard work of building a community out of a three-headed hydra of urban decay, suburban sprawl and Marion

Barry. They devote sizable blocks of time to such efforts, especially compared to the Lilliputian contributions of time spent by executives of megabanks, unions or other institutions that envision themselves too global to be local. There is, indisputably, negligible benefit to quarterly earnings reports from the continuation of this tradition of community service.

In St. Petersburg, a foundation which Nelson Poynter established now controls the newspaper. The *American Journalism Review* says many journalists consider it the nation's finest local newspaper. Nelson Poynter's successors, first Eugene Patterson and then Andrew Barnes and a winsome team of publisher Judith Roales and executive editor Paul Tash, have built the newspaper into a dominant Florida daily, rivaling the *Miami Herald* for influence and during some months exceeding the *Herald*'s circulation. The editorial page, edited by Philip Gailey, formerly of *The New York Times*'s Washington bureau, tilts decidedly more liberal than the predominantly Republican community, but that difference hasn't slowed the paper's growth.

Judith Roales and Paul Tash do not have the same profit expectations that are laid on public companies by Wall Street. The ratio of "news hole" to advertising lineage at the *Times* approximates 60/40, the reverse of the usual pattern at daily newspapers today. The *Times* strives for an operating profit of 15 percent, healthy for any business but not close to the 20 to 35 percent margins expected by many newspaper companies. While they see their own newspaper's culture as strongly committed to public service, they don't see the practical implications of that commitment as differing all that much from the projects of many local newspapers. "We all try to show that we care about our towns and cities," explains Judith Roales. "Some of us spend considerably more time and money on it, but just about all of us care a lot."

You cannot spend time around journalists without realizing that Judith Roales is right. Journalists do care. They have ideals, curiosity, a longing to contribute to a better understanding of the planet, hopefully its improvement. Ever buoyantly, they research the human condition. Bravely, they tell us things we would prefer not to hear.

Why, then, do we no longer see either the courage of the profession or the public service routinely performed by its leaders? Certainly, there are distractions. We are bombarded daily with evaluations of how the media has screwed up or infected public life with a new, nauseating virus. In one Sunday edition of *The New York Times* (March 22, 1998), for example, we learn the following—well, we can't call them "facts," so let's term them "points of view expressed with a conviction approaching moral certainty":

- In Maureen Dowd's column, Gary Hart says, "[I]t was a Washington journalism myth that people were demanding to know everything. There have to be some things between two people you don't want to know."

- In the *Book Review*, a reviewer of *Spin Cycle* by *Washington Post* media reporter Howard Kurtz believes that the book "should dispel any lingering myths about a liberal mainstream press eager to promote" President Clinton.

- In "Week in Review," Andrew J. Bleiler, Monica Lewinsky's former lover (when he was twenty-seven and she nineteen), and his wife, Kathy, felt forced to make a public acknowledgment of his extramarital affair with Monica because of overwhelming media pressure (100 media calls on their answering machine the day after Lewinsky was first publicly identified on January 21, 1998). The Bleilers' four-year-old son, we also learn, "still puts his stuffed animals inside the front door when we leave." According to Mrs. Bleiler, "he says, 'Bubba's gonna guard against reporters.'" The headline of the article terms the Bleilers "A Scandal's Road Kill."

- In the "Arts & Leisure" section, *60 Minutes* producer Don Hewitt states on his fiftieth anniversary at CBS that "the people who run television and the people who work for television, like me, got richer. But television got poorer." This demise, according to Hewitt, is mostly due to the failures of the executives in television's entertainment divisions. "Is there more news to cover now than there was when *20/20* first went on the air 20 years ago, news that is forcing them to do two editions of *20/20* a week?" he asks rhetorically. "Nothing has changed out there in the world. What has changed is that the entertainment divisions can't come up with any more Jackie Gleasons, Lucille Balls, Mary Tyler Moores, Carroll O'Connors, Alan Aldas. If you need programming, go find another Jackie Gleason." Instead the networks add more and more news shows, which tend to be cheaper to produce than entertainment shows and are usually assured at least respectable audiences, especially if promoted with breathless teasers.

Yet each of these published statements in the *Times,* presented with what Mark Twain called the "calm confidence of a Christian holding four aces," is endlessly disputable. Gary Hart is wrong: all kinds of people inside and outside of the Washington Beltway want to know if a candidate for President is being faithful to his wife or is spending weekends with his girlfriend. Similarly, even the prolific Howard Kurtz cannot put to rest the reality that some liberal-leaning journalists have promoted the Clinton agenda, not at least so long as Sidney Blumenthal and Eleanor Clift are still breathing. And neither the hapless Bleilers (who did not in fact *have* to hold a press conference) nor Don Hewitt (whose prosecutorial dramatics on *60 Minutes* presaged the higher entertainment quotient in news programming) would deny being contributors to the catastrophes they abhor.

There is no perfect understanding of the public's bundle of contradictory attitudes toward the media—or the media's own conflicted attitudes toward itself—any more than there is a perfect understanding of the First Amendment. There is, however, accretion. Some things have changed. There is less of a public service ethos than there used to be. There is greater bottom-line pressure. There is more careerism and celebrity preening among journalists themselves.

Several scourges currently blind the public from recognizing and properly valuing the virtuous side of the media's profile, its public service and its good work. This is more than a simple matter of bad news overwhelming good. A look at each of these scourges shows that the problems are deep-seated and that the public itself is implicated symbiotically at every stage. But any honest look also shows that the true scourges are often confused with misleading charges and false generalizations. To understand the public's folly—our own contribution to the very characteristics of the media that we dislike the most—each of these features deserves a closer look.

THE CRUNCH OF THE BOTTOM LINE

Michael Gartner, former president of NBC News, editor and co-owner of the *Ames* (Iowa) *Daily Tribune* and certifiable media mogul, is arguing with me. Gartner likes to argue. This befits a recipient of the 1997 Pulitzer Prize for Editorial Writing and a man whose tongue can clip a hedge. It is September 1995 and we are eating dinner in a Des Moines chophouse. I am annoyed that *The New York Times* has played the Disney/CapCities merger announcement so Big on its front page—with a huge multicolumn headline above the fold as if the merger were at least as significant as a cure for cancer. Why, I ask rhetorically, does the media have to treat themselves and especially their business activity as so damned important? Wouldn't our problems with the public shrink a collar size if we didn't present ourselves as so colossal, so momentous? Gartner disagrees. "It is important," he says flatly. Humility is not a green plant that thrives in this pasture of Iowa.

Gartner held the presidency of NBC News longer than any of his predecessors except the first occupant of the office, William R. McAndrew (1961–68). He notes that McAndrew, who died from a sudden fall down a flight of stairs, was the only president of NBC News who left the job with any grace and dignity. Gartner's time at the network was up when he slipped on an escalator and took the fall for *Dateline*'s scandalous staging of exploding General Motors trucks. His departure was ridiculously ironic. Throughout a long career from page-one editor at *The Wall Street Journal* to editor and president of the *Des Moines Register,* editor of the *Louisville Courier-Journal* and then NBC, his journalistic standards and practices have been the moral equivalent of a Lexus—they never needed repair or a trip to the shop for fine-tuning. Still, he does not seem exactly thrilled with the unceremonious way his tenure terminated. I remind him that when he first took the television job he gave a speech in New York and commented on two absurdities: One, that unlike the president of most organizations, he was not the most highly compensated employee, ranking somewhere around twentieth on the list. Second, he knew that if he did a bad job at NBC he would be fired; but he also knew that if he did a good job at NBC he would be fired. Networks are like that.

"I'm still on good terms with Bob Wright [president of NBC] and Jack Welch [chief executive officer of General Electric, NBC's parent]," he tells me. He should be. During his time at the network, a lot more than GM trucks exploded. He took the news division from a loss to a $30 million annual profit. He's proud of his downsizing and his financial accomplishments. He's also proud of launching *Dateline,* the first successful newsmagazine at NBC, and advancing equality for women in an industry that had a reputation for treating them shabbily. At the outset, he was wildly controversial, abused for being a "printhead" with no experience in television. His results brought them around, even the doubting affiliates. "I took Chris Wallace off *Meet the Press* and put on Tim Russert, not just another pretty face," he remembers. Content, he believes, counts. He has just finished producing a six-part series on property taxes for the readers of his Ames newspaper.

Death has touched Gartner since he left NBC. The heart of his teenage son, Christopher, stopped suddenly from the onset of diabetes. "You cry every day," he says. "It is like cataracts or glaucoma; where once the world was bright, everything is muted with haze." Some people, especially the dim-witted whom he used to suffer badly, might say that Mike Gartner wore arrogance like a cologne. If his cocksureness and prickliness have softened, his quick wit and feistiness have not.

Has Big Media lost its soul, and its audience, in a quest for profits?

He rejects the notion as simplistic. He doesn't like Andrew Lack, his successor as president of NBC News, giving a speech and worrying out loud if television has contributed to the dumbing of America. Lack has told the Radio and Television News Directors that "we have been abandoning the thoughtful audience and with it our credibility."

"That's just a gimmick, a PR gesture and kind of hypocritical," says Gartner. "There's nothing he can do to change it. Television is not a niche medium, it's a mass medium." And television rarely reviews itself. "It's at the mercy of print critics, who treat it like a soap opera. Most of them don't like news, they like numbers.

"Television news has to be so simple," he explains. "It's very difficult to take information in with two senses simultaneously. That's why we're a headline service with pictures. We can't get into nuance. When we add unnecessary words or conclusions—'It looks like the mayor has his hand in the cookie jar'—it just tends to be divisive and hurts our credibility." He remembers once saying to the late John Chancellor when the long-time NBC correspondent and anchor had graduated to *NBC Nightly News* commentator: "How come you can get in more facts in ninety seconds than all the rest of the show combined?" "Easy," said Chancellor, "there are no pictures. They're not allowed." "I never thought of that before," Gartner responded.

When he does ruminate about the television business, he is mostly struck by the defensiveness, the "inability of people in television to explain their own medium and their own insecurity about the medium." He distinguishes between those who have had bottom-line experience and others. "No one who has not had budgetary responsibility is qualified to speak." He spurns "high-minded" speeches from people like Ted Koppel who have not had to "deal in real terms" with a $350 million television news operation or even his $500,000 newsroom budget in Ames. Bob Wright, he says approvingly, would refer to some correspondents as "journalists with a capital 'J.'" You can hear the sarcasm discharging and you can sense his doubts about the usefulness of criticism of television news from the leading lights of anchordom when he notes that the "decline in the ratings for television news corresponds with the rise of the millionaire class of television journalist."

These are truculent words from a man whose journalism credentials begin with a capital "J." He is hardly the only person skeptical about the value of multimillion-dollar salaries for television talent. Celebrity journalism is a problem. It can make the speaker seem more important than what's being said. But aren't profit demands higher? Gartner refuses to demonize the corporate front office. Writing in his *USA Today* column in 1995, he stated: "It makes no difference if media are owned by corporations or families or individuals. What matters are the integrity and intelligence and intrepidness of those owners. . . . Not once did GE boss Jack Welch or anyone else at GE ask me to put something on the air—or not to." This kind of subtlety earns him easy knocks. "Corporate loves him," a television executive told the *Sacramento Bee* in 1993. "He's a bottom-line guy."[2]

In truth, Gartner demonstrates the possibility of being attentive—*loyal* is too loaded a word—to both the editorial and the business spheres. But profit pressures and preoccupations cannot be dismissed. They are a root cause of the public's cynicism toward the media. Balancing "church" and "state" has become a knotty assignment in recent years. The traditional tension between the creative and idealistic part of the communications business and the need to turn a profit has deepened during the past two decades with the arrival of heightened profit expectations. Profit margins, once deemed respectable at 15 percent, have been pushed north of 20 and even 30 percent in order to impress Wall Street analysts, institutional investors and portfolio managers everywhere. The judgments that corporate managers make toward the real core of their business—the editorial product—either are made with exquisite sensitivity to the journalistic conscience or the product suffers along with morale. No one has warned the public more loudly about the deterioration of the product at the hands of financial barbarians than journalist-advocates themselves—principally because they want to see some semblance of balance preserved in their ongoing dynamic with the accountants.

Former *Chicago Tribune* editor James Squires tagged the financial demands of Wall Street as the root of most evil in his 1992 indictment of the corporate managers at the Tribune Co., *Read All About It*. After Squires's subsequent stint as press secretary to presidential candidate Ross Perot, he concluded that "the media no longer have the character to resist manipulation by the political establishment because they can be stampeded toward a distraction or an irrelevancy simply by feeding them something that serves both the career interests of journalists and the marketing interests of business.³ At Indiana University, he later passed the torch to the next generation of "J" journalists by putting it concisely:

> Newspapering is a business.
>
> Television is a business.
>
> Media is a business.
>
> But journalism has never been a business. When you try to make it one, it becomes something else, entertainment usually, or pandering.⁴

Like Squires, Peter Prichard bagged a brilliant career, his as editor of *USA Today* and Gannett Co.'s chief editorial executive, when he grew weary of the preoccupation with the cost-accounting approach to journalism. Gannett draws as much static for being single-minded about financial results as any media company. *The Washington Post*, which likes to take regular shots at Gannett in this regard, describes the "Gannett corporate culture" as "celebrating the efficacy of driving up profits by bringing down expenses."⁵ Under Prichard's regime, the newspaper once known as "McPaper" developed a harder, more serious edge. John Quinn, the original editor of *USA Today*, used to like to joke that the paper had "given new depth to the definition of shallow." Quinn and Prichard evolved the paper. Gradually, they removed the glitz while keeping the color. Prichard began selecting topics for *USA Today*'s "Cover Stories" which were less light and lively and instead examined national problems more thoroughly. One special project of which he was especially proud was an enormous study of the devastation wreaked by handguns. The series overwhelmed readers with accumulated misery. It marshaled popular support for the Brady bill and other congressional initiatives to control the sale of firearms. It garnered awards and respect within the profession. But Prichard could feel the apathy of some of Gannett's senior executives: Ho-hum, how much did *that* cost and what did it really do for our stock price?

Eugene Roberts, an Emperor "J" (Upper Class and Uppercase), remembers that when he left the *Philadelphia Inquirer* as editor, Knight Ridder's Miami headquarters had installed a computer system that could produce weekly tracking results (rather than monthly). "It drove the operating people in Philadelphia crazy because it could produce for Miami a faster look at results than the local operators could get." Ultimately, he says, Knight Ridder established an accountant as publisher who put other accountants in various management positions, and soon the entire business side was managed by accountants who could analyze the revenue, but not produce the revenue. The preoccupation with profits leads, he is confident, to short-term thinking and the dismantling not just of newsrooms but of circulation departments as well. After making the *Inquirer* one of the most respected newspapers in the country, a consistent winner of Pulitzer Prizes and mentor to the most lustrous talent pool in the nation, Gene Roberts hung it up. Not quietly. *The New York Times* drew him back from semi-retirement at the University of Maryland Journalism School to a crowning position as its managing editor, and he was soon on the road warning of "a tragedy in the making for journalism and for democracy." The culprit? "Budgets so tight at all but a few newspapers that an editor must decide a year in advance how busy the coming news year will be." Many newspaper corporations were "managing their newspapers like chain stores with no sense of being important local community institutions." It was "time, high time," to hold them accountable,[6] to force a "financial commitment necessary to live up to our responsibilities."

The morning after I have consumed asparagus and scallops with Gene Roberts in New York and told him he may be canonized for speaking to the fears of so many in the profession, the *Today* show sends Katie Couric on a shopping spree on the French Riviera to the tune of Roy Orbison's "Pretty Woman." "Don't worry," she assures Bryant Gumbel (and all the viewers), the shopping bags were really filled with tissue paper, not expensive items. "Tell all the NBC accountants back in New York," she says, smiling, on air. And in Los Angeles, on the same morning, Times Mirror makes the surprise appointment of Mark H. Willes as its new chairman and chief executive officer. Willes, previously the vice-chairman of cereal giant General Mills, says he "intends to apply the consumer orientation of packaged goods companies like General Mills to the information business." *The New York Times* article announcing his appointment implies that Willes will cut the fat out of Times Mirror, which "has a reputation among Wall Street analysts for spending heavily on projects." The *Times* also suggests Willes will shore up a "sluggish financial performance . . . that brought sharp criticism from Wall Street and depressed the price of the company's stock." In time, with the closing of *New York Newsday*, staff reductions elsewhere and the resignation of the *Los Angeles Times*'s respected editor Shelby Coffey, Willes will become known as "Captain Crunch" or the "Cereal Killer," cheered by stockholders but distrusted by journalists, the corporate corollary to Gene Roberts. If American trends germinate in California, one media CEO tells me, it is perhaps no surprise that Tony Ridder in 1998 moved Knight Ridder's headquarters from Miami to San Jose.

Stock options and corporate attentiveness to earnings have now made at least three generations of media managers comfortable millionaires. They have not piled up anywhere near the wealth of entrepreneurs like Ted Turner or the Silicon Valley computer icons, but they are far more flush than most of them ever dreamed of being. The rippling spread of wealth from the fortunes of media companies has been democratic too. Middle managers and editors have prospered as well as all the pension funds, mutual funds and 401-K accounts that own Disney, General Electric, Knight Ridder or any of 100 other well-regarded media stocks.

Long-term, this public perception of the media as "a good business" (in which they can share the riches on an earnings per share basis) blurs the distinction between such remunerative investments and other consumer goods or retail businesses.

Ironically, much of the public—or at least the investing part of them—probably doesn't give a whit about the media's traditional attachment to the public interest—not if it will cost them money. When Katharine Graham was chairman of the Washington Post Co. in the 1970s and 1980s, she religiously preached about the feasibility and desirability of delivering, simultaneously, shareholder value and the highest-quality journalism. A decade later, the two objectives are not linked together very often, even in lip service. Corporate chieftains now sense that investment analysts and portfolio managers are not much dazzled by talk about expensive commitments to content or the community. "It just sounds like a rationalization for poor profit margins," says one well-known industry analyst. "Unless a dedication to quality is part of a company's branding or market niche, like the New York Times Co., it's basically irrelevant to valuing a mass-market media. How much of the public prefers *Masterpiece Theatre* over reruns of *Roseanne?*" This is, of course, the predictable insult from Wall Street, and any business executive in any industry who is guided by it has no more talent than those who just consistently underestimate the taste or intelligence of the public.

There will always be a big market for schlock. Institutions like the media, with a special heritage and constitutionally conferred role in American life, do not have to dedicate themselves to the lowest common denominator. At least not so long as they want to maintain a place of respect and privilege under the Constitution.

The crunch of the bottom line on the resources available to journalism actually has more to do with the investing public's expectations of media companies than it does with Mark Willes or any other corporate gladiator. It is interesting to speculate about what shareholder reaction would be if the board chairmen of the top twenty media companies committed 30 to 40 percent of their earnings or free cash flow to a project we might call DEPTH—"Directing Earnings to Praetorian Thoroughness and Humanity." Praetorians, of course, were the bodyguards in the Roman republic. Not a bad way to regard journalists today. As Jim Squires asks, "Where else, pray tell, are we going to get the truth?" Squires's fear (and it should be ours) is that "truth has the same relationship with the new world of information that Winston Churchill once claimed it had to one of his political opponents. 'He stumbles across the truth every now and then,' Churchill grumbled, 'but always recovers as if nothing had happened.'"7

"Where," I ask Matthew Storin, editor of the *Boston Globe*, "would you put the money if your owners said you could spend an additional 30 percent of your newsroom budget on editorial content."

"That's an interesting question," he says, especially since "everything else that's been tried has not stopped the loss of readership by daily newspapers." Storin would hire more reporters to cover Boston and its suburbs. Content would deepen and so, he believes, would reader loyalty.

Some variation of this theme—not quite so dramatic as a 30 percent increase in the newsroom budget, but impressive nonetheless, has occurred at two daily newspapers owned by the Newhouse family. In Newark, editor Jim Willse was given the dollars to add fifty reporters and expand the *Star-Ledger*'s local and state coverage. The paper is becoming the dominant force in New Jersey. Likewise, the *Plain Dealer*, under the tutelage of publisher Alex Machaskee, has led the renaissance of Cleveland, building a new office downtown, a new printing and distribution facility in the suburbs, adding seventy-five reporters and editors and, as a result, expanding its franchise throughout northern Ohio. Machaskee attributes the *Plain Dealer*'s advances to the Newhouses' farsightedness. "Enhancing our core product was the most essential component of our strategy," he said in a speech in Washington in 1996. The *Plain Dealer* ranks first among major metropolitan newspapers in circulation penetration in its home county with 54 percent penetration daily and 72 percent on Sunday. Circulation has not declined even though northern Ohio has been losing population. The Newhouse family, it is worth noting, owns its newspapers in a privately held company without the nagging of the investment community.

"COMPETITIVE PRESSURES": GREEN PENIS ENVY

The crunch of bottom-line imperatives has sea-changed the way the public regards the media. But another, related slogan, "competitive pressures," is really not much of a reason for explaining why the public's anger has deepened during the last two decades. Competitive conditions among the ever-expanding number of media outlets are generally overused as an explanation why reporters pursue stories of salacious interest or intrude unnecessarily into private lives. Consider the case of the green penis, a story so ribald and delicious it had no chance of escaping public attention. Three Baltimore television stations couldn't resist giggling through their news reports about the green penis.

The hilarity began in 1994, according to court records, when a lab technician in a Baltimore urology clinic asked one of the clinic's surgeons, Ronald Tutrone, to perform a vasectomy on him. The surgery was successful. But what supposedly happened next, according to the patient, snipped away the myth that all is deadly serious in the land of medicine. The surgery was performed around St. Patrick's Day in 1994. While the patient was still sedated, and perhaps inspired by the colorful Irish holiday, Dr. Tutrone painted his co-worker's penis with dark green surgical dye. He allegedly added a "smiley face" on the tip of the penis. To cap off the humor, Dr. Tutrone instructed a nurse to snap a photo of the penis and then invited other clinic personnel to view his artwork. Laughter all around. Clinic personnel allegedly started referring to the lab technician as "Mr. Greenbean" or "Lambchop." The dye was easily washed off. The humiliation wasn't. The lab technician left his job at the urology clinic and, about a year later, sued Dr. Tutrone, the clinic and other clinic personnel for fraud, invasion of privacy and battery. So much for humor in the workplace. In July 1996, a copy of the technician's lawsuit was faxed anonymously to three television stations in Baltimore. (Some believe that the patient himself faxed the lawsuit; others think it was his adversaries.)

Telling the story of this operating room practical joke does not raise serious legal concerns since it had become the focus of a lawsuit. Because the story would be based almost exclusively on public court records, the stations did not have to worry about a threat of liability from an invasion of privacy claim. (The Supreme Court has ruled that the media cannot be prohibited from publishing a rape victim's name, much less the identity of a victim of a practical joke who chooses to sue over it.) First Amendment law cloaks the media with a privilege: so long as they provide a fair and accurate account of what appears in court records, they cannot be held liable for either defamation or invasion of privacy.

The journalistic or ethical decision—as opposed to the legal decision— is a different and more delicate matter. Exposing the patient's lawsuit to the viewing public obviously expands the universe of those who learn of his embarrassment. It is a risk every litigant takes in our open judicial system. It is also a struggle newsrooms grapple with constantly. What the public does not see, however, is the editorial process that goes on in such situations; it can resemble needlepointing in the dark—a struggle to be precise but usually painful. Cynics assume that anything salacious in a court file can find a home on the air or in print. But people in newsrooms are cognizant of their power to exacerbate or magnify a person's pain or suffering. And they do not hesitate to beat up those of their colleagues who seem to be insufficiently mindful of the power of media to maim or wound. When *New Yorker* writer Lillian Ross disclosed in a 1998 autobiography her longtime affair with the very married editor of the magazine, William Shawn, *Washington Post* columnist Richard Cohen criticized her for being oblivious to the fallout. Cohen wrote:

> Some writers do think about the impact their work will have on others, and sometimes as a result, they refrain from writing. . . .
>
> Mostly, though, . . . if we were always to take someone's feelings into account, nothing much would be written. To a degree, we are in the

103

business of hurting people, although we insist it is they who have done the damage. . . .

I have hurt people, I know, for no other reason than I needed a column, or, sometimes, a better one. . . . I am bothered by that, but bothered even more by those journalists—and Ross seems to be one—who don't seem to be bothered at all.[8]

At WMAR, the newsroom debated whether they should report the antics of the vasectomy clinic and the conversion of a joke into a lawsuit. The story ran for two principal reasons. First, in an affidavit submitted in the lawsuit against the urology clinic, a witness had stated that other patients may have been unwittingly photographed while sedated. With that allegation, WMAR felt it had a sound journalistic justification for disseminating the story: to warn other potential "victims" that they might become "medical porn." One can ask if that reasoning is just an expedient rationalization to get a sensational story with "Helen, you won't believe this" humor on the air. But news organizations are always imprisoned by such self-doubts or potential criticism in covering the courts; they either report the juicy fruit and risk denunciation for "trivializing" the news or they define "news" to exclude such tidbits and risk denunciation for missing the passing parade of life.

Station WMAR's broadcast about the green penis could be a classic illustration of how local news outlets handle stories that can burn them at the same time as they provide "sizzle" to a newscast. The report first outlined the patient's lawsuit against Dr. Tutrone and the clinic. Then it added some of its own reporting in an attempt to supply the perspective of the combatants. WMAR reporter Scott Broom reached the patient's wife by telephone, but neither she nor her husband were willing to discuss the case on camera. Broom also interviewed Dr. Tutrone's lawyer, Neal Brown. Mr. Brown said the incident was a practical joke among close friends and that at one time the patient and his wife had been laughing along. He then said, "This case is really nothing more than using the court system and now you, the media, for legal extortion."

The "legal extortion" comment prompted yet another lawsuit. This time the patient sued WMAR, Neal Brown, Dr. Tutrone and others for libel, claiming the comment accused him of the crime of extortion. Eventually, Judge Barbara Kerr Howe of the Circuit Court for Baltimore County dismissed the defamation claim. In the context of a legal dispute, she said, the phrase "legal extortion" was "rhetorical hyperbole," a blunt statement of opinion that cannot give rise to a claim for libel. Station WMAR would have saved itself the time and trouble of a nuisance lawsuit if it had simply reported the bare bones of the patient's court filing against Dr. Tutrone and the clinic without any effort to add explanatory context. Little wonder that many local television stations favor a clipped, headline approach to reporting disputes rather than a more fulsome story that will inform viewers more coherently but runs the risk of embroiling them in the feud.

Ultimately, the most fascinating question about the green penis case—why did the patient respond to his colleagues' prank with a lawsuit—is posed and the viewer is left to wonder about the answer. The patient doesn't tell us why he didn't respond to the joke with a shrug, a witticism or even a retaliatory practical joke of his own. Private parts, it seems, are still deemed private even among a blasé hospital crowd. Or, perhaps, the lawsuit is a commentary on our litigious response to any affront. Or is the lawsuit a statement about the powerlessness of subordinates to combat a doctor's caprice? By any measurement, reporting on the lawsuit is "news," a remarkable event of potential significance that may tell us something about the texture of the social fabric. Would the story have been told in a less competitive age? Certainly. (Although a more delicate term than "penis" would probably have been used; Lorena and John Wayne Bobbitt broke the barrier on the mainstream use of the word.) Yet it will mostly be seen (and criticized) by the public as pandering—a media confection offered up to amuse, entertain and titillate rather than inform. Is this fair? Invasions of privacy and rude intrusions occur in everyday life—in operating rooms and everywhere else—not just on television. Yet the media and the slogan "competitive pressures" will be blamed for both transgressions simply because three stations chose to report on Dr. Tutrone's St. Patrick Day's joke.

THE CELEBRITY BLUR

If the owners of our major media companies (mostly us) are making more money at the expense of our belief in the value of the Fourth Estate's work, what about the nouveau riche journalists? Today, there are more millionaire stars in the field than ever before. Our pension funds are richer for the "branding" that the stars bring to their news products, but otherwise the media's celebrity culture hasn't helped us much. Hugh Sidey, Washington journalist for four decades, has perspective.

Hugh Sidey doesn't exactly dislike MSNBC's Brian Williams. He doesn't even really know him. He would probably like him if the two could just sit on the porch of Williams' Connecticut farmhouse and shoot the breeze. But Hugh Sidey seems not to like what he thinks Brian Williams represents.

It is January 1996 and Brian Williams is the new boy on the NBC block, covering President Clinton's first formal press conference in several months along with a smaller than usual assortment of other reporters assembled in the East Room of the White House. Outside, the fiercest winter storm since 1926 has dumped three feet of snow on Washington (and on the District of Columbia government's pretense to competence). The unplowed streets and treacherous ice have not deterred Hugh Sidey from attending. The author of *Time's* periodic column "The Presidency" has written about the American presidency for thirty-eight years. He is no stranger to Washington snowstorms (of all kinds) or to the far harsher weather that rages over the Iowa prairies where he lived as a boy. Today, as a kindness, he has brought a friend visiting from the Midwest to witness the spectacle of a presidential press conference. They get good seats, right down front, since the snow has apparently intimidated less hardier journalists. Sidey spots Brian Williams, who has also trudged through the snow to Pennsylvania Avenue. The television correspondent has reportedly received a new employment contract from his network that will pay him $1 million annually to cover the White House. The salary offends Sidey. But his resentment does not seem to flow from envy or the conventional disdain that print reporters often harbor for their broadcast colleagues.

"You know what that kind of money will make him do," he says darkly.

Hugh Sidey fears that Brian Williams will perform. Not report. His prejudice comes from the pride that his generation holds for a lifetime of reporting. Sidey has dispensed facts, insight and information. His *Time* column that generated the most mail described the death from blight of a giant old elm tree on the White House grounds. The current generation of Washington political correspondents tend to include themselves in their stories. Frequently, they even emphasize themselves rather than the trees around them or their news subjects. Daily news is delivered with "stand-up" commentary and the viewpoint of the correspondent, usually from the White House lawn, the Capitol dome, or another appropriate backdrop. The television image invariably makes the correspondents bigger than the backdrops—as if they were more important. But the high salary levels demand such self-justification. Journalism's star system detracts, necessarily, from reporting.

Perhaps Hugh Sidey would object less to this tyranny if he felt that it led to better critical analysis. But he obviously does not. Most prominent reporters, print as well as broadcast, don't stay on a single beat long enough to develop much context. Indeed, Brian Williams will not stay long at the White House, whisked away in 1997 to anchor MSNBC.

Ask Sidey about President Clinton and you will get a nugget of perspective laced with history:

"Dick Stroud—he's dead now—but, do you remember, he used to write the TR column for *The New Republic*. He was always quoting Calvin Coolidge. I asked him once why he was so enamored of Coolidge. He told me that Coolidge was President at a time when the country didn't really need a President and he had performed the assignment very well. Well, maybe in hindsight, the same will be said of Clinton."

Ask a nonveteran White House correspondent about Clinton and you will typically get an opinion assessing the future political repercussions of his recent actions. Or you may get a cold, savage psychological dissection of the man. There is nothing that bothers Hugh Sidey and journalists of his generation more than this willingness, at times even eagerness, of prominent journalists to rip into public officials with steely self-assuredness and self-righteousness. All the humanity, the roundness of a human being, is carved away to display one ugly misjudgment or imperfection. The public official becomes that flaw. The journalist is regarded by peers as perceptive.

As it turns out, Brian Williams, cursed with good looks and a Brokaw-like baritone, doesn't really deserve to be saddled with all the symbolic deadweight of the new era of star journalists. Actually, he's sort of a throwback. Bob Wright might even use the capital "J" on him. NBC had to "twist his arm," according to NBC News president Andrew Lack, to take the White House job. Williams didn't want to uproot his family from his wife's childhood home, a farmhouse in Connecticut, and he didn't aspire to the travel associated with covering the restless Clinton White House. So when Wright talked Microsoft's Bill Gates into footing most of the $500 million bill for the new cable channel, MSNBC, Williams leapt at the chance to resettle in Connecticut and cover stories that most interest him: political, government and business news. "I measure things by the journalism, as anachronistic as that sounds," he told the *American Journalism Review.*[9] His forays outside the MSNBC studio, mostly to audiences of journalists or journalism students, furnish plenty of evidence to support his self-portrait as a "TV dinosaur." "Don't speak for money and don't offer your opinions. It's like drugs," he tells the groups. "Jerry Springer has no business anywhere in a newsroom. . . . The fact that Jerry Springer has become so popular says a lot about our culture." To top it off, Williams doesn't even like the glorious nineties. "I think I'm the only skunk at the global garden party where everyone's talking about what a great time this is. I don't think the nineties are a good time at all. This is more an 'about me' decade than the eighties were. The United

States is intellectually and morally casting about, and it will take either an economic or a global crisis to get us out of it or to wake us up."[10]

It is not so much the personal qualities of celebrity journalists that rankle their less glittering colleagues. Most of the stars are so guilt-ridden by feeling undeserving of the power they possess that they work like Ritz-Carlton concierges at being genial. But who (except the agents and maybe the stars themselves) likes the *system* of celebrity journalism? Well, in a perverse way, actually, the public does. It's been created to bond with them. All the research from the consultants in television shows it. The essential product differentiation between stations or networks is the anchors. The news is basically the same. It all boils down to the anchors. The "J" people don't need this system or like it. Born of the entertainment culture, weaned on self-promotion, the star system showcases the gathering and delivery of news, rather than the substance of the product itself. Generally, it just undermines the clarity and authority of journalism. It creates a theatrical blur. "People see me on the street, and they think I'm Oprah," says R. W. "Johnny" Apple, a Washington bureau chief of *The New York Times*. This is kind of funny since, aside from being white and male, Johnny has loved many a good meal and could only resemble the talk show host if she were in need of one of her diets.

What is not so funny, and what has become a veritable hue and cry among journalists, is that the celebrity blur makes it virtually impossible for the public, which is not very adept at critical thinking in any event, to differentiate between "entertainment" royalty (talk show hosts, gossip columnists, social chroniclers and Don Imus) and "serious" bishops of the journalistic temple. It is difficult. Where does Geraldo belong? On which side of the fence is Sally Quinn? Dominick Dunne? Must Barbara Walters be schizophrenic if she interviews Academy Award nominees one week and the First Lady the next? The distinction is not all that useful, since market-driven media are supposed to be mixing "irresistible, entertaining" fare with more thoughtful food about the collapse of the Swedish social welfare system. Ben Bradlee, certainly an archbishop, coined the term "Holy Shit stories" at *The Washington Post* to describe the sweet spot where the ideas intersect, although the compass rarely pointed at Sweden. *Vanity Fair* epitomizes the blend every month and packages it with enough fragrance samples to make you dizzy. There are, to be sure, steps that news organizations could take to diminish the blur. The annual White House Correspondents Dinner has become a cattle call for Hollywood celebrities looking for a photo op and the chance to hear the President of the United States deliver one-liners like Bob Hope. Nothing forced the media companies who invite guests to this dinner (which once merely honored award recipients and saluted the President and his staff) to turn the event into a celebrity gawk. *Vanity Fair* even throws an "after-party" just like the Academy Awards and then publishes in its magazine a page of photographs of celebrities carousing with their journalist hosts. But deemphasizing celebrities in and around journalism is "a losing battle," thinks respected *Washington Post* reporter David Broder, who has been openly critical of the trend. "The people who make the hiring decisions keep hiring them and not just in television." When the *San Francisco Examiner* wanted a higher profile in Washington, they hired Chris Matthews, a former aide to Speaker Tip O'Neill, he points out. Jim Warren, Washington bureau chief of *The Chicago Tribune,* believes journalists would clarify what they stand for if they refused to "perform" at paid speaking engagements and spent more time digging good stories out of the courthouse and other venues.

Look what Warren and like-minded reporters are up against. The media blur blends into a pink-and-blue impressionistic haze when celebrities turn into authors, à la the entire cast of the O. J. Simpson trial, or when Washington political operatives reinvent themselves as journalistic "talent." The fog can cause high-speed accidents. As George Stephanopoulos distanced himself from his former employer in the early hours of the Monica Lewinsky scandal, his skepticism about the President's conduct deepened doubts about Clinton just as it scored high marks as a clever career move that fleshed out his new persona as a television commentator. News subjects morph into media stars faster than you can say Arianna Huffington, and all of fame's royalty feast together like moths around a streetlamp thinking they've found the sun. The fluttering can also be funny. Some sort of benchmark was set in 1997 at New York's Le Cirque restaurant, where Mark Fuhrman went to dine with his editor at Regnery Publishing, Richard Vigilanti, and Diane Sawyer after taping the second of two *Prime Time Live* specials intended by his publisher to rehabilitate Fuhrman and launch his book, *Murder in Brentwood*. (The strategy worked splendidly, the book becoming a best-seller.) Shortly after arriving at the restaurant, Fuhrman went to the men's room. Upon returning to his table, he told his companions: "I just saw Steven Spielberg in the men's room." Richard Vigilanti decided he needed to wash up and headed for the men's room. He arrived in time to hear Steven Spielberg tell a friend: "Gee, I think I just saw Mark Fuhrman."

The manufacturing or exploitation of celebrities by, for, in, and throughout the news media damages the media's reputation as serious, dispassionate journalists, and there is almost nothing they can do about it. As Daniel Boorstin has observed, the responsibility for making news is no longer God's. "There was a time," he wrote in *The Image: A Guide to Pseudo-Events in America*, "when the reader of an unexciting newspaper would remark, 'How dull is the world today.' Nowadays, he says, 'What a dull newspaper.'"

The media are dull at their peril. Two days after Dodi al-Fayed's death with Princess Diana, Matt Lauer struggled to maintain some dignity while interviewing Dodi's former girlfriend, the languid model and aspiring actress Kelly Fisher, on the *Today* show. The segment was appalling. Ms. Fisher offered the self-centered sentiment that "none of this" would have happened if Dodi had stayed with her. But is it realistic to expect Matt Lauer not to interview Kelly Fisher when she and her hard-charging lawyer, Gloria Allred, are announcing that she will drop her palimony lawsuit against Dodi? Is this news fit for *Today*? Is it even news? Sure. The morning shows are full of inconsequential froth as well as interviews with the Joint Chiefs of Staff and the ambassador from Iraq. The common denominator of the guests on the television morning shows is that they are almost always selling something: a new book, a CD, a political policy, a spin on the news, Christmas gift ideas. The pitches are delivered either by celebrities or by wanna-be celebrities like Ms. Fisher. Insipid or spellbinding (and it is not clear that producers prefer the latter), we lap it all up. Television bookers want to grab our attention, and poor taste can work just as well as probity sometimes. Our voyeuristic fixation with rich and glamorous stars in the entertainment, sports and political realms brings personal definition and drama to America's capitalistic dream. We rate the celebrities and wanna-bes today like Philadelphia teenagers used to rate new rock 'n' roll songs on *American Bandstand* with Dick Clark. Kelly Fisher gets a 2 on a 10-point scale; there's no melody and while the beat's not bad, you can't dance to her.

Television's endless self-promotion about its stars and its news programming has been as responsible as anything for the public's perception that the media is mostly about money. If I were king of television land, I tell a Phoenix station manager one day, we would ban all promos—those stupid, shrieking, hyperventilating, five-to-fifteen-second cymbal clashes designed to grab you faster than a stranger snapping a wet towel at your bare ass in a locker room. Not only are they annoying, they convince the public that we care more about rounding up audiences than informing them. This is especially true when the media all pounce and pound on a single story—such as Monica Lewinsky—where there really isn't much news after the second day, only a lot of rehashing, speculation and endless commentary. Drums roll and French horns promise "Crisis in the White House," but actually the only crisis is occurring in newsrooms where there is precious little news to report and overwhelming pressure to keep the story rolling along, just to hold an audience. Lewinsky's lawyer, William Ginsburg, became a national joke for going on too many shows when he had little to say, but at least some of the public's scorn is surely reserved for the media who were so undiscerning as to give him the airtime to blabber in the first place.

Banning promos would be a tough sell, even for an absolute monarch. My friend the station manager would prefer to muffle the carnival barker tone and elevate the informational content of promotional announcements. But he's not likely to be the first to try. His hesitation derives from a widespread cynicism in the industry about the hypocrisy of the public. The market research studies of any television station seethe with the stuff. "We want more international news, less blood and guts, and please hand me my copy of *War and Peace*," the surveys declare. In almost all markets, however, the news program which pops and crackles with crime reports captures the biggest audience. Why? Half of the blame falls on the public's shoulders, half on the media's. As Terry Connelly, a successful news director and general manager in numerous markets, analyzes it, there are two reasons why crime reporting predominates on *News at Eleven*: *immediacy* (what's happened since six o'clock) and *reportorial laziness* (the police radio provides a cheap and easy source of immediate drama). During more than two decades of experience in television news, Terry Connelly has seen one constant theme in viewer complaints: "There's too much 'negative' news." And he's seen one constant in programming: "Whenever a station has tried to do something about 'too much negative news,' the public rejects it out of hand." Viewers don't like it but they watch it. When Connelly arrived at WJLA in Washington, the top of the news was "all blood and guts." He deliberately changed the content. WJLA's ratings sank to a still lower third place in the market. Many reasons were offered for the station's being in the basement, but Connelly knows that the ratings could be juiced if he and Allbritton Communications were willing to do more cops, robbers and rapists. "We have to live in this community," he says. "It's not worth it." Stuart Zanger, a successor of Connelly's as news director of WCPO in Cincinnati, a station whose ratings glow as brightly as the journalism awards hanging on its newsroom's walls, doesn't believe "the reliance on crime—crime that is irrelevant to people's lives" leads necessarily to high ratings. In fact, while it may add a false sense of melodrama, it makes the newscast easily disposable. "The run-of-the-mill shootings, muggings, house break-ins—that sort of stuff—doesn't mean much to people," he told *Freedom Speaks*, the cable program produced by the Newseum in 1998. "When the newscast is over, people can't remember what they saw." It convinces them that their cities are as dangerous as ever, even as crime statistical measurements are declining. Yet anyone who doubts the depth of cynicism in television office suites about the public's viewing tastes should be told the story of Connie Chung when she was under contract to NBC in 1988. Inside NBC, they snickered and groaned when Connie produced a sixty-minute special called "Sex." It was terrible, everyone agreed. An embarrassment. It had no beginning, middle or end. Just titillation and lots of Connie. Then the Nielsens came in. The special ranked thirteenth among all television shows for the week, phenomenal for a one-shot program. The snickering stopped. Connie was asked to create more "documentaries." Interest at NBC waned in producing specials on "difficult" or "boring" subjects. A field unit previously assigned to produce a documentary on electric power began work on "Men After the Sexual Revolution." French philosopher Albert Camus once observed about the human tendency toward sloth that "if the essence of modern man could be summed up in a single sentence, it would be that 'he fornicated and read the newspapers.'" Today, that criticism might be renovated to "he fornicated and surfed the Net," which is more appropriate anyway since the Internet seems to be primarily used as the world's largest adult bookstore. If the public lapses into anywhere near the level of laziness that Camus feared, then it's *Entertainment Tonight* for all of us.

Wrestling with the public's hypocrisy leads broadcasters to a certain disdain and unhappiness with their own product and a fatalism that tempers their willingness to risk change or dullness. "Eight in ten Americans know who Tiger Woods is," Washington anchor Gordon Petersen says. "Fewer than two in ten know who the majority leader of the U.S. Senate is. . . . I don't know why I'm laughing—this is awful."[11] In cable, the cynicism is even worse, with executives shrugging and giving up because neither the public nor its representatives in Congress differentiate between good guys and bad guys. In 1994, James Kennedy, scion and chief executive officer of Cox Cable, told *Broadcasting & Cable* magazine:

> You know, I had our cable systems take all the really jazzy stuff off, the
> pay-per-view Spice, Playboy, that kind of thing. Then with the 1992

Cable Act, the good operators were hit just as hard as the bad operators. And I said to our guys, "You know, how big is the demand for that stuff out there?" They said, "It's really substantial; we're leaving a lot of money on the table." I said, "Go ahead. If that's what people want, let's give it to them." And we did that because ultimately I got tired of trying to be a good guy and operate our systems well and not put some of that junk on our cable systems and as far as the regulators were concerned, it didn't make a difference. They didn't consider good operators and bad operators. So I just said the hell with it, it's just a business, let's make money.[12]

Nobody knows the contributions of the media to the deteriorating relationship with the public better than the media itself. No profession, save perhaps the clergy, engages in more agonizing introspection than the media. Generally, this self-examination—or "self-flagellation" as it is commonly called by people skeptical of its usefulness—is done out of earshot of the public. The self-criticism is conducted regularly—some would say "obsessively"—within the profession. When it is done with the full blast of a twenty-four-inch gun, the industry stands up and applauds. Literally. The most galvanizing moment in journalism in recent years happened in the Waldorf-Astoria's Grand Ballroom in October 1997 when the Committee to Protect Journalists held its annual awards dinner to raise funds and honor journalists from around the world who had overcome beatings, arrests and imprisonment while reporting the truth. The committee's lifetime achievement award, the Burton Benjamin Memorial Award, went to ABC's Ted Koppel. With his boss, Disney chairman Michael Eisner, also chairing the dinner and listening, Koppel took aim and with these words received the evening's most sustained standing ovation:

> . . . We celebrate tonight the men and women whose dedication to the collection and distribution of facts threatens their very existence. When they antagonize those with money, political power and guns, they risk their lives. We, on the other hand, tremble at nothing quite so much as the thought of boring our audiences. . . . Our enemies are far more insidious. . . . They are declining advertising revenues, the rising cost of

newsprint, lower ratings, diversification and the vertical integration of communications empires.

. . . It is not death or torture or imprisonment that threatens us as American journalists. It is the trivialization of our industry. We are free to write and report whatever we believe is important. But if what is important does not appeal to the reading or viewing appetites of our consumers, we will give them something that does. No one is holding a gun to our heads. . . . We believe it to be sufficient excuse that we are giving the public what it wants.

. . . The most important events of the last couple of years have not been the O. J. Simpson trial and the death of Princess Diana.

JE REGRETTE

This is heresy, but I'm not sure Ted Koppel is right in one respect. The death of Diana, Princess of Wales, may actually have been one of the most important events of the last few years. It certainly was to the public, in ways that reached to the interior. Ten days after she died in an automobile crash with the lover portrayed as her new opportunity for happiness, *The New York Times's* Jane Gross found her appearing in hundreds of therapists' offices as women patients poured out their obsession with her death and their dismay that the men in their lives "hadn't a clue what so moved them." In a seminal piece of reporting, Jane Gross interviewed more than forty psychotherapists and gave us a glimpse at deciphering the most central, enigmatic question about the Princess's death: what explained the powerful cascade of emotion following her tragic end? Now this is reporting. The *Times* played the piece on its front page. We learned that "scores of therapists called Diana—at once frail and beautiful, flawed and grand—a perfect transference symbol . . . a blank screen on which women . . . (even women who disdain the celebrity culture) . . . could not resist projecting their fears and fantasies." The article illuminated the legibility of our lives.

This is the sort of explanatory journalism that tempers and restores the alchemy between the public and the media, for it is appreciated. Mostly, of course, Diana's death provoked disgust with the media, contempt for the "stalk-a-razzi" that chased her and a denunciation from her brother, the ninth Earl of Spencer, in Westminster Abbey. Moments after the funeral, Tom Fenton, the longtime chief European correspondent for CBS News, obviously moved, departed from merely reporting the procession of grief and issued a sort of personal, public apology for the media on-the-air. He spoke of how the media's coverage of the Princess had treated her like a soap opera. He said, "I regret it." He thought that the media had not covered her charity work. And he repeated, "I regret it." He told viewers that "we had wanted to go to Bosnia with her on the trip" to generate more widespread opposition to land mines, but that "the people who make the decisions had said 'no.'" And he repeated, "And I regret it." One hundred years earlier, across the English Channel, another journalist, Émile Zola, had used the same literary device of repetition with equal dramatic effect to accuse French officials of anti-Semitism in the false conviction of Alfred Dreyfus on spying charges. ("I accuse Lt. Col. Du Paty de Clam of having been the diabolical agent of a miscarriage of justice . . . I accuse General Mercier . . . I accuse the War Office . . .") Zola's "J'accuse" stands as one of the greatest manifestos of journalism. A century later, "J'accuse" has evolved into "Je regrette."

Nothing the media do offend the public more than the intrusive way in which they have come to do their work. No amount of rationalization about "competitive pressures" or the need for journalists to be aggressive or the public's hypocritical desire to snoop into the private corners of people's lives can justify some of the mindless, ill-mannered practices. True, the process of newsgathering is not as lovely as the end product. (Mike Gartner says, "Sausage makers are probably sitting around right now saying, 'Gee, what a messy process that newsgathering is; it gives us a bad name.'") Granted, provocation can be an effective tool to pry truth from the mouths of practiced liars. Yes, Horst Faas, the Pulitzer Prize–winning photojournalist, has a point when he says, "We followed Diana the last months of her life because she was off with a playboy and a future King of

England. If you float around the Mediterranean and take a prince along, that's big news."[13] But the chase, the stakeouts, the ambushes, the interviews done with misplaced prosecutorial zeal, the crush of photographers and videographers "doing their job" are all ultimately self-defeating. They have given journalists the image of vultures.

"They're just awful people, jackals, aren't they?" the president of an Ivy League college says to me one day.

"Well, no, they're not, but they have not imposed any order on themselves," I reply, ever the orderly lawyer.

Talk to anyone at the center of a media maelstrom and you will find that their chief complaint focuses on the chaos created by television's aggressive "bookers," news producers paid to be relentless. Working the telephones like boiler room telemarketers, they wheedle, cajole, promise, negotiate, do virtually anything to get you on camera. Lucianne Goldberg, the irreverent New York literary agent and author, who seemed to enjoy her supporting actress role in the Monica Lewinsky scandal (at least up to the point where she wanted to sue *U.S. News & World Report* for defamation), is characteristically blunt and funny:

"The print people weren't so bad. You could get rid of them. But the television news production people, my God! I think they all grew up in some concentration camp somewhere in Idaho, scrambling for bits of food."

Two months after Monica and Lucianne (and William Ginsburg and Linda Tripp and the whole cabal) burst onto the American consciousness, Lucianne had still not given any television interviews, other than one sidewalk photo opportunity outside her Upper West Side apartment in the early days of the unfolding story to quiet the baying hounds. Still, she says, *60 Minutes,* was sending fresh flowers to her apartment every week. "The place looked like a well-kept grave." The roses, the telephone calls, the gifts, the sweet and not-so-sweet seductions became more than a nuisance. They were obnoxious.

"At some point you just want to scream at them, 'Fuck off,'" she explains. "But when you do, they just get cheerful, and say, 'I'll call you next week.' It is impossible to embarrass these people."

Finally, she agreed to do a *Today* interview for Dan Abrams. "He was so honest, so direct," says Lucianne. "He said to me, 'Landing an interview with you would really help my career.' It was sweet."

Abrams and every other television correspondent will need more than candor (and good timing) to sign up interviews in the future. The burgeoning fragmentation of the cable, on-line and traditional television business will only exacerbate the competitive crush around news subjects. Eventually, those with something to say ("he was a good kisser") will simply sell the news interview as a commodity, not just to reap the cash but to grant an exclusive that will keep five hundred other requests at bay.

For years, the press has seen the institutional anarchy that pervades its newsgathering efforts as an endearing quality—cute dimples that hark back to *The Front Page* stage play where the newsmen were half handsome scoundrels, half saints. Today, the anarchy is as anachronistic as the "scoop." Few people outside of journalism itself care whether CNN or CBS is first on the air with a breaking story (the loser will be only minutes behind) or whether *Newsweek* or *U.S. News* gets an important new leak from the Secretary of State. Thoroughness, depth, accuracy, fairness, are the virtues the public seeks from the press, not speed, much less intrusiveness. Yet the media will not work together collaboratively and patiently to lessen the obvious problem. During the early presidential primaries, the networks will cooperate to send a "pool" camera crew and a young, relatively inexperienced assistant producer along with each candidate who seems to have a chance. It's a useful training ground for the novices. After the field narrows, the pools disappear, every campaign event turning into a staged photo op where the traveling press horde inevitably blocks the views of any party faithful still naive enough to show up and expect to see the candidate through the videocams and over the boom mikes. The major news organizations can't seem to even "pool" on routine, ordinary assignments. When *The Washington Post* called CBS in the spring of 1998 to see if they could share an intern for "grand jury duty" (standing in a hallway all day to watch who would enter the "Monica Lewinsky" grand jury room), CBS declined, saying it needed to use its own intern. There is no habit of cooperation and apparently no leader in the industry willing, in the words of the late Right Reverend John Walker, the Bishop of Washington, "to show that cathedrals can be built with small, daily acts of grace."

There is an opportunity here for the media to restore some of its lost credibility with the public. It will require not a dreaded and despised "monolithic" approach to reporting the news as much as peer pressure and an enlightened, longer view that change is both necessary and desirable. Basically, both the problem and the resolution are organizational, a skill which the media often profess to abhor but at which they are actually quite accomplished. They should not wait until a satellite truck runs over and kills the child of some stakeout "victim." Or until Congress, fed up with the anarchy, passes an "anti-paparazzi" bill or other "privacy protection." Already, in California, lobbying by a coalition of celebrities, the Screen Actors Guild and victims' rights groups has fertilized the 1998 enactment of the nation's first "anti-paparazzi" law. The legislation creates liability for "physical" and "constructive" invasions of privacy through photographing or recording a person engaging in a "personal or familial activity." Its vague, poorly drafted language will require years of litigation to understand. (The California law actually operates to encourage the use of unsupervised freelancers by news organizations). Whether or not the enthusiasm for this legislation spreads to other states, public sentiment is clear. There are elements of the relationship between the public and the media that cannot be changed, but bringing a higher level of civility to newsgathering is not one.

PART TWO

UNINTENDED CONSEQUENCES

6

The "Ride-Along"

There was a predawn chill in Baltimore on December 16, 1992—hardly surprising for this part of the country only days before Christmas. Most of the city slept at 3:30 A.M., but the Clarence Mitchell Courthouse was awake with the activity of several sheriff's deputies and some videographers just arrived from the city's three major television stations. For the cops and the camera crews, the chill was hardly noticeable. An adrenaline rush kept them warm as they prepared for a series of busts that would generate publicity for the cops and, with any luck, compelling pictures for the videographers.

To some, the edge in the air may have seemed a bit zealous. After all, this was just another planned bust of "deadbeat dads." Unpaid child support enfeebles the nation, but its offenders rarely climb to the class of *French Connection* drug cartels. Fathers (and mothers) withhold child support to vindicate the scars left over from a napalmed divorce or to escape obligations that are deemed unjust or oppressive. Whatever the reason, those who are charged with enforcing court decrees face the same overwhelming demands that burden other law enforcement agencies. Too many deadbeats; too few cops. For a helping hand, the enforcers have turned to the news media.

Cleverly, the Maryland Department of Human Resources had devised a publicity campaign called the "Ten Most Wanted" for at least three years before this cold December morning. It was designed to show the department's determination to apprehend and arrest deadbeats.

Internal directives noted in 1989, "[W]e believe that the publicity will encourage delinquent obligors who might imagine themselves appropriate candidates for a future Ten Most Wanted list, to pay their arrears and their obligations more consistently."[1]

On December 16, after the raid, the department would issue its seasonally adjusted "Holiday Ten Most Wanted for Child Support" list, complete with pithy diatribes: "If you know someone who is not supporting his or her children, then they are committing the greatest crime of all: denying their children the right to a decent life."[2]

Baltimore's Office of Child Support Enforcement and its sheriff had done their part by inviting the media along on the early-morning sweep. Ideally, there would be pictures of several suspects being manacled. There was no heavy-duty reporting here, just collecting visuals. Only one of the three television stations even bothered to send a reporter; the others dispatched cameramen who would perform double duty—shooting video and gathering any tidbits to pass on to "the desk" for redistribution to writers who would compose short narratives that would not overtax the limited "news hole" available in each newscast. Performing public service, after all, works best when everybody wins. The police sweep would be a good story for television: simple point, strong video, few words.

By 4 A.M., the cars and vans were rolling. WMAR's cameraman strained to use the fleeting passing headlights and streetlamps to extract names, addresses and any other newsworthy information from the cop-speak in the arrest warrants. For the most part, the night was as frustrating as reading by streetlight. With the cameras poised to videotape their moves, deputies dramatically piled out of their vehicles to arrest the first suspect. No one was home. They arrived at a second Baltimore residence. The suspect's mother was there, but no suspect. Deputies arrested a third suspect while he was on the job as a cabdriver—not very visual.

The fourth of the planned arrests involved Benjamin Bond. Deputies arrived at his mother's house, knocked, then pushed their way in. Mary

Bond admitted that her son was asleep in the basement. Without protest from Mrs. Bond, the three camera crews spontaneously followed the tracks of the deputies into the basement where Benjamin and his brother, John, were sleeping in their underwear. The cameras caught the mildly dramatic video of deputies leading a shackled and, by this time, fully clothed Benjamin from behind a curtain and up the stairs to the waiting patrol car.

It wasn't *The Untouchables,* but at least the night was not wasted. For the most part, the three television stations aired perfunctory reports. A WJZ anchor intoned a twenty-four-second report:

> Delinquent fathers were the target of a sheriffs' roundup in Baltimore City early this morning. Thirty-seven-year-old Benjamin Bond is accused of owing more than $6,000 in back payments. Forty-nine-year-old James Kearney was driving his cab when sheriffs found him. Kearney owes more than $12,000. Sheriffs are still searching for two other men—thirty-seven-year-old David Turner, who owes $14,000, and forty-year-old Leroy Knight, who owes $6,000.[3]

Hardly the stuff of Emmies or Du Pont awards, the coverage would nonetheless warn recalcitrant parents to pay up or face the possible embarrassment of a televised arrest. Yet, for all their social value, the news reports would cost the stations enough money to make everybody wish they'd devoted the night of December 16 to a sound sleep rather than to public service.

Ten months after the busts, a complaint and summons arrived at the front desks of WBAL, WJZ and WMAR, alleging trespass, invasion of privacy, conspiracy and denial of the Bonds' civil rights.[4] Benjamin Bond alleged that a judge had released him shortly after his arrest, finding that he was in "substantial compliance" with his repayment order. But Benjamin did not allege libel, which would have required that he prove the reports false. He may or may not have been significantly behind in his obligations, as the State of Maryland alleged, but the court was apparently satisfied that Benjamin was making satisfactory progress in paying them off. Benjamin's other brother, James, claimed that he repeatedly asked the news crews to leave, a contention flatly denied by all three stations. No one, said the stations, ever protested the presence of the cameramen.

Though the news reports were substantially true, and although the stations were basically doing their part to help enforce the laws and, just maybe, improve the lives of some children, two of the three stations settled the lawsuits within a matter of months, making confidential payments to the Bonds and avoiding the uncertainty of a lawsuit. The third station settled later. None of the stations contested the charges by asking the judge to decide, long before trial, if the Bonds had a case. There was a respectable legal argument—not a slam-dunk winner by any means, but convincing—that the news media do not trespass on private property or invade anyone's legitimate privacy rights just by accompanying law enforcement officials on their rounds, especially when news coverage of police work has such benefits to society.

Why did the television stations fold 'em, rather than hold 'em? Had the news media lost their nerve? Were they too defensive or just plain smart?

To some extent, the answer lies in an incident just a few months before Benjamin Bond's arrest. In Brooklyn, Tawa Ayeni and her four-year-old son, Kayode, were home alone during the early evening of March 5, 1992, when there was pounding on the door of their Flatbush apartment. Several Secret Service agents and Postal Service inspectors loudly announced that they were police conducting an investigation. Mrs. Ayeni, wearing a dressing gown, cracked the door slightly. According to her testimony, an agent shoved her in the chest while others rushed into the apartment and began searching bedroom closets.

Federal agents suspected Babatunde—Tawa's husband and Kayode's father—of credit-card fraud. A magistrate had issued a search warrant for any evidence in the suspect's home. When the agents arrived, Babatunde was nowhere to be found, and while they did not suspect his wife of any involvement in the fraud, they searched the apartment. Babatunde's presence was immaterial under terms of a search warrant that empowered officials to look for evidence. When the agents left, more than three hours after they started, their efforts yielded only a photograph of the young family to be used for identifying Babatunde. By any cop's standards, the search was a bust.

Much like the Maryland authorities who were facing a losing battle in the child-support wars, federal agents confront an insurmountable task to control credit-card fraud. The scams range from the theft of credit cards carried in the mail to counterfeiting. As the 1992 Christmas season approached, even as federal agents continued their investigation of Ayeni and his alleged cohorts, news releases trumpeted credit-card fraud as "a $3 billion per year industry [that] is growing faster than law enforcement officials can move to stem the tide."[5] But when the Secret Service, Postal Service and credit-card companies teamed up in Chicago to educate consumers, only eight people showed up at a seminar on security.[6] Was it any wonder that agents believed that press involvement was crucial to their efforts?

Hoping to enlist the media's help, and to generate some public awareness, agents agreed to let a CBS television crew join them in the search of the Ayeni apartment to videotape a segment for Ed Bradley's *Street Stories*. The crew, which arrived well after the search started and left long before its completion, videotaped an interview with one agent and about twenty minutes of the search, including agents pawing through personal effects, including photos, financial statements and letters. Briefly, the camera focused on a wall hanging, "Rules for a Happy Marriage," before returning to the search and the agents questioning Mrs. Ayeni.

Street Stories is now gone, but not its legacy. Though the CBS videotape was never broadcast on television, it aired in the chambers of Judge Jack Weinstein, a federal judge who sits in the Brooklyn-based Eastern District of New York and who has been described by a manual on federal judges as "a liberal with a strong civil rights record."[7] Weinstein had been a Columbia Law School professor and an author of legal treatises on evidence and the vagaries of civil procedure, the rules of litigating a civil claim. Then, in 1967, Lyndon Johnson called to offer Weinstein a place on the federal district court.[8]

If he had no reputation as a judicial activist before the late 1980s, Judge Weinstein earned his stripes when he presided over the Agent Orange case, a class-action toxic-tort suit filed by Vietnam veterans who claimed adverse health effects from the infamous defoliant used in the war. A 1989 book by Yale Law professor Peter Schuck, *Agent Orange on Trial*, detailed the judge's extraordinary efforts to bully the parties into settlement. A few years ago, the *New York Law Journal* said that the book "documented the management of a case by a very strong-willed judge— some say too much so."⁹ Nonetheless, in 1991, *The New York Times* was quoting "lawyers [who] variously say that [Weinstein] is brilliant and creative, energetic and compassionate, that his rulings blend scholarship with pragmatism."¹⁰

Judge Weinstein's involvement in the Ayeni case began not in any lawsuit against CBS, but in Babatunde Ayeni's attempts to obtain a copy of the videotape to use in defense of criminal charges eventually placed against him. CBS, following customary practice within the industry, resisted. The media have long opposed these attempts to press them into service as a sort of litigation resource or video library for the prosecution or defense. Reporters fear that they seem to take sides when their testimony or work product becomes the subject of a trial. And when confidential sources are involved, compelling reporters to testify or to surrender their notes, video- or audiotapes may reveal identities and dry up important sources of information. Some forty-three states, including New York, have passed "shield laws" or recognized a state common-law privilege to protect the press. Even where there is no shield law, states and federal courts widely recognize a qualified "reporter's privilege," grounded in First Amendment protection for newsgathering, to avoid testifying or turning over tapes, photos and notes. Neither New York's shield law nor the privilege was much help for CBS.

Babatunde did not challenge the validity of the search warrant, but he had diverse theories why he needed the tape, including a claim that the court should dismiss charges because of "outrageous government conduct." Judge Weinstein disagreed with Babatunde that the videotape would help him seek dismissal of his indictment. But the judge added:

> A Court . . . should be particularly careful in a criminal case not to fore-close or prejudge any defense that a defendant might present at trial. . . .
>
> . . . The legal relevance of the tape is that it proves that an exhaustive search of defendant's apartment failed to reveal a shred of evidence of credit-card fraud. This argument, of course, is one defendant would be free to make even without the tape. As a matter of law, defendant could successfully prove that his apartment contained no evidence of a crime without use of the tape. As a practical matter, however, the value of the tape to defendant's case in terms of its potential effect on a jury is ex-tremely high. The tape, particularly the statements contained within it, would provide defendant a window through which he could demonstrate to the jury with extraordinary clarity the government's zeal to arrest him and its failure to produce any evidence after tearing apart his home.
>
> Our juries are particularly vigilant to prevent gross overreaching and abuse by the government. . . . This tape, with the gripping pictures of a cowering wife and child and lack of any evidence supporting the govern-ment's case, is likely to be strongly relied on by the jury in weighing the government's charges. . . .[11]

As for CBS's privilege to resist Babatunde's subpoena, the videotape's possible benefits to the defense—slim as they might be—outweighed any interests that CBS might have. And besides, CBS could claim no privilege in its videotape *when it had no right to record it in the first place.*

Judge Weinstein's sensibilities were plainly offended by the search, al-though it seems unlikely that a federal judge would be surprised to learn that most police searches are every bit as intrusive and thorough. But it was the television camera that enabled the judge to view the search. Rather than praise or acknowledge this unique "window" on police ac-tions, Judge Weinstein turned his wrath on CBS and gratuitously invited the Ayenis to sue CBS:

Defendant does not seek damages from CBS at this time. This court could not, in any event, entertain such a request for relief in a criminal case. That CBS both trespassed upon defendant's home and engaged in conduct, with the connivance of the government, directly contrary to Fourth Amendment principles, however, bears upon the court's evaluation of CBS's newsgathering privilege. The First Amendment is a shield, not a sword. Even a reporter must accept limits on how far upon another person's privacy he or she may intrude. To both approve CBS's violation of defendant's privacy and rule that he is not permitted to see the private images that were taken from him in the course of that violation would be intolerable. CBS must give defendant the tape which records the images and sounds taken from his home without his permission while illegally within his home.[12]

Ayeni later pleaded guilty to one count of credit-card fraud, but his wife and young son accepted the judge's implicit invitation. When they sued CBS and a Secret Service agent, they struck it lucky by drawing as their purportedly impartial jurist none other than Jack Weinstein. Though Judge Weinstein had concluded already that CBS had (1) trespassed, (2) violated Ayeni's privacy and (3) entered the Ayeni home "illegally," the judge apparently suffered no compunctions about presiding over a *civil* case that, seemingly, he had prejudged.[13]

Since 1939, when the Supreme Court issued its watershed First Amendment decision in *Near v. Minnesota* and for four decades thereafter—until the mid-1980s, judges have built fortresses for free-press rights. Courts made it difficult for public officials or public figures to silence their critics,[14] for government to obstruct the media's scrutiny, even when scrutiny involved secret papers purloined from the Pentagon,[15] and for state legislators to dictate how far reporters could go in their crime reporting.[16]

Given the broad First Amendment protections available to the news media, anyone might have expected CBS to ask the court to dismiss the case on those grounds. But rather than a predictable First Amendment defense, CBS tried a subdued approach. Piggybacking on the govern-

130

ment's case, CBS argued that the network acted with the permission of government officials and should be entitled to the same "qualified immunity" that usually protects officials from suit.

The defense was the wrong tack for all defendants. Allowing cameras into the apartment, wrote the judge, was a violation of the Fourth Amendment's shield against unreasonable search and seizure—"the equivalent of a rogue policeman using his official position to break into a home in order to steal objects for his own profit or that of another."[17] The federal agents had no claim to qualified immunity and, in any case, a private corporation like CBS and a private individual like the *Street Stories* field producer would never be entitled to the defense.

To his blistering pronouncements against CBS in Babatunde's criminal case, Judge Weinstein added another quote that equated the media with, well, scum. "CBS had no greater right than that of a thief to be in the home," he wrote.[18] That was enough for CBS. The network agreed to pay the Ayenis an undisclosed settlement rather quickly after the decision.[19]

Was CBS's decision prudent or precipitous? Certainly, CBS could not count on appellate reversal of Judge Weinstein's denunciation of its news practices. Neither the federal appellate court in New York nor the U.S. Supreme Court has demonstrated enthusiasm for newsgathering cases in the past few years, and as the government would learn, the appellate court in New York showed no more sympathy than Judge Weinstein had for what some might have seen as public service journalism. After CBS's settlement, Secret Service agent James Mottola—the sole government target identified by the plaintiffs—appealed Judge Weinstein's decision to the federal appeals court based in New York. The appellate judges showed they could turn a phrase as proficiently as Judge Weinstein.

"A private home is not a soundstage for law enforcement theatricals," they harrumphed.[20] In order to justify a case against the agent, the appellate court agreed with Judge Weinstein that the network's photographs of the Ayeni home amounted to a metaphysical "seizure," violating the Fourth Amendment's prohibition on illegal searches and seizures. It was okay for the gendarmes to ransack the Ayenis' apartment; they just couldn't show the public what they were doing. As a price for hitching up with the media, Postal Service and Secret Service agents would have to face trial.

The bad news from the "soundstages" of New York was powerful persuasion for the three network-affiliated television stations in Baltimore. They might better pay Benjamin Bond than risk long and expensive litigation leading to perhaps nothing more than similar judicial attacks on their efforts to report the work of law enforcement officials.

Most lawyers and executives in the communications industry now sense that courts will not be receptive to the argument that news organizations have a privilege to accompany the police onto private premises to show the world how laws are enforced. The presence of reporters and cameras in some instances probably even discourages the use of excessive force by the police or resistance by suspects. Yet the undeniable public interest in receiving information about law enforcement activities has clearly been transcended by public cynicism about television news ("They just want sensational crime shots") and by an even more potent force, privacy.

Privacy interests have driven courts to paint a talismanic line at the door of a private residence. In the Ayenis' case, the courts disregarded such facts as Babatunde's guilt or innocence, or his wife's possible knowledge of his activities. Neither Judge Weinstein nor the appeals court exhibited much concern for the difficulties of law enforcement to warn the public about credit-card fraud, or Babatunde's personal responsibility for putting his family in publicity's way. Not long after the Second Circuit's decision, another federal appeals court ruled that courts should not ignore these factors. Significantly, the case was not "tainted" with the involvement of the news media. The search had nothing to do with cops enlisting the media for publicity purposes. Instead, police officers used a General Motors security agent to help them search a home for stolen GM tools and parts. What is the unavoidable lesson here? When the police come calling with GM, rather than CBS, courts must consider whether marrying a possible felon reduces one's

reasonable expectation of privacy. Or, put more tartly, automobile manufacturers have more rights to recover stolen parts than the media have
to render public service.

   CBS's expensive "ride-along" with the Secret Service hardly marked
the first time that media had been sued for trespass. And for a while in the
1970s, it looked as if the media might be forgiven their trespasses (at least
if they served some useful purpose). The high-water mark for the media's
right to report from private property came in 1976. A Jacksonville,
Florida, newspaper had published a gruesome photograph showing the
charred silhouette of a seventeen-year-old girl on the floor of the home
where the teenager had burned to death. The victim's mother was furious,
especially since she had first learned of the circumstances surrounding her
daughter's death from seeing the newspaper upon her return from an out-
of-town trip. She instituted suit against the newspaper for trespassing at
the fire scene. The Florida Supreme Court dismissed the claim, recognizing that the news media had a privilege to accompany firefighters and police in similar circumstances due to well-established "custom and usage"
in the news business. The court wrote:

> It is not questioned that this tragic fire and death were being investigated
> by the fire department and the sheriff's office and that arson was sus-
> pected. The fire was a disaster of great public interest and it is clear that
> the photographer and other members of the news media entered the
> burned home at the invitation of the investigating officers. . . . Many af-
> fidavits of news editors throughout Florida and the nation and affidavits
> of Florida law enforcement officials were filed in support of [Florida
> Publishing Company's] motion for summary judgment. These affidavits
> were to the general effect that it has been a longstanding custom and
> practice for representatives of the news media to enter upon private
> property where disaster of great public interest has occurred—entering
> in a peaceful manner, without causing any physical damage, and at the
> invitation of the officers who are investigating the calamity. The affi-
> davits of law enforcement officers indicate that the presence of the news

media at such investigations is often helpful to the investigations in developing leads, etc.[21]

What a difference twenty years make. In the Jacksonville case, *Florida Publishing Company v. Fletcher,* the court not only recognized but heralded the public-interest role of the media. In more recent cases, including *Ayeni,* the rule in the *Fletcher* case, and its underlying respect for the media's work, has fallen from judicial grace. *Fletcher* is missing from the decisions in the cases against CBS or Secret Service agent Mottola. Even in Babatunde's attempt to get the CBS videotape for use in his criminal defense, *Fletcher* deserved only a brief mention, and little explanation how it differed from Babatunde's case except a hint that *Fletcher* applied only to "scenes of recent emergencies and disasters"[22]—a distinction without much of a difference. Instead, Judge Weinstein relied heavily on other cases that seemed to fit more closely with his preconceptions:

> If the news media were to succeed in compelling an uninvited and nonpermitted entry into one's private home whenever it chose to do so, this would be nothing less than a general warrant, equivalent to the writs of assistance which were so odious to the American colonists.[23]

It made little difference that CBS had not argued that it had a right to enter a private home "whenever it chose to do so." Judges now simply take the media's ubiquity for granted.

By 1994, Judge Weinstein had plenty of fodder for the argument that the media had no place in a private home. Only a smattering of cases echoed *Fletcher's* preference for conferring a privilege on the media when gathering the news. A couple are instructive:

- When a reporter covered the tragic death of two children who suffocated inside a refrigerator, a New York trial court rejected the parents' claims of trespass on their property. There could be no liability, the court reasoned, where the report was of legitimate public interest and the reporter's intent was not to injure the parents. The 1970 case is among the last to remember that, historically, litigants could use trespass only to claim compensation for property damage.24 Activist courts have broadened the claim to allow for alleged emotional and reputational injuries.25

- In 1986, an Iowa trial court rejected a couple's claim that newspaper and television reporters invaded their privacy by photographing dead cattle on the couple's farm. The reporters were covering a sheriff's investigation into the deaths and the court agreed that the media did not trespass where they had damaged no property and had received the sheriff's tacit approval to visit the farm.26

Far more plentiful than these embers from the Jacksonville fire were judicial decisions that paved the way for Judge Weinstein to liken the media to thieves. Most of these precursors foreshadowed the view of one's home (or castle) as a delicate needlepoint pillow in need of protection from greasy hands, no matter how many tortured victims, Uzis or drugs resided within. You could hear the rising crescendo:

- In 1981, a New York state trial court let a homeowner maintain claims against television stations that had accompanied a humane society investigator on a search for mistreated pets in a private home. The trial judge seemed to leave hope for different results in other cases, particularly where a newsworthy event involved disaster, or where the media could prove the custom or usage offered as evidence in *Fletcher.*27

- In 1986, a California appellate court allowed a widow's trespass and emotional distress claims against NBC for videotaping paramedics' unsuccessful efforts to save her husband from a heart attack in the couple's home. While the case goes further than any previous to limit a First Amendment defense to trespass claims, at least until the Ayenis' lawsuit, the extreme facts of the case—the public broadcast of a health emergency—probably limited its effect.28 Yet don't all of us want to know the caliber and speed of effective medical care under such circumstances, and is it reasonable to expect media coverage without immunity from lawsuits?

- In 1993, a federal court in California agreed that a domestic abuse victim and her daughter could assert a claim against *Street Stories* for videotaping the victims in their home. A camera had accompanied a Mobile Crisis Intervention Team as it worked to help crime victims, including their efforts to calm the plaintiff and to help her build a case of spousal abuse.[29]

- In 1994, the Texas Court of Appeals allowed a ranching family to maintain a suit against a television station that escorted an animal control officer onto a ranch. The officer was investigating reports of malnourished horses. Although the court allowed the claim to proceed, it reasoned that only a jury could decide if the plaintiffs had established a case of trespass and infliction of emotional distress.[30]

Why have these cases ignored principles that deserve at least some consideration and weight? Are privacy interests so commanding in our dislocated, fearful world that they always trump personal responsibility and public interest? By and large, the cases of the last decade are so disdainful of the media that they disregard a criminal suspect's own responsibility for his family's loss of privacy, or the public's need to know the truths about what transpires behind closed doors.[31] Matthew Arnold once wrote that freedom is a good horse to ride, but it's a horse to ride somewhere. Our conflicted attitudes toward press freedoms are now leading us nowhere, or worse, in directions that endanger democracy by elevating our reliance on government.

The anthology of trespass litigation signals disturbing trends beyond the judiciary's growing hostility toward the news media. Up to the mid-1990s, the media had not been timid or tentative in asserting their rights to cover legitimate news events when they transpire on private property. Increasingly, however, the media's public-interest arguments are not only unsuccessful but astonishingly so. Respectable legal positions grounded in the public-service role of journalism are met with disdain bordering on ridicule and contempt ("thieves"!). It is hardly surprising, therefore, that judicial hostility to First Amendment arguments has led to a self-fulfilling fear and to the anomaly of cameras continuing to "ride along" while media companies hasten to compromise rather than defend challenges to their right to be free from trespass lawsuits.

In truth, of course, Judge Weinstein's vehemence has had more impact than his position properly allows. The decision of a trial judge does not truly rank as "precedent" in the Anglo-American system of justice, though the decision may be persuasive to other judges. Only decisions of appellate courts can bind the courts under them. But not long after Judge Weinstein's ruling, according to the Associated Press, the *FBI Law Enforcement Bulletin* warned police that they should not permit "[m]edia participation in enforcement activities that occur in private areas . . . "[32]

Police reticence and some degree of media self-censorship is undoubtedly reducing coverage of law enforcement work. And it is also certain that privacy proponents will exploit judicial antagonism to newsgathering by bringing "test" cases that seek to restrict the needed and natural cooperation between journalists and the police.

In Manhattan, federal judge Allen G. Schwartz ruled in February 1999 that a police tradition known as the "perp walk" violated the constitutional rights of a burglary suspect who was paraded before a local television station's cameras. The standard police practice, dating from even before Theodore Roosevelt was New York City's Police Commissioner, responds to the press's demands for a glimpse of criminals who have been arrested and showcases the accomplishments of the police. In his opinion Judge Schwartz criticized the practice for infringing on the Constitution's prohibition against unreasonable seizures. He concluded that the perp walk had been "conducted in a manner designed to cause humiliation" to the suspect, "with no legitimate law enforcement objective or justification." The judge ruled the suspect could proceed with a lawsuit against New York City for embarrassment and damage to reputation.

Similarly, in Colorado the American Civil Liberties Union has taken up the cause of one especially unsavory felon in order to advance the privacy rights of criminals. The ACLU's initiative, reminiscent of its attempt during the 1960s and 1970s to expand statutes permitting convicted felons to expunge their criminal records, is as misguided as its belief that expungement of records would aid rehabilitation.

The ACLU's spear carrier in Colorado is thirty-four-year-old Mark Robinson, now a resident of the Colorado prison system serving sentences for sexual assault on a child and sexual exploitation of children. He has sued four Denver television stations, both daily newspapers and various reporters for trespassing into his private residence. And what a home it was. So clean. Working bus stops and other places, Robinson enticed twenty-two teenaged girls, some as young as thirteen years old, to his home on the pretext of employing them in a cleaning service. He would then persuade the girls to pose nude.[33] Police had invited media cameras to accompany them on Robinson's arrest in the hope that additional victims would recognize the residence and come forward with their stories of Robinson's exploitation of them. The plan worked. Robinson pled guilty after substantial evidence accumulated from girls who had responded to the news coverage.

The ACLU case challenges the right of county and city police to invite the media to the arrest and search of Robinson's home. Presumably, the ACLU figures if it can win this one, it can win any case. If the ACLU can persuade Colorado courts to overlook the benefits that the public derives from permitting cameras to record Robinson's arrest, then no public-interest argument can open the door of a private home. The presumption of privacy becomes a sacred cow. The home becomes off-limits to the media even when the government has probable cause to enter. Wait until some police brutality or misconduct occurs within these sacred palaces of privacy. Then we will see how glorious this new body of law is. How odd to believe that people need protection from the media, but not the police.

In other places on the planet, people fear repression more than a camera lens. If there were a free press, they would gladly invite the media to witness police action. The intrusion is thought to be worth the protection of public scrutiny. But now in the land of the free and the brave, we punish the police for inviting this scrutiny willingly. We protect the scoundrel who uses a house as his home office for crimes. We flog the media for highlighting social ills that hide inside a private home. Our judiciary now deems it necessary to protect citizens from the media, with little regard for individual circumstances or the apparently remote possibility that television might just do something good.

In 1992, the Baltimore television vans had rolled along with the police to apprehend "deadbeat dads." By 1999 (after six more years of "reality-based" television newscasts), the Supreme Court of the United States squarely faced the issue of whether law enforcement officials could invite the media along on their crime-busting raids of homes. Two cases—one involving the search of a Montana ranch by federal wildlife agents and the other involving a police search for a fugitive at his parents' Maryland home—were combined by the High Court into a single argument. In Maryland, the media were still taking pictures of people in their underwear. As the parents of the fugitive were rousted from their bed, clad only in undershorts and a nightgown, the accompanying photographer snapped away. The fugitive son was not in the house.

At oral argument in March 1999, the justices were clearly appalled by the police-press collaboration. Justice O'Connor described the Maryland incident as "an amazing invasion" of the couple's privacy.

"Why do you have to take photographers into someone's house?" Justice Souter asked counsel for the law enforcement agents. "You can have a news conference when it's over."

When the counsel tried to explain that the presence of the news media prevents any possible police misconduct, Souter dismissed the idea as "fluff." Across the ideological spectrum, the justices saw only the privacy interests of a homeowner. The benefits to the public (and homeowners) of the media's presence were cast aside.[34] As syndicated columnist Dan Thomasson would write: "Everyone loses in this instance—the public, which ends up with only what the police want it to know; the police, who are unable to defend themselves against scurrilous accusations; and the press, which often must sort out the truth from sketchy, second-hand reports."

SPEAK INTO MY NECKLACE, PLEASE

Two months before TWA Flight 800 dove in a fireball into the Atlantic Ocean off Long Island, station WCPO was showing people in Cincinnati just how lax security measures were at the Cincinnati International Airport—and, by implication, any airport.

Still shiny from a major expansion that had made it one of the largest Delta hubs in the world, the airport was anything but state-of-the-art behind the scenes. Delta had contracted, for cost reasons, with a company to provide security, cleaning and baggage-handling services. Employees of the contracting company were naturally supposed to be carefully screened, since their unfettered access to the planes would make it easy for someone to place a bomb on board if he or she had a reason to do so. A three-month investigation by WCPO's I-Team discovered a "huge crack in the system." Delta's contractor was so "desperate" to hire workers for low-pay jobs that they performed ridiculously inadequate background checks, the WCPO report said. Viewers met Leroy Bradley, alias Stephen Toy, a former worker at the airport who had had the run of the place under a temporary security badge even though his prior work record had been falsified and his criminal rap sheet hidden. The company had not conducted a thorough enough check to learn that Leroy wasn't really who he said he was.

"I could have blown up an airplane," said Leroy.

WCPO's correspondent Laure Quinlivan then took viewers on a trip to see just how simple it was for virtually anyone to gain access to the planes by going to work for the contractor. The station sent one of its associate producers, Linda, to a job fair which the contractor was holding at a local Comfort Inn in nearby Erlanger, Kentucky. Linda carried a hidden camera in her purse. The conversation with an interviewer for the contractor was illuminating:

"I need you bad, I'll start you Monday. I need you to work bad," said the interviewer.

Linda expressed some amazement at how desperate he was for help: "You sound like you need people."

"Within the last two weeks, I've lost about a hundred people," said the man matter-of-factly.

"Why?" asked Linda.

"Because they all have felonies," said the man with a burst of candor that would have been unthinkable if he had known a camera was recording him.

He hired everyone in the room, the news report continued, but checked only one of the three previous jobs that Linda had concocted for her phony employment application. The one job reference actually checked by the company led to correspondent Laure Quinlivan, who posed on camera as Linda's former employer. "She only worked two months here" (not a year as specified on the application), said Quinlivan into a telephone. "Aren't you interested in her job performance?" she queried. "Believe it or not, no," responded the caller. Just to be sure the job reference was really horrible, Quinlivan added, "I think maybe she had a drug problem." The contractor still wanted Linda on her high-security job Monday morning.

Misrepresentation and hidden cameras had been used to cover a story that could not have been shown to the public otherwise. Was it important enough to justify the use of the clandestine camera? Indisputably. Another part of the report illustrated how security badges for workers weren't even checked before they were given access to the airport's service and maintenance areas. Equipped with a hidden camera in his Igloo lunchbox, one employee knocked on a security door and then breezed through unchecked when someone opened the door for him. Within a day after TWA Flight 800 exploded in midair, WCPO was able to do a further report that grew out of the I-Team's earlier work and that other local stations could only dream about broadcasting. (Indeed, a full twelve days after the crash, *The New York Times* published a front-page story, "Few Checks on Backgrounds of Ground Crews at Airports," which echoed WCPO's earlier reporting, including the quote, "This is the major hole in the system."[35]) The station told viewers frankly that it had still been debating "whether to tell you" the "airline industry's best-kept secret," but the fate of TWA Flight 800 had forced the issue. The secret? Even brand-new airports like Cincinnati's do not screen checked baggage for explosives on domestic flights even though the technology is available to do so.

This is the type of editorial decision making that goes on every day in newsrooms large and small, print and electronic. The public, however, rarely catches a glimpse, much less fully appreciates this decision making. WCPO had refrained from telling a dramatic, significant story out of a sense of responsibility, perhaps even a fear of criticism. ("Look at those idiots in the media—telling everybody that luggage isn't screened on domestic flights so some mad bomber can check a bag full of explosives and then not get on the plane.") These are tough calls. Reasonable journalists can differ on how to handle a situation or treat a story. When WCPO aired the luggage "secret," it also reported that the FAA had been "dragging its feet" in requiring the airlines to buy and use the expensive equipment to screen checked baggage. Would broadcasting the story earlier have motivated the FAA? Probably not much, but who knew? Tragedies like TWA Flight 800 seem to have more to do with sparking federal regulation than news coverage about yet another potentially dangerous situation. The public, of course, does not and cannot give the media credit for self-restraint—for stories it never sees. When, as here, the story emerges in the aftermath of carnage, there may be some who wonder whether the media have been accomplices in silence. In any event, the media is not likely to receive the benefit of the doubt for doing (or trying to do) the right thing.

But "doing the right thing" is exactly what the news executives at this local station are all about. In fact, those are the words that WCPO's former news director Jim Zarchin uses when he explains why he chose to work in television news. ("We wanted to make things right; we wanted to do the right thing.")

Surreptitious taping, however, whether or not done as part of award-winning public-service journalism, is not popular with the public. As with the public's (and the judiciary's) reaction to "ride-alongs," people tend to identify with the homeowner in his underwear or the guy who's candid when he believes he won't be held accountable but flannel-mouthed when he sees a camera or tape recorder. Hidden cameras smack of sneakiness. Two-way mirrors. Uncle Howard peering around a corner with his videocam to catch the unsuspecting, the compromised. The new generation of subminiature cameras—the "hat cams," "button cams," "lipstick cams"—are technology's gift to newsgathering. Used sensibly, they promise public-interest journalism at its most gleaming—exposing hypocrisy, fraud and deceit. They should permit us to look at reality more clearly. They can also be used to cover the inconsequential—how the towel man at the car wash will steal a five-dollar bill left on the dashboard. Somewhere in between lies the news story of social usefulness. A hidden camera set up at any fast-food restaurant (especially one on an interstate highway) might do wonders to restore table manners in America. Watching people eat in these places can be a new form of weight control—it takes you four days for your appetite to return.

PRIME TIME LIVE GOES TO COURT

From coast to coast, microcameras are revolutionizing consumer reporting. In West Palm Beach, for instance, station WPTV documented the fleecing of car owners by unprincipled mechanics. In Phoenix, station KNXV told of the unnecessarily expensive repair of videocassette recorders. Even when there is no outright fraud or deceit, hidden cameras can open a world of consumer reporting that is otherwise off-limits. The twenty largest supermarket chains didn't want to talk to ABC about their sales of shelf space to major manufacturers—so called "slotting fees"—a practice that is perfectly legal, but of indisputable importance to American shoppers. As *20/20*'s Brian Ross reported in November 1995:

> [I]n the last few years, slotting fees, almost unheard of just ten years ago, have come to involve billions and billions of dollars, blamed by many manufacturers for both driving up the price of what's on the shelf and keeping lots of new products off the shelf. And with some 15,000 new products this year . . . slotting fees are something everyone in the grocery business seems to know about, something only a few are willing to talk about. Wherever we went at this convention put on by the big supermarket chains, two public relations people followed to listen and to warn.[36]

So ABC gave a hidden camera to a Georgia manufacturer of a scrumptious barbecue sauce in order to document his difficulties in getting his product into New York stores. Viewers learned, most for the first time, that manufacturers pay $5,000 to $10,000 per item to get shelf space in a supermarket, regardless of product quality, cost or any other factor that consumers might find important. In one case, slotting fees added fifty cents to the cost of a package of cookies. The hidden cameras gave this *20/20* story its authenticity and power; a traditional report, where retailers refuse to talk publicly and brand secondhand reports as off-base, would pale by comparison. Hidden cameras undercut the "plausible deniability" that shields corporate and institutional interests, as well as swindlers and charlatans, from public accountability.

The successes of the hidden camera justify broad legal protection for its use in newsgathering. An uneven reception in the courts, however, suggests that the media will face the same judicial antagonism it has witnessed in the "ride-along" cases.[37] In North Carolina, a jury in 1997 awarded $5.5 million in punitive damages against ABC News for using hidden cameras to record questionable practices in a Food Lion meat department. Food Lion had sued ABC over a 1992 *Prime Time Live* report that depicted unsanitary conditions at Food Lion supermarkets, including rotten meat, fish, chicken and other food being dated again and put out for sale after their proper expiration dates had passed. The report included on-camera interviews with six former employees from different Food Lion stores who recounted claims of widespread unsanitary conditions. *Prime Time* producers conducted background interviews with dozens of other former and current employees, many of whom related corroborating tales. In order to verify the employees' stories, two *Prime Time* producers went undercover, accepting jobs at Food Lion deli and meat departments. When they quit two weeks later, they had hours of microcamera footage that graphically confirmed many of the worst allegations. Pictures of dirty equipment and floors and spoiled food formed the centerpiece of a disturbing report.

In the public arena, Food Lion fought back with a public relations campaign that vigorously attacked the veracity of *Prime Time Live*'s report. But in court, Food Lion sidestepped the issue of the program's accuracy. Instead, the supermarket chain battered the practice of undercover journalism itself, asserting that the producers had committed fraud by misrepresenting themselves and obtaining and conducting their supermarket jobs under false pretenses. The jury agreed, awarding Food Lion compensatory damages of $1,402, primarily for the cost of training the two undercover producers. It then awarded $5.5 million in punitive damages, apparently to send ABC a "message."

It is not clear what this message is supposed to be. The jury seemed most perturbed by the reporter's use of an assumed identity and false credentials, without recognizing that some element of duplicity is inevitable in this kind of reporting.[38]

The foreman of the jury in the *Food Lion* case, an amiable man from Greensboro, North Carolina, told *Good Morning America* after the verdict that the media needed boundaries. The jury felt that reporters shouldn't misrepresent themselves or use other deceptive practices to obtain the news, even when the "news" amounted to truthful reporting about serious health and safety violations at one of America's largest grocers. The foreman also said the case "wasn't about the First Amendment," which, of course, is like saying skiing isn't about snow. In fact, the lawsuit was actually one of the most pernicious attacks in recent years on the public's First

Amendment right to receive truthful information. Even narrowly construed, the decision's logical conclusion would almost totally insulate corporations and other powerful institutions from the eyes of undercover enterprise journalism.

Undercover journalism has an honorable place in American history. Nelly Bly's famous "Ten Days in a Madhouse," exposing deplorable conditions at New York's Blackwells Island Insane Asylum, was made possible only after she misrepresented herself to asylum authorities, pretending to be insane. Nearly one hundred years later, *Los Angeles Herald-Examiner* reporter Merle Linda Wolin posed as a poor illegal alien to report a sixteen-part series on sweatshop conditions. Hidden cameras, meanwhile, have exposed deplorable social conditions and wrongdoing, such as abuse at nursing homes and day-care centers, trafficking in babies and Medicare kickbacks.

Prime Time Live's exposé on Food Lion was consistent with this rich tradition. It was exactly the kind of television journalism we ought to want to encourage—a well-documented report on a subject of serious public consequence. If Food Lion believed it was genuinely wronged by *Prime Time Live,* it should have challenged the facts of the story—and the motives of ABC's journalists—in a defamation suit. Its strategy was to sidestep the facts of the report and attack instead the means by which some of those facts were obtained was a public relations coup. But it is also an ugly legal precedent which unless overturned will be a shot at the messenger that pumps lead right into the public's optic nerve.

Similarly, some courts have declined to open the door to businesses that do not open their doors to the public. A Los Angeles trial court refused to dismiss a case against *Prime Time Live* for videotaping private conversations inside a business that offered pricey psychic advice to the public through "900" telephone numbers. ABC had investigated suspicions that the "psychics" were phonies; the psychics complained that ABC covertly videotaped comments and aired them out of context to prove the network's premise that the service was a scam. As in *Food Lion,* the network needed to plant its reporter as an employee, but the psychics posted "no trespassing" signs and purportedly imposed a blanket "no visitors" policy on their facility. A trial ended in a $1 million verdict for the psychics.[39]

In Chicago, *Prime Time Live* fared slightly better in what should have been—but has not been—an influential decision written by one of the most well-regarded judges in the nation, Richard A. Posner, Chief Judge of the U.S. Court of Appeals for the Seventh Circuit. Appointed to the appeals court bench in 1981 by President Reagan and elevated to Chief Judge in 1993, Posner is among three judges quoted most often in other judicial opinions by their peers.[40]

The University of Chicago law school professor has been a progenitor of important legal trends, notably the "law and economics" movement that applies cost-benefit analysis to judicial decision making, even in the First Amendment area. ("After all, what courts are trying to do is maintain a marketplace for ideas and opinion," he says.[41]) He is a "prolific writer" whom admirers describe as "brilliant"; Supreme Court Justice William Brennan, for whom Posner once clerked, has praised him as "one of two authentic geniuses I have ever met."[42] (Justice William Douglas was the other.) The tribute is more than mere Brennan flattery; Posner ranked first among graduates from Harvard Law School in 1962.

In 1995, Posner handed ABC and *Prime Time Live* a victory of sorts, about as good a win as the media gets these days from the courts. The case involved an investigation into a Midwest eye clinic, operated by a Dr. Desnick, to determine if the clinic would recommend needless cataract surgery. ABC reporters and volunteers posed as would-be customers of the clinic. The clinic recommended surgery for the phony patients, unnecessary surgery according to ABC's medical experts. The clinic sued for libel and invasion of privacy based upon the intrusiveness of the hidden cameras and the misrepresentation of the reporters. Dr. Desnick claimed that the network's reporters had promised him they would not use "ambush" interviews or undercover surveillance.

Judge Posner's opinion hardly lionized the media. It did not sing about journalists as the stalwarts of democracy or keepers of the flame of freedom. Instead, Posner recognized the need for duplicity—both in newsgathering and in life:

> There must be something to this surprising result. Without it a restaurant critic could not conceal his identity when he ordered a meal, or a browser pretend to be interested in merchandise that he could not afford to buy. Dinner guests would be trespassers if they were false friends who never would have been invited had the host known their true character, and a consumer who in an effort to bargain down an automobile dealer falsely claimed to be able to buy the same car elsewhere at a lower price would be a trespasser in the dealer's showroom.[43]

Posner concluded that a business, opening its doors to the public, could not cry foul or claim invasion of privacy when reporters entered under pretext.[44] And then, having ruled in ABC's favor out of dispassionate, analytical realism, he cut loose with a blunt assessment about how much honesty people can reasonably expect from reporters:

> Investigative journalists well known for ruthlessness promise to wear kid gloves. They break their promise, as any person of normal sophistication would expect. If that is "fraud," it is the kind against which potential victims can easily arm themselves by maintaining a minimum of skepticism about journalistic goals and methods.[45]

Personal feelings about what scum buckets might populate the media obviously didn't blind the judge to reaching an intellectually honest result. You don't have to like or admire the media, Posner seemed to be saying, but it is wrong to cripple newsgathering by denying them legal protection for the tools of their trade:

> Today's "tabloid" style investigative television reportage, conducted by networks desperate for viewers in an increasingly competitive market . . . constitutes—although it is often shrill, one-sided, and offensive, and sometimes defamatory—an important part of the market. It is entitled

to all the safeguards with which the Supreme Court has surrounded liability for defamation. And it is entitled to them regardless of the name of
the tort . . . and, we add, regardless of whether the tort suit is aimed at
the content of the broadcast or the production of the broadcast. *Desnick
v. American Broadcasting Cos.,* 44 F. 3d 1345, 1354.

Distaste for the media, Posner would say, cannot lead to disdain for
the First Amendment freedoms we have given them to bring us the information a free people need. Unfortunately for America, Chief Judge Posner is an oasis in the judiciary.

7

A Fine Day for the Government

Each of us—even the hedonist or the egoist or the most insensitive lout—possesses *bikezel,* the word the Zulu tribe in South Africa uses to describe the spirit that alerts us to danger. Sometimes we call *bikezel* "intuition" or "experience" or "a hunch." It signals us when a child is about to go over the edge, when a co-worker is about to quit, when a friend is about to announce that she is getting divorced. "That we are surrounded by deep mysteries is known to all but the incurably ignorant," the Nigerian novelist Chinua Achebe has written.[1] *Bikezel* is one of these mysteries.

There is a sense of dread in what might be called the First Amendment tribe these days. The members of this community include media people, lawyers, educators and true believers, ranging from judges to librarians and artists. They are united by a belief in the transcendent value of language and art and an abhorrence of governmental attempts to "protect" people from free expression, whether it is cigarette advertising or Robert Mapplethorpe photographs. They know, with Aeschylus, that wisdom does not come from information alone but from the pain which accompanies experience and which "falls drop by drop upon the heart." Some of these people see a python lying dead ahead on the American path. It is a snake engorged and empowered with the public's venom toward the media. Quietly, it is already choking the breath out of what Justice William Brennan saw thirty years ago as our "profound national

150

commitment to the principle that debate on public issues should be un-inhibited, robust and wide-open."[2] Objective evidence tells us the danger exists. *Bikezel* tells us it will prey on us more voraciously in the future.

In case after case after case during the past ten years, a slow drumbeat of dull defeats has accumulated in the body of First Amendment law governing the news media. The ride-along cases are emblematic. None of these defeats, on an isolated basis, are so shocking or patently unreasonable as to sound a general alarm. Taken together, however, they create an unmistakable trend: First Amendment law in this nation is stagnating. At a time when the new world information order calls for a brave adaptation of existing First Amendment law to the possibilities of a new age, the expansion of First Amendment rights has not just ground to a halt but is actually retreating. Records brimming with information that should be open to the public have been sealed. Newsgathering has been affirmatively discouraged. Confidential sources have been needlessly identified. Prior restraints and trumped-up, intimidating libel cases that should have been dismissed preemptively have become grueling endurance contests. Sometimes, they are settled for hundreds of thousands or millions of dollars. Video cameras are regarded as vampires except when they record men getting kicked in the testicles or dogs carrying birthday cakes for *America's Funniest Home Videos.*

To some extent, the stagnation of the law has been masked by the lack of a stunning, dramatic disaster. No landmark First Amendment case from the Warren or Burger Court has been overturned. Yet, while a ludicrously unconstitutional piece of congressional grandstanding called the Communications Decency Act has been struck down as an indecent limitation on free speech on the Internet, no major First Amendment cases have been significantly advanced. Several have been eroded around the edges. "The biggest news from the Supreme Court of the United States in the First Amendment area during the past decade has been the Court's silence,"[3] says my colleague Bob Sack, the distinguished longtime counsel to *The Wall Street Journal,* whom President Clinton named to the U.S. Court of Appeals for the Second Circuit in 1998. The silence has been

151

mistakenly greeted in some news media quarters with relief. (These people anticipated far worse.) The judiciary's silence reflects nothing more or less than the same cold disdain that permeates the public. If the judiciary's overarching attitude toward the media in recent years could be summed up with a single maxim, it would be: "Why should we give them any more First Amendment rights? They can't use the ones they have now with any responsibility."

REVELATION AT THE BOCA CLUB

This sense of chip-by-chip erosion can be detected both objectively and subjectively. In the latter category falls a defining moment which occurred at the Boca Raton Resort and Club in the winter of 1996. Sprawling over 356 acres of lush gardens on both the Intracoastal Waterway and the Atlantic Ocean, the Boca Club calls up the grandeur of the past. High-ceilinged salons, tiled fountains, lonely, endless corridors, give the older part of the hotel a chill amid the humidity and mildew. As if the surroundings were not illusion enough, the management has arranged in the bar for roaming magicians to entertain the guests. In season, the hotel fills up with a steady tide of conventioneers, businesspeople with spouses availing themselves of a long weekend wrapped in yesterday's splendor.

On one such January weekend, an American Bar Association group collected the protagonists of the famous Pentagon Papers case together again to share reminiscences. The occasion marked the twenty-fifth anniversary of the Supreme Court's famous 6–3 ruling that the United States government could not prevent *The New York Times* and *The Washington Post* from publishing classified Pentagon documents about the Vietnam War. The losing party, namely the government, was cheerfully represented by Whitney North Seymour, the U.S. Attorney in New York at the time and an appointee of the Nixon administration. He was outnumbered. Two of the *Times*'s lawyers on the case, James Goodale and Floyd Abrams, were there, as was the newspaper's former executive editor Abe Rosenthal. Judge James Oakes from the U.S. Court of Appeals for the Second Circuit provided a semblance of neutrality until you remembered that he had dissented from the decision of that court upholding the government's effort to prohibit publication of the papers. The *Times*'s current counsel, George Freeman, moderated, but he didn't need to use a cattle prod. Twenty-five years of pent-up explanation spewed forth.

The *Times* men were candid:

"I don't like anything militaristic," declared Rosenthal, "I'm not a lefty. I'm anticommunist, antifascist. I'm against all militarists. I don't even like doormen."

"I have always been a Nixon-hater," confessed Goodale. To him, the government and the news media clashed over the Pentagon Papers because "Nixon was trying to 'get' the Eastern establishment."

The *Times*'s greatest fear, strange in hindsight, was that the papers were a hoax. When the classified documents had been leaked to the *Times*, Rosenthal's "terror was that some kids at Harvard were writing all this." Authenticating the papers became as important as "making damn sure—or at least as much as we could be—that we would not endanger the security of the United States."

Prosecutor Seymour would have none of it. It was "absolute and pure nonsense" that Nixon was conducting a "political vendetta against the *Times*," he said. Nor was the publication of the papers any sort of "brilliant journalism."

"It was just an instance of receiving a gift [from disenchanted Pentagon bureaucrat Daniel Ellsberg] and deciding what to do with it," he sniffed.

As for endangering the country, the former warriors found common ground. "The government's real concern about the Pentagon Papers," said Seymour, was that they described various Cold War diplomatic efforts with supposedly neutral countries in Europe, the Middle East and elsewhere. According to the government's lawyer, "no one gave a damn about the ancient history of Truman's attitude toward Vietnam." In fact, Abrams believed that the government readily understood that the great bulk of the information contained in the papers could not possibly imperil national security. "Ninety-five percent [of the Pentagon Papers] could have been declassified," Abrams thought.

Rosenthal remembered the government's agitation the same way. "Kissinger was screaming about us endangering U.S. relations with the Australians or the Chinese. Who cares? It wasn't the *Times*'s function to protect diplomatic relations."

There was also general agreement about one other point: the Pentagon Papers decision from the Supreme Court had grown, over time, to assume far greater importance to the average American than initially seemed likely. When the confrontation between the government and the media had erupted accidentally as yet another unpleasant wart of the Vietnam War, the newspapers' success in court had been largely due to the overreaching cloddishness of the government. The would-be censors in the Nixon administration were unable to make a convincing argument in court mostly because so much of the information they were trying to secrete from public view didn't even deserve to be classified.[4] (President Nixon himself used to joke that the government's system for classifying documents was so crude that even the White House menu was classified.) But the case has come to represent much more than the dismal failings and absurdities of the classification system. Two and a half decades later, Judge Oakes saw the opinion as embedding in First Amendment law a prohibition against prior restraints that is virtually absolute. Scholars agree. Indeed, Professor John Calvin Jeffries, Jr., of the University of Virginia's Law School faculty, has questioned[5] our devotion to what Justice White termed "the concededly extraordinary protection against prior restraints enjoyed by the press under our constitutional system."[6] To Jeffries, the doctrine of prior restraint after the Pentagon Papers case is so overblown and "so far removed from its historic function" that it is "entirely" unhelpful in weighing what the late Justice Blackmun called, in dissent, "the broad right of the press to print and the very narrow right of the Government to prevent."[7] The Pentagon Papers case was a high-water mark for First Amendment freedoms. The tide has been receding ever since.

In 1971, it was the ideological center of the Court, composed of Justices White and Stewart, as well as the liberal wing of Justices Black, Douglas, Brennan and Marshall, that accounted for the substantial, but tapered 6–3 victory handed the newspapers. The three dissenters, it should be remembered, were neither antimedia nor reactionary. Chief Justice Burger would later champion and expand First Amendment rights for the media in a number of landmark opinions.[8] Justice Blackmun would later author *Roe v. Wade*. And the well-respected Justice John Marshall Harlan, a sixteen-year veteran of the Court, criticized the "frenzied train of events" and "almost irresponsibly feverish" haste with which the Court dealt with the case.[9] Justice Harlan and his fellow dissenters had no doubt about the magnitude of the issues. Harlan termed them "as important as any that have arisen during my time on the Court." But all were offended by the "precipitate timetable" for their decision making, and both Blackmun and Harlan, in separate dissents, felt constrained to quote Justice Oliver Wendell Holmes's admonition that "great cases, like hard cases, make bad law."[10]

Sitting amid the reflected glory of the Boca Club, listening to the voices from the Vietnam era, the younger audience could not help but wonder whether the Pentagon Papers controversy would play out the same way today. What if the government sought on national security grounds to prevent publication of leaked information about, say, American efforts to destabilize a Chinese (or born-again Russian) communist regime? And what if the government's traditional overreaching in this area could not be relied upon? That is, what if the government's argument for a prior restraint focused not on the 95 percent of the leaked documents that were improperly classified (as in the Pentagon Papers situation), but instead on the 5 percent that were legitimately top secret? Would a Supreme Court composed of conservative intellects like Justices Scalia, Thomas, and Chief Justice Rehnquist be able to attract another vote from centrists O'Connor, Kennedy, Souter or Stevens or procedural sticklers Ginsburg or Breyer in order to adopt a different approach? Would abstruse arguments over the separation of powers, so bothersome to the dissenters in the 1971 case, dictate greater deference to the power of the executive branch in the field of foreign affairs? Wouldn't the public's comparative lack of sympathy for the media benefit the government's case? In a dangerous world where Americans prize their comfort and global dominance and are no longer afflicted by an unpopular war in a Southeast Asia jungle, wouldn't the public value government secrecy over the need for a press with the power to check official misuse of power?

As the twenty-fifth anniversary celebration of the Pentagon Papers precedent concluded, someone from the nineties posed the question to some of the panelists from the seventies. Would a new clash between media and the government come out the same way today? Floyd Abrams admitted it was difficult to "see exactly where the votes would come from" to win the Pentagon Papers case today, but thought we should have faith that somehow it would end up the right way. Other answers came reluctantly, but a consensus was clear. You cannot pluck cases from one historical epoch and plop them into another time and place. But with that caveat, yes, it would be different today. The facts of a new case would be meaner, and the government would almost certainly do better.

JOHN GRISHAM GOES TO COURT

We do not need predictions, however sensible but inevitably speculative, to detect the stagnation of First Amendment law or realize that many liberties the public and press take for granted are really constructed of plaster, not bedrock. One or two wrecking balls could easily crumble existing prior restraint law and give the United States government greater leeway to conduct operations under the sort of veil drawn around the British government by the Official Secrets Act. Will it happen? If an economic downturn or world crisis should make Americans more dependent upon governmental leadership, or even if technological and scientific advances continue to create an expectation that we need government supervision of the marketplace to assure equal access to such "entitlements" as health care or educational opportunity, then it seems indisputable that people are more likely to regard the government (rather than the media) as a friend and protector. How rapidly attitudes will have changed in a quarter of a century.

There are abundant indications all across America that people will support the idea of curtailing their own access to public information when it bumps, even gently, into some governmental priority. This is especially true if the odious television camera is involved. Only a decade ago, when technology had produced tiny camera eyes to record unobtrusively what transpired in America's courtrooms, state after state welcomed television coverage of judicial proceedings. Now, states are retrenching and even star reporters like Nina Totenberg have misgivings about the wisdom of camera coverage. "Every person I respect in television believes cameras shouldn't be in court," she says. This is more than just post–O. J. Simpson traumatic stress disorder. "I know the intellectual arguments [for their presence in court] are sound, but my tummy tells me it's wrong for reasons I can't fully articulate."

John Grisham can. The best-selling author of legal thrillers like *The Street Lawyer, The Client* and *A Time to Kill* remembers the day in 1996 when he asked a judge to gag him. He hadn't tried a case in seven years. He'd been writing novels, making movie deals, moving from Oxford, Mississippi, to a horse farm near Charlottesville, Virginia. He felt rusty. ("I'm just as nervous as you are. I've got the jitters," he would tell the jury in his opening statement.) Worse, half the media buzzards of the Western Hemisphere had showed up in Brookhaven, Mississippi, to watch Mr. Zillionaire Author perform magic (or, maybe, fall flat on his skinny ass).[11] The trial would be irresistible grist for the celebrity mill. Like the heroes in his popular fiction, Grisham would be chasing justice for a victim of careless capitalism—in this case for the widow of a railroad brakeman who had been crushed to death in a switching accident between two railcars in 1991. John had tried wrongful-death cases before. He'd been a trial lawyer (as well as a state legislator) in Mississippi before the success of *The Firm* rocketed him into publishing's ozone. This case against the Illinois Central Railroad was as ordinary as any he had ever handled. Now, however, the interest in him was somewhat keener.

That was the problem. How would he do justice for his clients if, outside the courtroom, thrusting microphones were endangering his teeth and reporters were asking him what he planned to wear to court tomorrow. In view of his fame, he told the judge, it would be a whole lot better for the proceedings if the court placed a gag order on the participants in the trial, including the lawyers. The media birds could be easily scattered with a "the judge said we can't talk." Judge Keith Starrett of Lincoln County Circuit Court obliged. (He also instructed Grisham to stop giving autographs to dazzled fans after court had recessed for the day.) Similarly, Judge Starrett denied a request to permit broadcast camera coverage of the trial. Mississippi gives judges broad discretion to exclude cameras from the courtroom, and, like fire ants at a picnic, they are routinely zapped. No trial has yet been broadcast in Mississippi. The judges are determined to keep cameras out. Interestingly, Judge Starrett did allow a closed-circuit camera to relay the proceedings to a nearby room where an overflow army of reporters was camped. John didn't find the cameras distracting during his three-day trial, but he was always aware of their presence.

"The mixture of lawyers and cameras is a foul one," he firmly believes. "Cameras in courtrooms make actors out of lawyers and stars out of ordinary witnesses. It's a chance to perform. There's a heightened level of awareness—people outside the courtroom are watching, so those inside feel compelled to add an extra dose of drama."

Grisham laughs when he recalls how the legions of reporters gradually slipped away as his civil case became boring, "as most civil cases do." He thought some of the witnesses were "genuinely disappointed" when they realized their testimony would not be viewed outside the courtroom. He asks himself, "Would they have testified differently with cameras present? I don't know. It's possible. I caught one crucial witness in a number of inconsistencies, and he grew quite hostile. His face turned red and his fists were clenched. It was obvious the poor guy was not being completely truthful, and there was no place for him to hide. I think he might have snapped with the extra pressure of a camera recording his fiasco for the community to see before dinner."

And Grisham has no illusions about his own vanity or susceptibility to grandstanding. "I had him on the ropes, bloody and staggering. With the added energy of a camera capturing one of my finest moments, I might have pounded harder. In fact, I am sure I would have handled him even rougher."

Then he grows pensive and resolute.

"People discuss things on the witness stand that they would never mention in normal conversation. That's the nature of a trial. A courtroom should be a private place, solemn and dignified—a place where people can reluctantly tell their secrets without the world listening.

"Courtrooms should not be the stages that television has turned them into."

There is more here than just a gracious Southerner talking. Grisham reflects a prevailing sentiment throughout the land. There's no tougher expert court reporter than Nina Totenberg. She has covered celebrated cases and the Supreme Court for National Public Radio and, later, ABC for more than two decades. Nina once took on a spouses' session at a federal judicial conference with an address entitled "The Media: The Folks You Love to Hate." Afterward, the spouses were dribbling foam from their mouths and discussing how to knot the world's slowest strangulating noose. Nina does not shy from controversy. Her reporting about marijuana use ended Judge Douglas Ginsburg's nomination for the High Court, and former senator Alan Simpson once imitated a hot-spring geyser from his native Wyoming when he erupted over her Clarence Thomas reporting after a *Nightline* appearance. Nina now openly wonders whether televising trials jeopardizes the judiciary's effectiveness. "Archie Cox used to speak of the mystique of the courts," she says. "Part of their authority derives from their difference, their introverted nature."

John and Nina have respectable and influential allies, including Max Frankel, the former executive editor of *The New York Times,* and Charles Nesson of the Harvard Law School faculty. The camera is "a different beast" than a reporter's pen, Frankel has maintained for some time, and it "is transforming our involvement with justice."[12] "The camera corrupts not because it lies but because it magnifies images and issues. . . . And by inviting us . . . to second-guess the justice system, it saps that system of its sovereignty."[13] Nesson agrees, arguing that the accuracy of jury verdicts is not nearly as important as their credibility.[14] Cameras and all the color commentary that accompany celebrated cases make us feel better informed than jurors. Thus, the jury's privileged position evaporates and the "awesome majesty" of the courts begins to resemble Hans Christian Andersen's naked emperor on parade.

As persuasive as these views are—and they are all the more attractive coming from such thoughtful, knowledgeable people as Grisham, Totenberg, Frankel and Nesson—there should be no mistaking that they seek a fundamental limitation on a freedom that has been deeply ingrained in Anglo-American traditions for centuries—the right to public judicial proceedings. The right has been seen by our Supreme Court as belonging not just to a criminal defendant but to the public as well. "People in an open society do not demand infallibility from their institutions," Chief Justice Burger wrote in 1980, "but it is difficult for them to accept what they are prohibited from observing."[15] "Fine," say the opponents of camera coverage in courtrooms, "let the reporters in, but exclude the cameras. Give us filtered viewpoints that we can discount if we wish; just don't give us unfiltered reality." As the world records itself (and sees itself) more and more visually with every passing year, this notion will soon seem as antiquated as un-air-conditioned buildings in tropical climates. This is not to say Grisham and company do not have a point, only that technology marches on, changing our expectations.[16] Refusing to rely on cameras to record the reality of American justice seems like turning off the air-conditioning during the summertime in Washington as a way of shrinking the federal government.

What is really needed here is a tailored, more inventive approach where judges would become more learned on the subject of controlling television coverage in their courtrooms. The hapless Judge Lance Ito has been roundly criticized for not "managing" media coverage of the Simpson trial (as well as for not managing the proceedings themselves). Yet Ito or any judge has almost no training and precious little experience dealing with the potential downsides of camera coverage. Admonitions to jurors and witnesses, or even a frank two-way conversation, are rare. Rules about trial participants capitalizing on or exploiting their "performance" in the courtroom have not been considered. Stern lectures about "playing to the camera" could be as customary as other jury instructions, but courts have done little in this area. The country is full of former television journalists and network executives who deliver "media training" services to the needy, mostly corporate executives fearful of getting skewered by a rapacious interviewer. They learn how to answer questions like "Tell me, Mr. Gold-cufflinks, how do you justify making $12 million in salary, bonus and stock options last year when you're paying your Jamaican workers twelve cents an hour?" Or "How do you feel when people accuse you of making coffeepots that explode and kill people?" Some of these media trainers, like Judy Leon at the Powell Tate agency in Washington, are superb, worth every penny as they help hone a message and give news subjects a modicum of control in a situation where the media has most if not all of the cards. In court, of course, judges do in fact have most of the control, but when it comes to camera coverage, they act as paralyzed as any other victim of the lens. It would be interesting for the National Judicial College in Reno or the Federal Judicial Center, the educational arm of the federal courts, to embark upon programs to teach judges how they can effectively use cameras for their judicial purposes (and public purposes) while, at the same time, limiting undesirable side effects.[17] The courts ought to hire their own media consultants. The television industry would work with the judges (and probably even fund them) faster than you can say "V-chip."

But that enlightened approach is the opposite of what is actually happening across the nation. The hostility toward camera coverage has spilled over to other areas, with judges curtailing access to all kinds of information in the courts out of a general unhappiness with the media. The results are counterproductive.

Everyone, for instance, ought to know about Steven Alan Miller. Steve is a helluva guy. Just one little problem, though. He can't seem to stop himself from belting back a few drinks and then sliding behind the wheel of his pickup truck. When he tried it in April 1994 in Naples, Florida, local sheriff's deputies caught him driving 72 mph in a 45 mph zone. Miller's face was flushed, his eyes were watering, and—surprise—there was a bottle of vodka and a can of orange juice on the front seat. Miller is no dummy. He refused to take a Breathalyzer test. But his erratic driving and the ingredients for a screwdriver were enough for the police. They arrested him for reckless driving and driving under the influence.

Miller was all set to go to trial a year and a half later, when the *Naples Daily News* learned that he had twenty-one previous arrests and fourteen convictions for drunk driving. Not surprisingly, article after article appeared in the local press about Miller, his past and the state of the law that allows someone with Miller's history to cruise the highways. In response to the extensive coverage, Miller's counsel asked the court to "gag" everyone involved in the case by ordering them not to speak to any news media until after a verdict had been rendered.

When the court held a hearing on the gag order request, it started with Judge Elmer Friday saying that he was "shocked" by news reports about the trial. "I rather suspect they no longer teach constitutional reporting in journalism schools, based on what I have seen in this county," Judge Friday said. "I'm not convinced there has been a responsible handling of this matter by the media. There's been a field day at the expense of the constitutional rights and privileges of citizens." Judge Friday then announced that he was going to enter a gag order reaching further than the one Miller had sought—not only would participants in the trial be prevented from speaking to the news media, but the media were not going to be permitted to speak to anyone about the facts of the case.

Down to the courthouse galloped the *Daily News*'s lawyers. They made fairly familiar constitutional arguments: gag orders against the media have been all but outlawed by the Supreme Court. Other techniques such as a change of venue or close questioning of prospective jurors can ensure a fair trial, the High Court believed.

Judge Friday reconsidered. He decided not to restrict the media's right to cover the trial. As he announced his decision, however, the judge added the standard lament of all trial judges faced with assuring an accused criminal a fair trial: "I'm distressed as a judge by this kind of conduct by the press. I want more responsibility."

The Miller case entered jury selection. Less than a week later, *Daily News* editor Colleen Conant (later the editor of the *Boulder* [CO] *Daily Camera*) called her lawyers again. This time, the judge had refused to allow the newspaper's reporter into the courtroom to hear questions being put to potential jurors. In fact, the door had been locked, and guards would not even let the reporter into the room to register the paper's objections.

This was too much. A 1983 Supreme Court decision had already faced the same situation and had ruled that the First Amendment clearly requires voir dire to be open to the public. Managing editor Phil Lewis trudged to the courthouse himself, only to stand outside the locked doors while his lawyers drafted and faxed a motion to the court and headed for the courthouse. In the end, the court begrudgingly agreed that the law required it to open the voir dire, but in issuing his decision, Judge Friday once again took the opportunity to complain about reporting in the Miller case, claiming that "[t]he right to a fair and impartial trial in this community is under attack" by the news media.

The Naples newspaper had successfully protected the right of the public to witness the trial of Steven Miller, but the court's open hostility toward the media overshadowed any perception of "victory." Should a local newspaper need to call on a SWAT team of First Amendment attorneys to reargue well-established constitutional law, especially when they are merely trying to report on a criminal trial of concern to the community? Increasingly, the answer is yes. It's a fine day for the government.

JOIN THE CLUB

Judge Friday isn't the only magistrate ticked off at the press. But at least in the Naples story there was a happy ending. The public eventually knew about Steve Miller's trial.

The public isn't faring so well elsewhere. The evidence aggregates from around the nation:

"Thank You, NBC, We'd Just As Soon Not Know"

It is axiomatic that whatever resources a news organization must spend to rid itself of nuisance lawsuits, it can't spend on reporting the news or anything else. Media executives charged with calculating news budgets, and then meeting them, most often see the cost of nuisance litigation through the proverbial green eyeshades, measuring how the money handed over to their defense lawyers could have been allocated to two or three additional reporters. They also know that the true cost of litigation isn't just the money; it's the disruption to an ongoing news operation—the unproductive time devoted to depositions, document review and conference room huddles with counsel usually over some news story of a year ago that hardly anyone remembers, much less cares about. There's not even any grand principle at stake, unless you call refusing to be nickel-and-dimed into economically expedient settlements a lofty ideal. Since 1980, many states and the federal courts have tried to prevent the unfairness of nuisance lawsuits by awarding sanctions and attorneys fees to deserving defendants. Winning them in media libel cases, however, no matter how frivolous or meritless the claim, has become virtually impossible. You would have an easier time extracting a seven-year-old's baby teeth with pliers.

There couldn't be a more craven lawsuit, for instance, than the one filed by former congressman Craig A. Washington against the *Houston Chronicle* and NBC's *Dateline* in 1995. It was simply spiteful. Congressman Washington's constituents in Houston had declined to return him to Capitol Hill after the newspaper and *Dateline* had reported on shenanigans with his House of Representatives' expense money. (He had rented federal office space from his ex-wife at a suspiciously high rate, hired as his staff counsel a former law partner who owed him money, and hired the mother of his out-of-wedlock child to be his special events coordinator.) Public officials, like Congressman Washington, have an uphill burden in a libel case. They are saddled with the requirement of proving that a false statement of fact was made recklessly, not just carelessly. Congressman Washington had a hard time even finding a false statement in the NBC broadcast or the *Chronicle's* editorial. (He conceded that the facts in a *Chronicle* news article were true.)

The network and the newspaper moved to dismiss the case and requested sanctions. Federal judge James Robertson made fast work of the nonexistent claim. He found that the congressman couldn't "bear his burden" of proving falsity and that the statements in the editorial were "very clearly opinion." But sanctions? An award of attorney fees for NBC's and the *Chronicle's* time and trouble? Oh no. All of a sudden the media victims became the bad guys. "I think in some sense the defendants have brought this hearing on themselves by asking for sanctions," said Judge Robertson with reasoning that caused counsel's jaws to drop in the courtroom. Then, amazingly, he took a further potshot at the press.

A "robust press" and a "robust plaintiff's bar" just "deserve one another," the judge suggested blithely. As he strode off the bench, he seemed not to have noticed that he had just equated accurate news reporting about a congressman's questionable financial transactions with the filing of a wasteful, spurious lawsuit.

"Now We've Got 'Em Right Where We Want 'Em"

Everyone always wants to know what the media knows. Before the high-water years of First Amendment law in the early 1970s, they used to ask for sources and unpublished information regularly. Prosecutors, criminal defense attorneys and other litigants treated newspapers and television stations like the reference room at the public library. Need a videotape of an automobile accident? Subpoena the footage from the local station. Did an accused give a jailhouse interview about the crime? Subpoena the reporter for the information—published and unpublished. Did press reports about a crime justify a change of venue to a place where jurors were less knowledgeable about the incident? Subpoena all the local media to produce copies of their actual coverage. This appetite for news material and testimony from reporters began to make the press look like the research arm of law enforcement. Besides the disruption to ongoing operations (reporters couldn't be covering the news if they were sitting around the courthouse waiting to testify), this overreliance on the media to do the legwork and the homework that could be done by others also endangered the media's appearance of neutrality or impartiality. It didn't take long for reporters to hear from people with stories to tell: "I'm not talking to you. You'll just tell the cops." Even if sources felt the reporter would fall on his pen and languish in jail before revealing a secret identity, they didn't want to run the risk of disclosure if the law provided the press with so little protection from prying.

In 1972, the Supreme Court responded to these efforts to "annex" the news media as "an investigative arm of government" by handing down *Branzburg v. Hayes*.[18] The 4–1–4 *Branzburg* decision was not as equivocal as the splintered vote suggested. As Harvard's Laurence Tribe has summarized, "lower federal courts have consistently read the case to support some kind of qualified privilege for reporters" to protect their sources and unpublished information.[19] Justice Powell's critical swing concurrence boiled the essence of the new reporter's privilege into a single sensible sentence:

> [I]f the newsman is called upon to give information bearing only a remote and tenuous relationship to the subject of the investigation, or if he has some other reason to believe that his testimony implicates confidential source relationships without a legitimate need of law enforcement, he will have access to the court on a motion to quash [the subpoena] . . .

For twenty years after *Branzburg*, a vast number of subpoenas directed to reporters were quashed. Steadily, throughout the nation, federal and state courts built up substantial protection not just for reporters' confidential sources but also for the central notion that the news media ought to be independent from government's law enforcement activities. Except when every other alternative avenue had been exhausted, and only when a compelling need existed for the reporter's testimony, judges were honoring the idea that newsgatherers should not be co-opted (or harassed) by prosecutors or defense attorneys looking for an easy (and cheap) way to assemble evidence for a case.

And then, in the mid-1990s, the slippage began. Suddenly, courts were no longer inclined to give reporters the breadth of First Amendment protection that had become customary during the two previous decades.

In New York, the influential Second Circuit Court of Appeals signaled the future directions of the judiciary when it reversed course on more than twenty years of law that had established the reporters' privilege in limestone, if not granite.[20] The about-face came in a strange and ironic case involving Bruce Cutler, the lawyer for reputed Mafia magnate John Gotti. Cutler had been hauled before a federal judge on charges of violating a gag order by making statements to the press during Gotti's criminal trial. As part of his defense, Cutler subpoenaed notes from reporters with whom he had spoken and the unused videotapes, or "outtakes," from news organizations. The Second Circuit refused to quash the subpoenas, brushing aside First Amendment arguments and the Circuit's own precedent with ease. The Cutler decision merely presaged a trend. "The drift became clear," says George Freeman, the chief editorial lawyer for *The New York Times.* "Unless a confidential source of information is involved, the courts are having less and less sympathy for the First Amendment arguments." Instead of stretching the law to protect journalists, judges are demanding more and more testimony from them, particularly in criminal cases. The results put some reporters exactly where a lot of people would like to see them—behind bars.

That's the last place *Miami Herald* reporter David Kidwell thought his work would land him when he went to interview John Zile, an accused murderer, in a Florida penitentiary. Zile had already confessed to killing his seven-year-old stepdaughter when Kidwell visited him in prison, posing as his friend in order to gain admittance. Zile talked about his role in the crime—how he had spanked and disciplined little Christina because he was "furious" with her. When she started to cry, he covered her mouth with his hand. She died of asphyxiation. Zile and his wife hid her body in a closet in their apartment for several days and then Zile buried her behind a shopping center in Tequesta. Zile's wife was convicted of first-degree murder for failing to intervene to prevent her daughter's death and is serving life in prison without parole. Zile's initial murder trial ended in a mistrial when one juror, concerned about a possible death penalty, declined to agree to a first-degree conviction.

Kidwell had not been called by prosecutors during Zile's first trial. His story added some color and drama to the confession that police already had from Zile, but the inconsequential details weren't material to the case. By the retrial, prosecutors had changed their minds. Now they wanted Kidwell's testimony. Belts and suspenders this time. Kidwell demurred. He couldn't be both an arm of the prosecution and an effective reporter. If potential sources perceived him as a covert investigator for the state, they wouldn't talk to him.

Judge Roger Colton sentenced him to seventy days in jail for contempt of court. As Kidwell later told the court:

> I want you to know I've struggled with this decision for months. I've spoken to friends and colleagues and ethics experts across the country, searching for a way out, looking for a cohesive argument as to how I can maintain my professional convictions and stay within the law.
>
> I haven't found one. I have spoken with other reporters who won't interview criminal defendants anymore for fear of subpoenas. I have spoken with editors who suggest we systematically destroy our notes. I have spoken with media attorneys who say the law has abandoned us.
>
> All of this only helped firm my resolve. I don't want to go to jail. I'd rather go back to work this afternoon. But either way, when I do go back to work, I have to know I'm free to pursue all sides of a story without interference from the government, that I can represent myself as fair and impartial and know it's true.
>
> I know the law is against me. The courts have retreated from the idea that these principles are worth protecting. I'm convinced I cannot allow my ethics to retreat with them.

John Zile was convicted without David Kidwell's testimony. He is serving a life sentence.

Kidwell spent fifteen days in jail and was released pending appeal of his contempt conviction. The Florida Court of Appeals was utterly unsympathetic to him. "The reporter here," wrote the court, "has made no plausible showing that even non-confidential sources will dry up if not protected by a qualified privilege." Whatever benefit of the doubt reporters may have been given on this issue in the past (and "proving a negative" is always speculative enough to warrant a little faith), judges are no longer inclined to cut journalists any slack, even when they are as earnest and in as much obvious agony over professional ethics as Kidwell clearly was.

Florida is a microcosm for what has been happening nationally, says Jane Kirtley, executive director of the Washington-based Reporters Committee for Freedom of the Press, an organization that has conducted the most thorough and comprehensive research into the subpoenaing of reporters during the past two decades. "Judges don't appreciate the need for journalists to be independent, and they're not prepared to embrace the notion that journalists need legal protection in a wide variety of situations simply to be able to gather the news. They don't get it. They simply don't get it."

Instead, Kirtley believes the data show a revulsion over newsgathering practices, a preoccupation with the process of journalism rather than its product. That process is endlessly debatable. In the recent court decisions, you can see that judges, no less than the public, are "deeply offended at some level." They get hung up on the unremarkable and incidental fact that Kidwell lied to get into the jail to interview Zile. "Can I trust her?" a source invariably wonders about a reporter. Judges have transposed the question to "Do I approve of what this reporter has done?" Under the First Amendment, it is—for public officials, even those in the third branch of government, even those whose black robes and high bench set them apart from elected officials—the fundamentally wrong question to ask.

Nine hundred miles off the Florida coast, in the islands treasured by the European discoverers of America, a horizon of the coming clash between government and the press could be seen in 1998 and 1999.

Superficially, it was possible to dismiss the fury between Pedro Rosselló, the Governor of Puerto Rico, and *El Nuevo Día,* the commonwealth's largest newspaper, as a local storm. Americans tend to treat

Puerto Rico like that. Exotic. Distant. Irrelevant. No matter that Puerto Rico, if we were smart and lucky enough to incorporate it as the fifty-first state, could give us a window on Latin America. We would then have the opportunity to absorb an invigorating culture and the language which a third of Americans themselves will speak in ten to twenty years.

The fight between the Governor and the newspaper teaches us a more immediate lesson. In a climate where the public harbors ambivalent or worse feelings toward the press, government officials can exploit those feelings. The experience in Puerto Rico is all the more chilling because however "arrogant" or "overbearing" Governor Rosselló may be—and both adjectives are frequently used to describe him—he is not stupid. Rosselló is media-savvy. He used some of the same political and media consultants as President Clinton and enjoyed a friendship with the Clinton White House. He is a thoroughly modern governor, popular among his peers. He has served as chairman of the Democratic Governors Association, chairman of the Southern Governors Association and an adviser and fundraiser for the Gore-2000 campaign. Rosselló aspires, it is said, to become a member of a Gore cabinet. Secretary of Health and Human Services would fit nicely, since he was a pediatric surgeon prior to taking up politics.

Similarly, the other protagonist in the San Juan drama, *El Nuevo Día*, cannot be reduced to an aberration. It is certainly not especially disliked in its market. Quite the contrary. It is the newspaper of record in the commonwealth, generally respected on the island for its journalism and its benevolence. The newspaper's strength derives in part from the reputation of its owners, the Ferré family. The Ferrés could be said to be the first family of Puerto Rico. The grandfather, Don Luis Ferré (now ninety-five) is a former governor, statehood advocate and arts patron who is revered throughout Puerto Rico. His sister is a nun whose public charities qualify her as the Mother Teresa of the island. His daughter, Rosario Ferré, is one of Latin America's most well regarded novelists. His son, Antonio Luis Ferré, is publisher of the newspaper and an enlightened and successful businessman whose advice is sought by the wise. Antonio Luis's five children are all actively engaged in the family's businesses, including the newspaper and Puerto Rican Cement Co., Inc., a New York Stock Exchange company and the leading provider of the building material prized in the Caribbean for its resistance to hurricanes.

As a newspaper family, Antonio Luis Ferré and his children also resemble their peers. Purposeful as the Sulzburgers, modest as the Scrippses, smart as the Grahams, the Ferrés assemble talent around them. Jerry Tilis, a former senior advertising executive for Knight Ridder and now a consultant to several metropolitan newspapers, observes that he has never seen a newspaper operation with such a consistently high-quality work force as *El Nuevo Día*'s.

The two-year legal dispute pitting the newspaper against the Governor began in April 1997 when *El Nuevo Día* published a critical assessment of the first one hundred days of the Governor's second term. The next day all government advertising, from eighteen different government agencies, was canceled or withdrawn from the newspaper. The editors had been told earlier that the Rosselló administration was growing increasingly irritated with their news coverage of scandals in the telephone company (then owned by the commonwealth) and the management of water resources. But, they did not expect this kind of retaliation. Soon, the paper's reporters began encountering obstacles in obtaining information ordinarily available, and Puerto Rican Cement Co., Inc. began experiencing unprecedented regulatory problems, including cancelations of previously approved construction permits. In meetings with senior members of the Rosselló administration in the summer of 1997, the editors believed they were offered a "deal": "lower the newspaper's tone" and the government would respond in kind.

The editors rebuffed the offer and began speaking out against what they felt was a clear-cut attempt by the government to coerce favorable news coverage. National media, including *The Washington Post*, drew attention to the controversy, and national and Inter-American press organizations began condemning the Rosselló administration.

In December 1997, convinced that the retaliation was continuing unabated, *El Nuevo Día* and the cement company filed a major civil rights lawsuit in federal court in San Juan, charging violation of First Amendment rights under the civil rights statute that is often used in discrimination cases (42 U.S.C. § 1983).[21] The Governor and his aides promptly hired eleven law firms in San Juan, Miami, Washington, Boston and Philadelphia, all at public expense, to defend the case. They denied any wrongdoing, claiming that the actions against the newspaper and cement company were legitimate regulatory policy-making or enforcement activities. They also argued, astonishingly, that the government itself had a First Amendment right of "free speech"— and that it should be able to place its advertisements wherever it deemed appropriate. The First Amendment was written, of course, to protect people from the tyranny of a censorious government—not to give government free speech rights. But, never mind. The public officials enlisted Alan Dershowitz, late of the Claus von Bulow, O. J. Simpson and Clinton defense efforts, to advance this hare-brained theory.

The litigation did not go well for the public officials. First, the federal trial judge, José A. Fusté, and then the U.S. Court of Appeals for the First Circuit (to which appeals from Puerto Rico are taken) denied the Governor, his chief of staff and press secretary qualified immunity. In short, they could be held personally liable for damages suffered by the newspaper and the cement company.

"It would seem obvious," wrote the Court of Appeals from Boston in a major First Amendment decision, "that using government funds to punish political speech by members of the press and to attempt to coerce commentary favorable to the government would run afoul of the First Amendment."

"Obvious?" We should be grateful that the federal Court of Appeals sitting in the Boston harbor that once witnessed a colonial tea party still finds such a fundamental principle "obvious." It had not been so "obvious" in other governmental corners or the Court would never have had to rule at all.

On the eve of trial in May 1999, after each side had spent millions of dollars slugging away at the litigation, the parties reached a settlement. The Governor publicly stated his belief in free press principles and issued an Executive Order ensuring that government advertising would be bought on a rational basis using standard industry criteria unrelated to news coverage. The cement company's projects proceeded. "Our objectives in bringing the lawsuit have been achieved," said Antonio Luis Ferré. "Both the newspaper and the cement company can conduct their businesses without government interference or pressure. This case was about big principles, not big money."

In one sense, Antonio Luis Ferré was correct. In reaching a settlement, the newspaper and the cement company gave up the prospect of a multimillion-dollar damage award. The award would have probably come from the public treasury, a drain that didn't interest the civic-minded Ferrés. Yet, in another sense, the case had been costly to prosecute: two years of considerable expense and disruption. At the lawsuit's conclusion, you could not help but wonder whether less public-spirited publishers than the Ferrés would be willing to undertake such a fight for principles. We must hope that they will continue to do so, for the brazenness of the government's arguments shows us that public officials will be more shameless than ever about using the public's antipathy toward the press for their own advantage.

The experience in Puerto Rico also illustrates dramatically the new paradigm for governmental manipulation of the press. Today, many news enterprises, from NBC and ABC to *Slate* at Microsoft, are part of large corporations, the components and cousins of which can be vulnerable to all types of government pressure. One of the most important legal precedents established in the *El Nuevo Día* case was Judge Fusté's recognition of the right of an affiliated company (Puerto Rican Cement Co., Inc.) to sue derivatively for the damages it suffered due to the infringement of the newspaper's First Amendment rights. The precedent will be useful in warding off a twenty-first-century form of governmental manipulation of the press. That manipulation will be made all the easier if the public believes that the news media ought to be put in its place anyway.

8

"Hello, Houston. We Have a Problem"

Juror Lovella Norman, a retired Sears saleswoman with a nice grand-motherly neatness, didn't have qualms about voting to saddle *The Wall Street Journal* with the biggest libel verdict in American history—a total of $222.7 million.

"They need punishing," she told *The American Lawyer*'s Susan Beck after she and her six fellow jurors unanimously awarded the bonanza in March 1997 to a defunct Houston securities firm run by two flamboyant bond traders.[1] Some of Lovella's disdain was reserved for *Journal* staff reporter Laura Jereski, who had authored the offending article. Jereski had steadfastly maintained the substantial truth of her article throughout her trial testimony even though it was demonstrably flawed with errors. So did her editors, at least when they weren't suggesting that they hadn't all that much to do with Jereski's article in the first place.

Lovella also felt sorry for Laura Jereski: "I really did. But . . . [then I decided] I'm wasting my sympathy, because I don't believe she cares." The *Journal*'s tough trial strategy (its counsel told the jury that the plaintiffs were scoundrels who sold "toxic waste" investments to unsuspecting pension funds) only succeeded in convincing Lovella and her colleagues that the staff was unapologetic for its mistakes and arrogant.

Eventually, trial judge Ewing Werlein, Jr., threw out the $200 million in punitive damages levied against the newspaper but left standing a $20 million award in actual damages and a $20,000 punitive damage award against Jereski personally. The judge found that while there wasn't sufficient evidence to prove that the *Journal's* management had acted in reckless disregard for the truth, there was enough evidence for the jury to conclude that Jereski was at fault and that her libelous article had led to the securities firm's collapse. "It's just a serious matter to destroy a company like that with falsehoods," Lovella said.

Sometimes, as the saying goes, "it's better to be lucky." About a year after the jury's whopping verdict, while the case was on appeal, the *Journal* received an anonymous telephone call about the possibility of new evidence. After a year of more wrangling, Judge Werlein found that relevant audiotapes of telephone conversations were not produced by the plaintiff investment firm, and that the withholding of those audiotapes constituted misrepresentation and misconduct warranting a new trial.

Dow Jones's lucky escape from a debacle in Houston cannot be written off as an aberrational shotgun blast from a Texas jury. Not with libel plaintiffs collecting six- and seven-figure verdicts and settlements on a regular basis after 1996.[2] Local prosecutors are the luckiest, or most savvy, bunch. Philadelphia district attorney Richard Sprague finally dunned Knight Ridder for more than $20 million (and uninsured to boot) after almost two decades of litigation. A Waco prosecutor won $58 million and collected more than $10 million from an A. H. Belo television station. The hapless Richard Jewell settled with NBC for $500,000 without even filing suit against the network and then used his new wealth to fund his lawsuit against the *Atlanta Journal & Constitution,* claiming that he was unfairly portrayed as the mad bomber of the Summer Olympics. A doctor in Cleveland, and even parents of a drunk driver who killed two pedestrians in Wilkes-Barre, have received settlements in lieu of media companies enduring the agony and uncertainty of a trial. Appellate courts in the 1980s could generally be counted on to rectify and reverse irrational jury excesses. In the 1990s, however, media companies no longer had the same confidence or winning track record in the appeals courts. For plaintiffs, the libel business has never been more brisk or lucrative.

Nowhere is it written in modern American libel law that the media is supposed to win every case, although one could be forgiven for thinking so given the track record over the thirty-five years since the landmark *New York Times Co. v. Sullivan* revolutionized the law in 1964. During the 1960s, 1970s and 1980s, winning libel plaintiffs could be counted on two hands. Most public officials and public figures resigned themselves to the glum reality that they didn't stand a chance in libel litigation. The legal deck was too heavily stacked against them. In 1984, prominent plaintiff's lawyer John Walsh explained the basic problem for the rich and famous. Walsh had served as counsel to such "mad as hell and I'm not going to take it" corporate executives as Mobil Oil president William Tavoloureas (who unsuccessfully sued *The Washington Post*) and former Bendix dream team William and Mary Cunningham Agee (who unsuccessfully threatened to sue columnist Richard Reeves and dozens of newspapers that carried his column). At a Washington symposium honoring the twentieth anniversary of the Sullivan decision, Walsh spoke wistfully but without whining about the "bites of the apple." Under the Sullivan doctrine, the media are given so many "bites" or opportunities to whittle away a libel plaintiff's case. Almost no one could survive the gauntlet.[3] One way or another, the media get the "breathing space" for mistakes and outright falsehoods that Justice Brennan's decision of the Court in *Sullivan* saw as necessary for the rigorous pursuit of truth in a democracy.

The good justice never had any illusions about the painful practical implications of his bold theory. Bill Daugherty, a friend of Brennan's from summers on Nantucket, remembers storming back to his house on North Wharf from Main Street, where he had just bought that morning's *Boston Globe* at The Hub and read what he felt was a terribly unfair and inaccurate news report about his role in a controversial investment scheme. Brennan stopped his obviously agitated friend on the sidewalk and asked why he was fuming. Bill Daugherty let loose with enough invective about the "irresponsible" *Boston Globe* to make a Coast Guard seaman blush the color of a cooked lobster.

"Yes, that's awful," said Brennan solicitously. "And I suppose it's really all my fault. I wrote the opinion which lets them get away with all that."

Brennan's famous charm soothed his friend that morning. As he continued walking back home, Bill Daugherty also understood that Brennan expected him to tolerate the mistakes of journalism—so long as they were merely stupid, careless or ignorant and not calculated or deliberate. That is the expectation and the bravery of Brennan's *Sullivan* doctrine. It is the reason that First Amendment advocates saw the decision when it was handed down in 1964 as an occasion for "dancing in the streets," as Alexander Meiklejohn, the Yale philosopher and educator, then ninety-two years old, told Harvard's Harry Kalven.

The confidence and uniquely American optimism of the *Sullivan* doctrine lie in its central premise: we must tolerate some false speech in the search for truth. Embodied in this notion is a realistic view of journalism: truth comes not in daily news cycles, or even long, "in-depth" investigative reports, but instead through the full torrent of news that rushes past us incessantly, the river without a mouth.

I learned this lesson from no less a monument of journalism than Turner Catledge, the former executive editor of *The New York Times*, who was willing to testify under oath that his newspaper did not deal in the currency of truth. Catledge, a man of the Mississippi soil who had returned to his roots after his retirement from the *Times*, had been willing to lend his dignity, grace and authority for the defense in a libel trial. The offending article had appeared in a "People" column in the *Memphis Commercial Appeal* and had already been branded as "false gossip" by the U.S. Court of Appeals for the Fifth Circuit by the time Turner Catledge agreed to testify. The salacious tidbit had reported in 1972:

FLICKERING FLAME: Back in 1957 Anita Wood, who came from Jackson, Tenn., to Memphis to sing on TV, was Elvis Presley's "No. 1 girl." This week as Elvis closed his month-long show at the Las Vegas

Hilton, Miss Wood stopped by the hotel for what appeared to be a "re-union" of two old friends. Elvis recently filed for divorce from his wife of five years, Priscilla. Miss Wood is divorced from former Ole Miss football star Johnny Brewer.

Not much about the item was accurate. Anita was not divorced from Johnny, and she had been nowhere near Las Vegas for a "reunion" with Elvis. (Her lawyer conjured up quite a scene with those quote marks.) The sourcing for the story had seemed plausible at press time. After three trials, two trips to the Fifth Circuit and one final stop at the U.S. Supreme Court, the *Memphis Commercial Appeal* ultimately won the case, but by then the sourcing didn't seem anything but sloppy. The three trials, each won by Mrs. Brewer, were particularly painful for the newspaper.

Each morning for several weeks during the last trial, I walked to a federal courthouse, bleached blindingly white, in Vicksburg, Mississippi, a town which had seen one of the fiercest battles of the Civil War. Turner Catledge, the newspaper's expert witness on the journalism in question, walked along with me some of those mornings. He probably sensed, as I did, that the trial was not going well for us. The jury wasn't buying anybody's explanations for the mistakes. After a lunch break one afternoon he suggested:

"When I go back on the stand, why don't you ask me whether *The New York Times* prints truth." Properly coached by my witness, I acquiesced.

"Mr. Catledge," the question came when we resumed, "does *The New York Times* print truth."

"No," the witness responded proudly. "It's not always attainable. Accuracy is a goal. Any newspaper deals in facts, in accuracy. But truth, that's another thing altogether. When *The New York Times* publishes truth, it is only inadvertent, almost an accident sometimes."

The jury should have been stunned. They weren't. Probably a libel trial is not the right moment to lower expectations of *The New York Times.* Turner Catledge had a number of mornings during that trial in Vicksburg to teach a young libel lawyer about the possibilities of journalism. And I remember him telling me, and I believe it today, that there is an element of paradox in the *Sullivan* doctrine. Paradox, he would remind me, overwhelms us by seeming to present obvious contradiction, but in reality paradox expresses a great truth. For Turner Catledge, for many of us, the *Sullivan* doctrine is grounded in a theory of truth that is broad and sensible and distinctively American. That theory encompasses the bold idea that falsity is a means of ascertaining truth. Unlike the common law which we inherited from England and which has no tolerance for falsity, the power of our constitutional libel law rests not on the need for government to protect people from false information, but on the conviction that people are capable of discerning the difference between truth and falsity.

"Without *New York Times v. Sullivan*," concluded Anthony Lewis in his 1991 book, *Make No Law: The Sullivan Decision and the First Amendment*, "it is questionable whether the press could have done as much as it has to penetrate the power and secrecy of modern government, or to confront the public with the realities of policy issues . . . The complexities of libel law are the price of a decision that has greatly enlarged the freedom of the press and of all Americans."[4] Lewis also correctly observed that the Sullivan decision began "a sea change" in First Amendment law.[5] In the years following the decision, he demonstrated, "the Court resoundingly vindicated the promise of the First Amendment." Almost a decade after Lewis made that observation, however, it can now be shown with equally abundant evidence that courts, including the Supreme Court of the United States, are no longer inclined to continue that "vindication" by updating and expanding First Amendment rights, even when the press is acting as the public's surrogate.

"WHERE'S *RIVERSIDE PRESS-ENTERPRISE* III?"

The stagnation of First Amendment law in the 1990s can be seen in the deterioration of the *Sullivan* doctrine's effectiveness, the retrenchment in the scope of the reporter's privilege, the judicial hostility toward cameras and the antagonism toward the media's very presence virtually anywhere. It can also be detected in the stillness of the air at the Supreme Court.

In 1980, the court fashioned out of whole cloth a brand-new First Amendment right belonging to the public, and what Justice Burger then termed its "surrogate," the press—a right to attend and observe criminal trials. This new right had nothing to do with cameras in the court. It merely guaranteed the public the right to have the media attend criminal trials to be the public's eyes and ears. Three subsequent decisions in the 1980s, two of them growing out of cases brought by the *Riverside* (CA) *Press-Enterprise,* expanded this new First Amendment right. In swift succession, the High Court mandated a presumption of openness for such critical parts of the judicial process as the voir dire examination of jurors and the preliminary hearings of criminal defendants (which are usually the only opportunity to hear the quality of evidence against an accused since approximately 90 percent of all criminal prosecutions end when plea bargains make trials unnecessary). This new First Amendment right arrived as part of the "sea change" in the Court's approach to the "promise" of the first sentence in the Bill of Rights. The rationale used for manufacturing the new right also promised that future cases might expand it to create a constitutional right of the public and press to have access to all sorts of government records and proceedings. In mock horror and obvious disapproval, Chief Justice Rehnquist described this possibility as a sort of "constitutional sunshine law." Rehnquist was not an admirer of the new right. Others were. Justice Stevens saw it growing out of a broad First Amendment "right to receive information." And the intellectual godfather of the new right of access, Justice Brennan, saw it applying to any proceeding that traditionally was open to the public and where openness benefited the Republic. Obviously, this reasoning could be applied to open under the Constitution (rather than under state or federal statutes) all sorts of legislative or administrative meetings and hearings and perhaps records as well. After the two *Riverside Press-Enterprise* cases, constitutional lawyers reasonably expected more Supreme Court decisions opening other parts of government to public inspection.

But after 1985 the well ran dry. The Court has not uttered a word about its bold new First Amendment right since then. There has been no third case from the *Riverside Press-Enterprise* or anywhere else.

It is fair to ask whether the stagnation in First Amendment law is due to factors other than a reflection of the public's scorn for the media. One favorite theory, especially in the 1980s and early 1990s, was that a new generation of politically conservative judges and justices, appointed during the twelve years of the Reagan-Bush administrations, is retreating from the activism and precedents established by older, more liberal jurists. This theory, which might be labeled the *People* magazine analysis, became conventional wisdom at about the time when the deteriorating relationship between the public and the media coincided with philosophical shifts occurring in both the country and the courts. As America grew more conservative, the lack of advances in First Amendment law seemed a natural and probable consequence. In an August 1989 op-ed column in *The Washington Post,* headlined "The Media Under Siege," New York publishing lawyer Martin Garbus warned that "Supreme Court conservatives want to give the states an ability to limit the boundaries of what have been considered fundamental rights," particularly free speech rights.[6] This theory collapsed with the weight of time and events. By 1998, Floyd Abrams was writing in the *Columbia Journalism Review* in an article entitled "Look Who's Trashing the First Amendment":

> [T]he First Amendment . . . is indeed under attack again. But this time its most consistent attackers are on the left. And many of its most powerful defenders are on the right.[7]

In truth, judicial or political philosophy is a miserable bellwether for predicting how an individual judge will react to a particular First Amendment case. Long before Kenneth Starr became the nemesis of the Clinton White House and an independent counsel cheered by the Republican right, he was the Court of Appeals judge who in 1984 brilliantly synthesized decades of confusing, contradictory law governing editorial commentary and forged one of the most remarkable First Amendment decisions of his times. Starr's opinion for the entire D.C. Circuit Court of Appeals in *Ollman v. Evans and Novak* was worthy of Justice Brennan. It was just as expansive and rigorous as any First Amendment opinion written by either of Starr's liberal Court of Appeals counterparts, Richard Arnold of the Eighth Circuit or Gilbert Merritt of the Sixth Circuit. Likewise, one of the few judges on the D.C. Circuit who did not join Starr's opinion in *Ollman,* but who concurred and wrote separately with a zest and sympathy for First Amendment values that has not been seen since in American jurisprudence, was Robert Bork. Bork, of course, is more commonly remembered as President Reagan's nominee for the Supreme Court who was deemed too conservative by a Democratically controlled Senate to be confirmed. Yet, ironically, Bork showed more solicitude for the media, and perspicaciousness about the gathering storm likely to rage around it, than virtually any other public official in America. He favored in *Ollman* the broadest possible protection for authors because of what he foresaw as "a freshening stream of libel actions which often seem as much designed to punish writers and publications as to recover damages for real injuries."[8] This trend, Bork believed, could threaten the "free, and frequently rough, discussion" encouraged by the Constitution. He looked at the road ahead and worried that "an upsurge in libel actions, accompanied by a startling inflation of damage awards, . . . threaten[s] to impose a self-censorship on the press which can as effectively inhibit debate and criticism as would overt governmental regulation that the First Amendment most certainly would not permit.[9]

Within the academic community, there is also another theme—although not quite an explanation or theory—that bears on the erosion of First Amendment law.

Most First Amendment scholars don't disagree that little has happened in First Amendment law affecting the press during the last ten years. But they wonder if the dearth of activity isn't somewhat attributable to a doctrinal shift—i.e., a new ideological orientation in First Amendment law that emphasizes permissible regulation of speech and deemphasizes that "traditional, liberal commentator position promoted by the American Civil Liberties Union (ACLU)," as University of Virginia professor Ted White describes it. White points out that the focus of First Amendment scholarship has changed in the past ten years, to an attitude that he describes as "retrenchment." Legal scholars have stopped writing about *rights* under the First Amendment and focus instead on *responsibilities*—i.e., examining the type of governmental restrictions on speech that are permissible under the First Amendment. Thus, for instance, noted antipornography activist Catharine MacKinnon pushes a ban on pornography because it contributes to male domination. She dismisses those who oppose her in the name of free speech because she believes that the only reason to value free speech over a woman's right to be free from persecution by pornography is to perpetuate male power. Mainstream scholarship is moving away from the marketplace-of-ideas concept of the First Amendment—where voicing any idea (other than one that threatens imminent harm) is considered inherently valuable because it adds to the public discourse—toward a belief that the voicing of certain ideas should be restricted because their very expression threatens our idea of a civilized society.

The political correctness movement, proliferating hate-speech codes and the theories of legal scholar Cass Sunstein reflect this shift. Sunstein argues that the First Amendment has been usurped to protect "speech that has little or no connection with democratic aspirations and that produces serious social harm."[10] This "mistake" can only be corrected, according to Sunstein, by the government exercising the "reasonably broad power to regulate (among other things) commercial speech, libelous speech, scientific speech with potential military applications, . . . and certain forms of pornography and hate speech."[11] Even protecting the good name of beef and vegetables becomes important to Sunstein, as he showed in a *New York Times* op-ed on the occasion of Oprah Winfrey's defense of a libel lawsuit brought by Texas cattlemen. "Narrowly interpreted laws that protect products from libel can do a lot of good, and they aren't unconstitutional," he wrote in January 1998.[12]

This "Sunstein/MacKinnon shift" from an expansive to a restrictive view of freedom of speech incorporates the idealized notion of the First

Amendment as protector of minorities from the will of the majority. But now there is a twist. The "victim" in First Amendment cases has changed from the "maverick" or outcast, such as the hooded Ku Klux Klan member or the scurrilous publisher, to the big media company with enormous economic power. When American Nazis sought a permit to march in Skokie, Illinois, the typical liberal commentator's gut reaction was, "Everyone hates the Nazis, but this [type of speech] is what the First Amendment is all about." Today, the questionable "speaker," typically a big company with money, lawyers and economic and political clout, is viewed as being able to protect itself without special help from the Constitution. In short, media "victims" today look as if they can take care of themselves since they are controlled by what Justice White called (with characteristic disdain) "a few powerful hands operating very lucrative businesses."[13] Indeed, many First Amendment cases today, such as the "must carry" wars between broadcasters and cable operators, can be seen as reducing the amendment to a battle for the bottom line.

Then, too, the past ten years have not witnessed the sort of repression present in the Vietnam or Watergate era. Blatant, raw censorship provokes a strong response. The methods by which slick public officials regulate speech now is more insidious, a product of the object lessons of repression. We have drawn further away from crude censorship, but closer to a dangerous zone of suppression as we have slowly migrated toward an economy where media and entertainment companies are as interrelated with government and politics as politicians and celebrities at a Hollywood fund-raiser. The greatest threat to First Amendment freedoms today may be clever governmental manipulation of regulated industries aimed at influencing the editorial content of sister companies. Newspapers that once felt tolerably vulnerable to government's heavy hand because of the ownership of broadcast licenses have been replaced by networks owned by parent companies which are regulated by the Nuclear Regulatory Commission or the Environmental Protection Agency.

Academic scholarship tends to reflect court decisions or political crosscurrents somewhat more than it influences them. Governmental regulation of hate speech, condom advertisements or flag burning inevitably becomes more interesting to academics than the newsgathering problems of the press simply because judges are dealing with them as actual cases. In the end, the Sunstein/MacKinnon shift is more likely an intellectual justification or rationale for what is going on in American society instead of a cause of anything, including the stunted growth in First Amendment law.

THE MIKVA EXPLANATION

The day after Abner Mikva announced his retirement as counsel to President Clinton in September 1995, *The Washington Times* gave its readers a little explanation for the resignation. The newspaper reported:

> When Mr. Mikva took the White House job, he noted that he had recently remarried and liked to set aside time for tennis.[14]

Mikva relished telling people that *The Washington Times* article had caused him serious problems at home. His wife of forty-seven years wanted to know why she had not been invited to his recent wedding.

The *Times*'s error was corrected five days later. It was not the first time Mikva had been forced to find some humor in the press's coverage of him. When he had been a congressman from Illinois, editorials in the *Chicago Tribune* used to refer to him as "Airhead Ab." When he was Chief Judge of the D.C. Circuit Court of Appeals, intense press coverage regularly portrayed him as presiding over an alley full of scrappy cats, judges who hissed at each other with ideological division and clawed each other daily. When he finally completed his life's assault on the separation-of-powers doctrine by moving down Pennsylvania Avenue to serve as White House counsel for President Clinton (after the suicide of Vincent Foster and the politically disastrous tenure of Bernard Nussbaum), he was mocked for wanting to supervise a kindergarten of novice lawyers.

Just before Chief Judge Mikva left the bench, he was assigned randomly, with Harry Edwards and Patricia Wald, two well-regarded judges appointed by President Carter, to hear the appeal of a libel case against *The New York Times Book Review.* Deciding the case should have been a cakewalk. It was not.

The weirdness around the case began with a *Times* review of a book written by Washington, D.C., author Dan E. Moldea entitled *Interference: The Influence of Organized Crime on Professional Football.* The review, written by veteran *Times* sportswriter Gerald Eskenazi, offered positive comments about *Interference,* including that "there is some really hot stuff in here . . . " but concluded that despite its strengths, *Interference* was marred by "too much sloppy journalism to trust the bulk of this book's 512 pages—including its whopping 64 pages of notes."[15] Eskenazi supported his opinion with illustrations from the book, including Moldea's misspelling of several prominent sports figures' names and his mischaracterizations of certain people and events in football lore. As book reviews go, the *Times* critique was relatively straightforward. Other reviewers had treated *Interference* more harshly. The *Philadelphia Inquirer,* for example, had written: "The germ of a compelling story is there, but in Moldea's hands the germ grew into a virus."[16]

Nearly a year later, Moldea sued the *Times,* disputing the *Review*'s conclusion and quarreling with its examples. Cheered on by authors who had been similarly unappreciated by the *Times Book Review,* Moldea nevertheless was unable to persuade the federal district court that his case deserved a trial. Judge John Garrett Penn dismissed his lawsuit on an early motion, finding that the review's conclusion of "too much sloppy journalism" was "an unverifiable opinion," and that each example used in the review was "either a supported statement of fact or a nonverifiable opinion."[17]

None of this was terribly surprising. "How can an author sue over a bad review?" people would ask me when they learned of my work on the case for the *Times.*

"Of course, it's unusual," I'd reply. "But Moldea is claiming the review made false statements of fact about him and his book, and while he can't sue over opinions evaluating the book, he can *theoretically* sue if the review made false statements of *fact*." I would hasten to emphasize the *theoretically*, because the lawsuit was, in our view, nonsense.

Moldea disagreed. He appealed the dismissal to the D.C. Circuit Court of Appeals and took to the hustings. At the huge annual American Booksellers Association convention in Los Angeles, he and his lawyer debated the merits of his claim with me on a well-attended panel program. What interested me most about the afternoon was not the reprise of the legal arguments, which sounded the same familiar melodies as the courts were hearing, but instead the responsive chords which Moldea was finding with the audience of authors, publishers, bookstore owners and affiliated denizens of the book world. Whenever Moldea would rant against the power of the *Times Book Review* to make or break a book with a positive or negative review, the audience would nod in agreement as if a flashing "Nod Now" sign had been turned on from the podium.

This disapproval of the *Times's* alleged power is closely related to the fear and loathing which many businesses—from restaurants to Microsoft—harbor toward the unchecked and unaccountable power the media allegedly have to define or shape public attitudes. These powers are undoubtedly overstated. Publishers, for instance, know that glowing reviews do not generally help a book's sales and that the best-seller list is routinely filled with works that critics have panned, if they've even bothered to review them at all. But, no matter. Our strong egalitarian impulses at the end of the twentieth century suggest that free expression can be exercised vigorously by powerless people yearning for equality, but when the powerful speak, it had better be with sobriety bordering on unctuousness, or preferably, blandness and banality.

The *Times's* review of Moldea's book was pungent and succinct: *Interference* had "too much sloppy journalism." When oral argument began in the D.C. Circuit Court of Appeals, Judge Mikva made it clear that worse things had been said about him. Judges Edwards and Wald, however, were clearly troubled by the sting of the review. And Edwards even critiqued the critique, lambasting the review as poorly crafted. To me, the review seemed pretty well constructed, really quite classic, certainly not half-baked.

Within four months, Harry Edwards and Pat Wald stunned the literary world and much of the rest of the country by reversing the trial court's dismissal of Moldea's lawsuit. In a decision of potentially far-reaching impact, the two judges decided that "too much sloppy journalism" wasn't a personal subjective opinion but a factual statement that could be proven true or false. Mikva dissented. Editorial writers and commentators went wild. The decision was trashed as "driving a truck through a small opening in the law of libel" and "greatly impairing the ability of opinion writers to speak their mind."[18]

The *Times* moved for reconsideration by the full Court of Appeals, arguing that the "destabilizing" decision "undermined two centuries of jurisprudence protecting literary criticism" and "placed at risk virtually every unflattering review by disregarding the wealth of common law and constitutional authority that recognizes the necessity of considering context in assessing the actionability of language." Former judge Kenneth Starr wrote a friend-of-the-court brief on behalf of a group of publishers to try to persuade his former colleagues on the D.C. Circuit bench that the Edwards/Wald decision was an aberrational departure from basic Anglo-American law.

On May 3, 1994, a second decision came from the three-judge panel of Mikva, Edwards and Wald. This time, the decision was unanimous. Again written by Judge Edwards, it began poignantly:

> I often have been struck by Justice Stewart's concurring statement in *Boys Markets, Inc. v. Retail Clerks Union, Local 770,* a case in which the Court reconsidered and overruled an earlier decision. Justice Stewart remarked that "[i]n these circumstances the temptation is strong to embark upon a lengthy personal *apologia.*" This remark has special poignancy for me now, because it underscores the distress felt by a judge who, in grappling with a very difficult legal issue, concludes that he has made a mistake of judgment. Once discovered, confessing error is relatively easy. What is difficult is accepting the realization that, despite your

best efforts, you may still fall prey to an error of judgment. Like Justice Stewart, I will take refuge in an aphorism of Justice Frankfurter:

> Wisdom too often never comes, and so one ought not to reject it merely because it comes late. . . .

Then Judge Edwards delivered the thunderbolt:

> After careful consideration of the *Times'* petition for rehearing and Moldea's response to that petition, we are persuaded to amend our earlier decision. The original majority opinion was generally correct in its statement of the law of defamation. Unfortunately, that opinion failed to take sufficient account of the fact that the statements at issue appeared in the context of a book review, a genre in which readers expect to find spirited critiques of literary works that they understand to be the reviewer's description and assessment of texts that are capable of a number of possible rational interpretations.
>
> In light of our reconsideration of this case, we hold that the challenged statements in the *Times* review are supportable interpretations of *Interference,* and that as a matter of law the review is substantially true.[19]

A mistake had been acknowledged, graciously and openly. It is a rare thing to see in public life. When it happens, it makes us regard the person confessing the error with new awe. The self-correction in *Moldea II,* as it came to be called, preserved the substantial protection afforded commentary and criticism under our libel laws, but it raised a significant question: Why had the mistake occurred at all? What had prompted two world-class judges to lose perspective? Judges speak through their opinions, but there was no answer in *Moldea II*—only repeated murmurs that the area of law was "very difficult."

After leaving the bench, Judge Mikva provided an insight. In a speech at Georgia State University's Law School in October 1994, Mikva spoke candidly about *Moldea,* which he described as the most important First Amendment case decided by the D.C. Circuit during his last term. For those looking for a behind-the-scenes explanation for the astonishing about-face of his colleagues, Mikva offered the following warning:

> A feeling is abroad among some judges that the Supreme Court has gone too far in protecting the media from defamation actions resulting from instances of irresponsible journalism.[20] . . .
>
> I've been a judge for 15 years, and now that I've taken off my robes, one of the first things I must say is—Watch Out! There's a backlash coming in First Amendment doctrine.

It would be reassuring to believe that judges in the next century will overcome the natural passions they share with the public and, like Harry Edwards and Patricia Wald, self-correct mistakes born of a disdain for the modern media. It would be hopeful to think that judges will be able to maintain the equilibrium and sense of humor of Justice Harry Blackmun, who in 1995 addressed a dinner honoring him after his retirement from the Supreme Court by saying:

> Oh, the media, they're always referring to *Roe v. Wade* and my work for women and homosexuals and that's all they ever mention. And they'll put it on my tombstone and never mention anything else I've done. And, oh, so what!

The line drew laughter and relief, but it bears mentioning that Justice Blackmun made the remarks to an audience of media people at a dinner sponsored by a media-backed organization. There is nothing so attractive as forgiveness.

There will be such moments ahead. But they will be overwhelmed by angrier, colder responses.

In the winter of 1998, a caravan of vans and trucks carrying millions of dollars' worth of equipment owned by the world's media companies surrounded the federal courthouse in Washington. They laid siege to the grand jury operating inside. On most days, nothing much happened. No White House lawyers or witnesses appeared. No friends of Monica's. Just a grim encampment of restless camera crews, reporters and still photographers waiting and watching. They lounged in beach chairs, drinking designer coffees and flavored waters, grateful to El Niño for warm temperatures. Inside the courthouse, people ridiculed them, spoke of them with disgust. "I'd like that job," said one juror, "just sit around all day getting paid good money. Not bad." "They're kind of pathetic," a clerk of the court offered, "but, boy, they sure do eat big lunches." The security guards usually set up barriers to pen them in, segregate them. On the third floor of the building, in the terrazzo-and-marble hallway outside the grand jury room, reporters lined up behind a blue velvet rope to peek at people exiting the elevator and heading within five seconds into the grand jury room. "I like it," Court of Appeals judge David B. Sentelle observed during the first week of testimony on the Monica Lewinsky matter. "It's like hogs in a pen."[21]

"Your clients are lazy and mindless," another Circuit Court of Appeals judge scolded me. "There's news happening in Washington, but it's not here. Why don't they go to the SEC? Not enough redundant pictures? It's lunacy for them to be camped here." He repeated the word for emphasis: "Lunacy."

And then he delivers the sort of warning I hear privately from judges all the time. "They're so dim-witted. Don't they understand that someday some nice lady like Betty Currie will bring a test case and then there will be new legal restrictions on the media? More test cases and more restrictions will follow." The judge's prediction is almost certainly right. Remember the picture of Betty Currie, President Clinton's personal secretary, scared to death as she was mobbed and crushed by cameras outside the federal courthouse? It evokes the sort of negative stereotype that will eventually provoke some media victim to sue—probably for invasion of privacy, assault, harassment or outrageous intrusion. The case will seek reasonable limitations on the right of a media pack to physically swarm around a news subject, even in a public place. It will point to the court-approved sanctions placed on paparazzo Ron Galella at Jacqueline Onassis' request in 1973. The court found then that in zealous pursuit of photographs of Mrs. Onassis and her young children, Galella had endangered their safety and intruded into their right to a certain amount of peace and quiet by jumping in front of John Kennedy Jr. while he was riding a bike in Central Park, following Mrs. Onassis too closely in an automobile and swerving near her in a motorboat while she was swimming. For these excesses and for such pesky antics as bribing doormen and romancing a family servant in order to learn about the family's movements, Galella was ordered by the New York federal court to observe the following restrictions:

(1) any approach within twenty-five (25) feet of defendant or any touching of the person of the defendant Jacqueline Onassis; (2) any blocking of her movement in public places and thoroughfares; (3) any act foreseeably or reasonably calculated to place the life and safety of defendant in jeopardy; and (4) any conduct which would reasonably be foreseen to harass, alarm or frighten the defendant.[22]

Hardly any reasonable person in the communications industry objects to a voluntarily imposed set of professional guidelines echoing the Galella rules of the road. But none currently exist. And news organizations as well as the paparazzi have steadily intensified the anarchy. It is just a matter of time before a court imposes order.

Corralling and curtailing the physical effronteries of camera crews is just one of many initiatives that news organizations must take to restore their authority on First Amendment issues with courts and, more broadly, with the public. One cannot read the devastatingly furious words of Judge Susan Webber Wright, the Little Rock judge who heard Paula Jones's sexual harassment case, without sensing that time has run out. In denying the request of media organizations for access to discovery materials in the *Jones* litigation, Judge Wright called the media "disingenuous," "inaccurate," "callous" and "driven by profit and intense competition." "Stories without attribution and based on gossip, speculation and innuendo fly through media outlets with blinding speed," she wrote. She would not reward the "saturation of the public" and the "media's profiting therefrom" by opening up records—even records where private matters were redacted—for the public's edification.[23] Blinded by her fury over the media's exploitation and "profiteering" from the *Jones* case, the judge simply cut off all information about an important case grinding through the public justice system. At another point in American history, her response would have been more measured, more respectful of the public's right to receive information about serious charges against the President of the United States and more receptive to arguments made by the caretakers of First Amendment freedoms. She might even have remembered the words of Albert Camus, the French writer, who wrote, near the end of his life after enduring two world wars in Europe: "A free press can of course be good or bad, but most certainly, without freedom it will never be anything but bad."[24]

What is being forgotten these days by judges—and many of the rest of us as well—is that First Amendment freedoms were not conferred on the press at the dawn of the American experiment by founding fathers impressed with the press's devotion to public service. Quite the contrary. James Madison saw the press as "chequered with abuses" and Thomas Jefferson deplored "the putrid state into which our newspapers have passed, and the malignity, the vulgarity, and the mendacious spirit of those who write for them." In fact, the founding fathers "had no very clear idea what they meant by" the First Amendment's guarantees, according to Professor Zechariah Chafee, who wrote the earliest study on free expression. David Anderson, the leading scholar of the origins of the press clause, concludes that while history yields meager insight on the framers' intent, it is remarkably clear that they valued press freedom much more deeply than the clause in the First Amendment which guarantees freedom of speech. The speech clause, Anderson explains, was "an afterthought." The press clause, on the other hand, was central to liberty, essential to provide "a necessary restraint on what the patriots viewed as government's natural tendency toward tyranny and despotism."[25] Thus, the origins and justification for the First Amendment's special place of honor for the press cannot be said to be founded on the press's "public service" role. Any historical basis for that claim is "at best uncertain and imprecise," says Robert M. O'Neil, the former president of the University of Virginia and now director of the Thomas Jefferson Center for the Protection of Free Expression in Charlottesville. It is, instead, undoubtedly more helpful to see the free press guarantee, as Justice Potter Stewart did, as "a *structural* provision of the Constitution," one designed to "create a fourth institution outside the Government as an additional check on the three official branches." Seen in that perspective, First Amendment freedoms should not depend so much on the public's approval of the press's work, or on the press performing public service, as on the recognition that as awful as they may behave at times, we are much better off relying on them than on government for our liberties.

9

The Credibility Breakfast

The mighty voices of the Eastern High School Choir are belting out "The Impossible Dream" to begin "The Credibility Breakfast." This is not the right music for a devotional meal organized to bring editors to battle. The leadership of the American Society of Newspaper Editors (ASNE) has billed the breakfast as a major event at its 1998 annual convention in Washington. It will launch a new four-year campaign to restore the credibility of the nation's newspapers—to make the "believability of newspapers the central concern of our newsrooms, ahead of profits. Ahead of what corporate thinks of us," as the organization's president, Sandra Mims Rowe, the editor of the Portland *Oregonian,* says with resolve. Still, the music is wrong. But for the ecclesiastical limitations, "Onward, Christian Soldiers" would be more appropriate.

"Haven't we been talking about 'credibility' forever?" Chuck Lewis, the friendly head of Hearst's Washington bureau, grimaces as he heads toward the ballroom. This is the same line you hear from any editor with more than 3.2 years of experience. But it flows more from defensiveness than weariness. Actually, they have been talking about credibility for a long time. Ten years earlier, at the same journalists' convention that saw Donna Rice bolt for the door, terrified of the beast, William Burleigh, then head of the E. W. Scripps Company's newspaper division and later

Scripps's CEO, delivered a keynote address calling for a focus on "our fundamental responsibility to be accurate, fair, credible and balanced."

One should never underestimate the earnestness of journalists. Inside the ballroom, with the choir crescendoed and the army fed, Sandra Mims Rowe launches into a battle hymn of astonishing effectiveness.

"If this is a time when the destructiveness and tawdriness of mass media hang like a curse over even the best-intentioned newspaper editors, it is also a time when changing values and new media players should prompt us to seek higher ground," she says. This seems to be a suggestion that newspapers don't have to ape Matt Drudge or dress up as a bearded lady in order to compete for attention on the carnival midway of the Internet. Then Ms. Rowe takes aim:

> As [our] profits have hovered near all-time records, many companies have not invested in journalistic training significantly enough to demonstrate their commitment to the highest standards. Nor have beginning salaries at most papers become competitive with those in other professions. It is now left to editors to provide the leadership *within* their companies, to demonstrate the true relationship between quality journalism and long-term success in the marketplace . . . We must stand unflinchingly for what we believe—with owners and publishers.[1]

Rowe is correctly targeting corporate honchos and their preoccupation with revenue growth and expense control. "Credibility is not about selling more newspapers," she declares. "It is about building the quality and integrity of our news."

She is pointing the way home. Not just for journalism but for the frightened communications businesses as well. The executives of the media companies are sweaty-palm anxious. At the turn of the century, the old paradigm of the mass media commanding a mass audience is fading. Newspaper readership is flat or declining. Television audiences are shrinking so steadily and the cost of entertainment programming is escalating so stubbornly that the major commercial networks would be unprofitable without their ownership of local stations in major markets. Fresh cable channels, from MSNBC to HGTV (Home & Garden Television) and Arts & Entertainment, are balkanizing television viewership. The new Yukon of the Internet soaks up the limited time that people have to absorb news, information and advertising messages. The new paradigm for the media business is "niching"—cultivating a fragment of the world with a specialized product appealing to a specialized interest or audience: newsletters on health or investing from the robust Phillips Publishing International; the Food Channel, now run by a former president of CBS News; the new "daily edition" on-line of *The Wall Street Journal* which entitles the reader to a twenty-four-hour pass to the newspaper's interactive edition—sold in early 1999 for $1.95 as opposed to 75 cents for the newsprint edition or $59 per year for the Internet edition (which is about one-third the cost of a print subscription). The economics of the World Wide Web may be weird, but no periodic surfer will go untapped.

In fact, the mass media, whether newspapers, magazines, television or radio, are marooned on an isthmus where the tides are lapping away the single thin connection to the mainland. In the 1990s only the new breed of "sexsational" stories—the John Bobbitt, O. J. Simpson and Monica Lewinsky melodramas—permit them to cobble together something temporarily resembling a mass audience. Both the public and journalists sense the contrivance. Certainly, part of the explanation for the contradictory attitudes in 1999 toward President Clinton ("he lied to us but we approve of his performance in office") was the public's realization that the media were using "sexsation" to corral an audience. And the exhaustion and disgust with the impeachment process was as palpable with journalists as with people in Trenton or St. Louis. "What if they gave a scandal and nobody came?" asked Linda Greenhouse, longtime Supreme Court correspondent for *The New York Times*, after the impeachment farce concluded. The rhetorical question summed up the fervent hope of many Washington journalists that their editors would reduce reliance on "sexsation" to seduce an audience. After all, the public's boredom with the Oval Office scandal after a few months showed how hard it is to sustain "sexsational" ardor.

Sandra Rowe is not the only leader in the media to tap into the high anxiety within her business and insist that companies devote more money to journalism and journalists (as opposed to technology and mergers). The Radio and Television News Directors Foundation has embarked on a three-year project from 1998 to 2000, the "Journalism Ethics and Integrity Project." The effort will conduct eighteen regional forums for the public and journalists to discuss electronic journalism. "Reinforcing core journalism values" and training on "ethical decision-making skills" are both the buzzwords and the objectives for these sessions. Other groups with a similar sense of urgency and nearly identical goals have sprung up on an ad hoc basis. With one mass mailing in September 1997, Bill Kovach, the head of Harvard's Nieman Foundation, and Tom Rosenstiel, the former media reporter for the *Los Angeles Times,* rounded up 1,076 members for a new organization called the Committee of Concerned Journalists. The committee declared itself "worried about the future of the profession." It was hell-bent on "creating a national conversation among journalists about core principles." The "conversation" would have three purposes: to renew journalists' faith in the principles and function of journalism; to create a better understanding of those principles by the public; and "to inform ownership and management of the financial as well as the social value" of the principles. "We must clarify what journalism means— and remind ourselves why we were called to it in the first place—or it will cease to mean anything," the committee announced ominously. Unsurprisingly, given the mood, the committee quickly collected journalists ranging from authors David Halberstam and Alex Jones to editors like John Carroll of the *Baltimore Sun* and Jane Healy of the *Orlando Sentinel* and local news directors like Lucy Himstedt from Montgomery, Alabama.

"We wouldn't have gotten all these people five or six years ago," says Tom Rosenstiel, now director of the pointedly named Project for Excellence in Journalism. Rosenstiel believes that when the media's credibility problems with the public began to creep onto the radar screen some fifteen years ago, the reaction among journalists was "let's fix it." This business model coincided with the push inside companies to have journalists become better MBAs, to enlist them in the battle to sustain profit margins in the face of shrinking revenue bases. Bonuses were tied to financial, not editorial, performance. A cultural change swept through newsrooms everywhere. The advertiser, not the reader or viewer, became the paramount concern. The shift in the syllogism had a corrosive effect on journalists. "Nowadays," says Rosenstiel, "when the public is angry with the press, the journalists' reaction is 'I agree with them.'" Hence, the arrival of the Committee of Concerned Journalists. "We need to reclarify the distinction between movies, talk radio and journalism," according to Rosenstiel. This will not be an easy assignment so long as Don Imus hobnobs on-air with network anchors and CNN correspondents drop into films like *Contact* (with Jodie Foster) for cameo appearances. Yet, the task is not so much to restore the image of journalists to the stereotypical portrayal in *The Man Who Shot Liberty Valance* (hard-drinking rascals who on good days rise above themselves). Rather, journalists want to recover a sense of their own importance, even centrality, to the larger universe of the communications world.

It is interesting where the money is coming from to support this "recapturing" of the profession. It is not, in the main, gushing from the media companies. Instead, it is cascading in million-dollar grants from what might be collectively termed "the billion-dollar foundations"—the Pew Charitable Trust in Philadelphia, the Freedom Forum (formerly the Gannett Foundation) in Washington and New York, the Robert R. McCormick/Tribune Foundation in Chicago, the Knight Foundation in Miami, even the Ford Foundation. Many of the assets of these wealthy foundations derive, of course, from the estates of journalism's barons, Colonel McCormick, for instance. In effect, the capital gains of the past are being plowed into restoration projects for the future. "There is an enormous amount of change facing communications companies," says Vivian Vahlberg, Director of Journalism Programs for the Robert R. McCormick/Tribune Foundation. "We're trying to provide the tools to steer journalism through these changes so it can emerge intact at the other end." The research of all the billion-dollar foundations shows a consistent disconnect between the public and journalists; as Vahlberg describes it, "the public didn't believe journalists were living up to their own standards and values while journalists feared that the public didn't care about or want any values," just entertainment. Listening to the zeal of both the foundation executives and the leaders in journalism, you know that this new movement represents much more than just what Wall Street calls a "technical correction." At the heart of the movement lies a simple theme (as well as an implicit threat): journalism is the product offered by media companies and unless it is practiced and produced at its best, the franchise will fail.

Among the top-ranking executives of some media companies, there is growing recognition that the new emphasis on content and journalism's "values" and "principles" will be as important as anything to holding on to the franchise. Gary Pruitt, president and chief executive officer of Mc-Clatchy Newspapers, the Sacramento-based company which in recent years has acquired both the Raleigh (N.C.) and Minneapolis newspapers, is convinced. Better training of journalists will enable them to deepen their understanding of complex subjects, and this greater depth in journalism's coverage, he believes, is the key to "protecting and expanding our brands and franchises." Pruitt has long thought that "people seldom grasp the difficulty" of a journalist's job. "We expect reporters to comprehend complicated subjects and then condense and distill and write about them for people with much less understanding, all under time pressure and with the expectation that no mistakes will be made. And usually the stories are controversial, so people will be picking at the nuances."

This is the kind of empathy that journalists like hearing from their CEO stallions. At forty-one, Gary Pruitt is among the most impressive thoroughbreds of a younger generation of professional managers at media companies. Carefully groomed for a competitive track, he has no intention of letting McClatchy's newspapers slide into oblivion. For all the talk about "hot" Internet and cable news outlets, he and his peers in publishing believe that newspapers, protected and enhanced with Web sites, will remain the dominant mass medium in local markets for years to come.

"Newspapers command the sole remaining mass audience," he says. "They're not subject to the same fragmentation and scads of new competitors as television or the Internet." Actually, newspapers' lead over the No. 2 advertising outlet in each market—usually a network affiliate—is actually growing. While they've seen some erosion in circulation, the drop has been nothing like television's where *Seinfeld's* share of the television audience in 1995 was equal to the share for *The Dukes of Hazzard,* a program that was the twentieth most highly rated show by Nielsen in 1978. Pruitt believes that as long as "we focus on preserving newspapers' market share, as opposed to profit margins," no new media will be able to eat their lunch. In essence, newspapers will move upmarket—the choice of the better educated—as television gravitates downmarket.

This reasoning runs counterclockwise to the viewpoint, trendy for more than a decade, that newspapers will become musty relics in the new Information Age, the analog in the communications world to railroads in transportation. The conventional wisdom seems mostly wrong because the Information Age is not termed, as Librarian of Congress James Billington notes, the Knowledge Age. It is knowledge, content, journalism, that Gary Pruitt and his fellow back-to-the-futurists are counting on—even bean-counting on—to secure the fortunes of their shareholders. "Newspapers with their breadth, context and depth are diamonds," he says. "The Internet is cubic zirconium." Delivery systems may change, he suggests, but content will always be king.

For journalists intent upon demanding higher salaries, better training and more time for more thorough reporting, the front offices of America's communications companies are not necessarily wholly occupied by receptive bosses like Gary Pruitt. Velociraptors in accountants' clothing lurk not just in shadows but behind mahogany desks. They would just as soon devour or at least downsize journalists as listen to "The Credibility Breakfast." But these are the true dinosaurs. The more they underfund their product, the more they dissipate their business and invite extinction. These dinosaurs do not hear the march of a "new professionalism" headed down their corridor.

"I reject a construct that suggests that *only* commercial goals are important, that the obligations of the journalist in a democracy do not have an *equal* importance. I will not permit myself, my journalism or my company to be defined only in terms of those commercial goals," says an avatar for the new movement, Maxwell E. P. King, who stepped down from serving as editor of the *Philadelphia Inquirer* from 1990 to 1998 to return to in-depth reporting, "devoting six months or more to one story." He has since left to head the Heinz Foundation in Pittsburgh. Max King is not naive. He knows that his hope for what he calls "this battle for a new professionalism" rests almost entirely "on the willingness of journalists to take some risks with their own security."[2] There is power behind this calling. What is at stake is one's own self-respect.

Max King and like-minded journalists—and there are many of them—will have the support of the billion-dollar foundations. By 1999, the Freedom Forum had fully inflated its Free Press/Fair Press balloon, a multiyear campaign to explain the new (and the old) professionalism to the public.

"We're so poor at explaining ourselves," says Peter Prichard, the Freedom Forum's president in Washington, "so the public judges us by what they see as our occasional despicable behavior. If I were an editor again, I'd write a regular column just about the craft."

The Freedom Forum has pumped millions of dollars into its project after a series of roundtable discussions with community leaders in San Francisco, Phoenix, Portland (Oregon) and Nashville during 1998 produced "depressing" results. "It's horrible out there," moans Prichard after participating in the roundtables. "Community leaders have given up on local television. They just see it as limited to fires and floods. And the local television people are in total denial."

In earlier decades, this self-analysis would have been done by media companies themselves (to the extent that it needed to be done at all). Now the media foundations like the Freedom Forum are undertaking the work. They are doing more than merely delivering rude messages to boardrooms. They are designing programs (and programming in a joint cable-television venture with PBS) that will redefine "fairness" as news coverage that is important ("a rollover wreck on I-17 will preempt serious coverage every time," the executive director of Greater Phoenix Leadership, Inc., had told the roundtable). If news organizations spent as much time worrying about "fairness" as they do about "accuracy," Robin Mc-Neil has suggested, the media's stock with the public would rise.

The Freedom Forum's Robert Giles is "reasonably optimistic" about the benefits that are likely to flow from the foundations' work. "The public is more discriminating about the media than a decade ago," he says. "And much of the media is poised for change." Some of the motivation for this willingness to embrace change is certainly self-preservation.

Giles and Prichard both remember the chilling prediction offered by Rabbi Emanuel Rose at their Portland roundtable. Rabbi Rose expressed his "great disappointment" about the lack of accuracy and context in news coverage and in the priorities of editors. "There may come a time when a judge somewhere makes a ruling that cuts back on our First Amendment rights," he said to a quiet group. "When that day comes, I will both cry and cheer at the same time."

Notes

Prologue: A Dangerous New Season

1. Al Neuharth, *Confessions of an S.O.B.* (Doubleday, 1989).

Chapter 1. The Canyon of Distrust

1. See *New York Times Co. v. Sullivan,* 376 U.S. 254, 270, 272 (1964).
2. *Westmoreland v. CBS, Inc.,* 601 F. Supp. 66, 68 (S.D.N.Y., 1984).
3. *Ibid.*
4. *Ibid.*
5. The Freedom Forum's exhaustive review and assessment of polling in this area during the last fifty years found an exasperating lack of correlative data. Few questions were asked consistently, so a comparison on trends or attitudinal shifts over various decades is not easy to measure.
6. Times Mirror, "The People & the Press: A Times Mirror Investigation of Public Attitudes Toward the Media, Conducted by the Gallup Organization," January 1986.
7. *Ibid.,* p. 3.
8. *Ibid.*
9. The American Society of Newspaper Editors, "Newspaper Credibility: Building Reader Trust," April 1985.
10. Times Mirror, "The People & the Press" (1986), p. 20.
11. *Ibid.,* pp. 20–21.
12. *Ibid.,* pp. 28, 67.
13. "The Press and the People—A Survey," *Fortune,* August 1939.
14. Times Mirror, "The People & the Press" (1986), ASNE (1985), p. 10.
15. ASNE (1985), p. 13.
16. Times Mirror, "The People & the Press" (1986), p. 19.
17. See, e.g., George Gallup, *Gallup Polls Public Opinion 1938–1971* (Random House, 1971).

18. Times Mirror, "The People & the Press" (1986), p. 23.
19. *Ibid.*, p. 25.
20. *Ibid.*
21. *Ibid.*
22. *Ibid.*
23. Interview with author.
24. Times Mirror, "The People & the Press: Part 2," September 1986, p. 19.
25. Interview with author.
26. Norman J. Ornstein and Michael J. Robinson, "Why Press Credibility Is Going Down," *Washington Journalism Review,* January/February 1990, p. 34.
27. Michael J. Robinson and Andrew Kohut, "Believability and the Press," *Public Opinion Quarterly* 52 (1988): p. 1740.
28. Richard Harwood, "Virus in the Newsroom," *The Washington Post,* August 12, 1990, p. C6.
29. *Ibid.*
30. Times Mirror Center for the People & the Press, "The People, the Press and Their Leaders," 1995, p. 7.
31. Times Mirror Center for the People & the Press, "The People, the Press & Politics: The New Political Landscape," October 1994, p. 141.
32. *Ibid.*
33. Times Mirror, October 1994, p. 160.
34. Linda Fibich, "Under Siege," *American Journalism Review,* September 1995, p. 16.
35. *Ibid.*, p. 20.
36. *Ibid.*, p. 6.
37. *Ibid.*, p. 12.
38. *Ibid.*, p. 7.
39. American Society of Newspaper Editors "Timeless Values: Staying True to Journalistic Principles in the Age of New Media." Prepared by the Harwood Group, April 1995.
40. Linda Fibich, "Undser Siege," *American Journalism Reviews,* September 1995, p. 3.
41. *Ibid.*, September 1995, p. 8.
42. *Ibid.*
43. *Ibid.*, p. 15.
44. *Ibid.*, p. 10.
45. *Ibid.*, p. 11.
46. *Ibid.*
47. March–April 1995, p. 25.
48. *Ibid.*, p. 27.

49. Adam Gopnik, "Read All About It," *The New Yorker,* December 12, 1994, pp. 84, 86.
50. *Ibid.*
51. *Presstime,* November 1995, p. 28.
52. *Ibid.*
53. *Ibid.*
54. *Ibid.,* p. 29.

Chapter 2. From Benchley to Brill, Luce to Levin

1. See Stanley L. Harrison, "Bibliography of Press Criticism by Robert Benchley (Guy Fawkes) for *The New Yorker,*" *Journalism History* 19:1 (Spring 1993), pp. 26–27.
2. Robert Benchley (Guy Fawkes), "The Wayward Press: Good Old Days," *The New Yorker,* June 30, 1928, p. 32.
3. *Ibid.*
4. *The New Yorker,* June 14, 1930, p. 36.
5. Robert Benchley (Guy Fawkes), "The Press in Review: A Front Page Crisis," *The New Yorker,* August 13, 1927, p. 28.
6. Robert Benchley (Guy Fawkes), "Intermission," *The New Yorker,* March 8, 1930, p. 40.
7. Robert Benchley (Guy Fawkes), "The Wayward Press: The Public Servant," *The New Yorker,* June 8, 1929, p. 32.
8. *Ibid.*
9. Robert Benchley (Guy Fawkes), "The Wayward Press: Summer Heat," *The New Yorker,* June 14, 1930, p. 36.
10. Robert Benchley (Guy Fawkes), "The Wayward Press: The Power of the Press," *The New Yorker,* December 6, 1930, p. 56.
11. *Ibid.*
12. William Randolph Hearst bought into the commercial real estate vision of his urbane editor Arthur Brisbane, and in the 1920s bought huge parcels of real estate in the upper Fifties between Eighth Avenue and Park Avenue. He purchased the Ritz Tower Hotel at Fifty-seventh Street and Park Avenue, which he sought to refurbish into another Claridge's, and built the Ziegfeld Theater and hotels like the Warwick and Lombardy near Sixth Avenue and Fifty-fourth Street. He and Brisbane collected various underdeveloped lots on the West Side and low-rent shops that lined Seventh Avenue. The Manhattan properties would have made the Hearsts one of the richest families in the world had they

not been forced to liquidate them in 1937 under pressure from their banks. See, e.g., Lindsay Chaney, and Michael Cieply, *The Hearsts: Family and Empire— The Later Years* (New York: Simon & Schuster, 1981), pp. 265–68.

13. Ken Fellata, "Annals of Communication: Awestruck," *The New Republic,* September 11, 1995, p. 12.

14. *Ibid.*

15. *Ibid.*

16. Lewis Lapham, "Gilding the News," *Harper's,* July 1981, pp. 31–39.

17. *Ibid.,* p. 39.

18. *Ibid.*

19. Lewis Lapham, "Notebook: Trained Seals and Sitting Ducks," *Harper's,* May 1991, p. 10.

20. *Ibid.,* pp. 10–11.

21. *Ibid.,* p. 15.

22. Robert Benchley, "Quiet Please," *The New Yorker,* January 10, 1931, p. 32.

23. See The Commission of Freedom of the Press, *A Free and Responsible Press,* "The Hutchins Commission: Its Times, and Ours," 1947.

24. See Stephen Bates, *Realigning Journalism with Democracy:* "The Hutchins Commission: Its Times, and Ours," Annenberg Washington Program, Communications Policy Studies, Northwestern University.

25. See John Sweeney, "Media Arrogance Spoils Fun," *The News-Journal (Wilmington, Delaware),* January 7, 1990, p. K3.

26. *Ibid.*

27. *Ibid.*

28. *Ibid.*

29. Howard V. Hong and Edna H. Hong, eds. and trans., *Søren Kierkegaard's Journals and Papers,* Vol. 2 (Indiana University Press, 1970), p. 485.

30. See Richard Harwood, "The Cost of Celebrity," *The Washington Post,* January 8, 1996, p. A17. As an author and social observer, Fallows has an acute sense of timing. In 1989, as American paranoia with Japan was ascending, he published *More Like Us: Putting America's Native Strengths and Traditional Values to Work to Overcome the Asian Challenge* (Houghton Mifflin, 1989). Using the knowledge he gained from living in Japan with his family during the late 1980s, he composed an original comparison of the American and Japanese cultures, concluding that "America should be moving away from the Japanese model, not toward it." The book was seen in some quarters as Japan-bashing, although if anything, it simply faithfully reported what Fallows had discerned in Japan and followed some logical conclusions deftly to their destinations.

31. Ross Anderson, "What James Fallows Needs Is a Good Local Newspaper," *Seattle Times,* February 14, 1996, p. B4.

32. PBS, January 22, 1996. Also participating on the program were Eric Alter and Michelle McQueen.

33. David Remnick, "Scoop," *The New Yorker,* January 29, 1996, pp. 38–42.

34. *Ibid.,* p. 40.

35. *Ibid.*

36. *Ibid.,* p. 42.

37. Ellen Hume, "Something's Rotten," *Columbia Journalism Review,* March–April 1996, pp. 49–52.

38. *Ibid.,* p. 49.

39. *Ibid.*; see e.g., Patterson, *Out of Order* (1993), Jamieson, *Dirty Politics* (1992), and Schudson, *The Power of News* (1990).

40. Hume, "Something's Rotten," p. 49.

41. *Ibid.* Some prominent journalists have departed political reporting for labors more directly designed to improving the political process. Michael Oreskes, for example, left *The New York Times,* where he had been a rising editor and former presidential campaign reporter to join the Free TV for Straight Talk coalition, a group dedicated to encouraging the free use of television time by political candidates.

42. Dan Quayle, *Standing Firm* (HarperCollins, 1994), p. 41.

43. ASNE Survey (1985), p. 97. Media people don't agree with the way the public sees it. When asked their biggest complaint about the way their own news organizations cover the news, 25 percent objected to a lack of sufficient resources/personnel to cover the news the way it should be covered; "sensationalism" ranked fifth as a principal concern, chosen by only 10 percent. *Ibid.*

44. J. A. Thalheimer and J. R. Gerberich, "Reader Attitudes Toward Questions of Newspaper Policy and Practice," *Journalism Quarterly* 12 (1935), p. 268.

45. Charles E. Swanson, "The Midcity Daily," *Journalism Quarterly* 26 (1949), p. 24.

46. Raymond F. Stewart, "Surveys of Reader Attitudes Toward Newspaper Combinations," *Journalism Quarterly* 30 (1953), p. 318.

47. George Gallup, *Gallup Polls: Public Opinion 1938–1971* (Random House, 1972): Vol. 1, p. 85, and "The Press and the People—A Survey," *Fortune,* August 1935, p. 70. Swanson's 1949 study has findings that typify some of the inconsistencies that result from specific questioning. Part I of the study revealed that only 36 percent thought that newspapers were generally fair to both business and labor interests, but 76 percent believed their own local newspaper to be so and 84 percent thought their own local newspaper was less distorted than other newspapers. Part II of the study indicated that more than local loyalty was

at work; overwhelmingly, the public rated newspapers "good" or "fairly good" in response to various questions regarding the press's performance in being fair or unbiased. Polling methods have improved with each decade in eliciting less superficial, "top of the head" responses.

48. See, e.g., Sidney Kobre, *The Yellow Press and the Gilded Age Journalism* (Florida State University, 1963), p. 46.

49. Dana's *Sun* was the nineteenth-century equivalent of the "light and lively" read, filled with one-sentence stories (called Sunbeams) and one-paragraph briefs in such columns as "Life in the Metropolis." See Kobre, *Yellow Press,* p. 31.

50. *Ibid.*, p. 28.

51. *Ibid.*, p. 30.

52. *Ibid.*

53. See William Randolph Hearst, Jr., and Jack Casserly, *The Hearsts: Father and Son* (Roberts Rinehart Publishers, 1991).

54. Tony Sutton, "Remember the Reader! Hearst's Ideas Remain Fresh Even Today," *The Quill,* May 1995, p. 33.

55. Chaney, *The Hearsts,* p. 36.

56. *Ibid.*

57. Vance H. Trimble, *The Astonishing Mr. Scripps: The Turbulent Life of America's Penny Press Lord* (Iowa State University Press, 1992), p. 5.

58. *Ibid.*

59. Susan M. Kingsbury, Hornell Hart and Associates, "Measuring the Ethics of American Newspapers: A Spectrum Analysis of Newspaper Sensationalism," *Journalism Quarterly* 10 (June 1933–December 1934) (six-part series).

60. Some historians and journalism professors believe that Hearst's influence on U.S. policy has been overstated and that post–World War I revisionist history attributed to him a bigger role than he actually deserves. Early historical accounts of the Spanish-American War do not refer to yellow journalism or its impact. See, e.g., Michael Schudson, *The Power of News,* p. 23, citing Lewis L. Gould, *The Spanish-American War and President McKinley* (University Press of Kansas, 1982).

61. The notion is hardly novel. In 1913, Rolfe Arnold Scott-James wrote: "We accept the daily paper as a matter of course, just as we accept trains and restaurants. Many persons display their only active feeling about the Press by expressions of contempt; they consistently use it and abuse it; their whole stock of current information is derived from it, but they continue to speak of the 'Daily Liar.'" *The Influence of the Press* (London: S. W. Partridge & Co., 1913), p. 15.

In 1938, George Seldes wrote that "thousands of Hearst readers hate his views but buy his newspapers." Seldes, *You Can't Do That* (Da Capo Press, 1938), p. 100.

62. Hazel Dicken-Garcia, *Journalistic Standards in Nineteenth-Century America* (University of Wisconsin Press, 1989), p. 229.

63. William David Sloan, *The Media in America* (Publishing Horizons, 1989), pp. 257–58.

64. Letter to H. N. Rickey and W. B. Colver dated March 2, 1910, published in Oliver Knight, ed., *"I Protest," Selected Disquisitions of E. W. Scripps* (University of Wisconsin Press, 1966), pp. 269–71.

65. Quoted in Trimble, *The Astonishing Mr. Scripps*, p. 69.

66. Silas Bent, *Newspaper Crusaders: A Neglected Story* (Whittlesey House, 1939), p. 40.

67. *Ibid.*

68. *Ibid.*, pp. 15–16.

69. Kobre, *Yellow Press*, p. 67.

70. *Ibid.*

71. *Ibid.*, p. 76.

72. Trimble, *The Astonishing Mr. Scripps*, p. 231.

73. *Ibid.*, p. 230.

74. "As a political crusader Hearst was more nearly unique, for although he often ran for office and sat in Congress from 1903 to 1907, he was not animated by personal desire for office but was a candidate, I am confident, as a part of his newspaper adventures. His politics was as neutral as a pair of socks, suitable either for the Right or the Left. For years he was left wing and semisocialistic, but the time came when he was to root vigorously for Andrew Mellon's proposal, while Secretary of the Treasury, that a retail sales tax be imposed. . . . He had supported William Jennings Bryan and had branded Mark Hanna in cartoons with the dollar mark, yet he pumped up a ballyhoo for Mellon for President. His agility in the about-face was acrobatic." *Ibid.*, pp. 47–48.

75. Sloan, *The Media in America*, p. 278.

76. Stephan Lesher, *Media Unbound: The Impact of Television Journalism on the Public* (Houghton Mifflin, 1982), p. 29.

77. *Ibid.*

78. *Ibid.*

79. Sherilyn Cox Bennion, "Reform Agitation in the American Periodical Press, 1920–29," *Journalism Quarterly*, 48 (1971).

80. James Melvin Lee, *History of American Journalism* (Houghton Mifflin, 1923), p. 451.

81. W. A. Swanberg, *Luce and His Empire* (Charles Scribner's Sons, 1972), pp. 53–55.

82. Luce's initial partner, Briton Hadden, had worked at Pulitzer's *New York World* after college.

83. James D. Squires, *Read All About It,* pp. 16, 28.

84. *Newsweek,* March 13, 1967.

85. *Ibid.*

86. Swanberg, *Luce and His Empire,* p. 124.

87. "The Woman Behind the Women: Why Did They All Hate Clare Boothe Luce?" *The New Yorker,* May 26, 1997, p. 70.

88. Henry Grunwald, *One Man's America: A Journalist's Search for the Heart of His Country* (Doubleday, 1997), p. 549.

89. Connie Bruck, "Jerry's Deal," *The New Yorker,* February 19, 1996, p. 55.

90. Quoted in John Kabler, *Luce: His Time, Life, and Fortune* (Doubleday, 1968), pp. 112–13.

91. *Ibid.,* p. 156.

Chapter 3. Dan Quayle Meet Hillary Clinton

1. Dan Quayle, *Standing Firm* (HarperCollins, 1994), p. 9.

2. *Ibid.,* p. 42.

3. Quayle's fatalism seems to have been cast in stone after an August 1989 interview with Diane Sawyer on *Prime Time Live.* The "setup" to the interview was a series of Quayle jokes. Then Sawyer asked him about his "easy" life. "I was fuming," Quayle wrote in *Standing Firm,* but "joked about all the work I was providing for comedians" (*Ibid.,* p. 132). "The media had put too much of their own credibility into creating the caricature to abandon it now. Getting a fair shake was hopeless" (*Ibid.,* p. 124).

4. Bob Woodward and David Broder, series on Dan Quayle published in *The Washington Post*—beginning January 5, 1992, asnd concluding January 12, 1992.

5. *Ibid.,* p. 60.

6. *Ibid.,* p. 11.

7. David Maraniss, *First in His Class* (Simon & Schuster, 1995), p. 246.

8. *Ibid.,* p. 342.

9. James Stewart, *Blood Sport: The President and His Adversaries* (Simon & Schuster, 1996), pp. 37–38.

10. Connie Bruck, "Hillary the Pol," *The New Yorker,* May 30, 1994, p. 91.

11. Walter Isaacson, "We're Hoping That We Have Another Child," An Exclusive Interview with the First Lady, *Time,* June 3, 1996.

12. Mona Charen, "Talk of Adoption Is Hillary Clinton's Latest Version of Femininity," Creators' Syndicate, Inc., published in the *St. Louis Post-Dispatch,* June 2, 1996.

13. Quoted in David Saltonstall, "Hillary Clinton says she hopes for another child in magazine interview, First Lady said she and President discuss adoption," *Austin American-Statesman,* May 26, 1996.

14. *Partners & Adversaries: The Contentious Connection Between Congress & the Media,* Elaine S. Povich, Freedom Forum, March 1996, p. 137.

15. Peter Baker, "Hillary Clinton Bemoans Influence of 'Right Wing' Media," *The Washington Post,* January 18, 1998, p. A11.

Chapter 4. The Girl from Yesterday

1. Tim Gallagher, Memo from the Editor: "Here's a Donna Rice Story That Won't Make You Laugh," *Albuquerque Tribune,* November 26, 1988.

2. Jon Nordheimer, "Woman in the News; an Actress in Turmoil: Donna Earle Rice," *The New York Times,* May 5, 1987, p. A1.

3. Gail Sheehy, "The Road to Bimini," *Vanity Fair,* September 1987, pp. 130–94.

4. Chuck Conconi, "Personalities," *The Washington Post,* March 20, 1989, p. B3.

5. Bob Swofford, "Credibility Sessions Tackle Sex Scandal, Corrections," *The American Editor,* May 1998.

Chapter 5. The Public Service Quotient

1. Chris McConnell and Paige Albiniak, "Putting a Price on Public Service," *Broadcasting & Cable,* April 6, 1998, p. 70.

2. Bob Wisehart, "NBC Pays Price for 'Bottom-Line' News," *Sacramento Bee,* February 15, 1993.

3. James D. Squires, "Newspapers Have Lost Their Zeal to Educate the Public About the Real Issues," *ASNE Bulletin,* November 1992.

4. James Squires, "Journalism.COM: Press Responsibility in a New Millennium," Roy W. Howard Lecture, Indiana University School of Journalism, October 6, 1997.

5. Lloyd Grove, "The Latter Day Gordon Peterson," *The Washington Post,* June 16, 1998, p. E1.

6. Eugene Roberts, "Corporatism v. Journalism: Is It Twilight for Press Responsibility?" Press Enterprise Lecture, Riverside, California, February 1996.

7. Squires, "Journalism.COM

8. Richard Cohen, "Plundered Secrets," *The Washington Post Magazine,* June 14, 1998, p. 7.

9. Marc Gunther, "The Cable Guy," *American Journalism Review,* January–February 1997.

10. Brian Williams, speeches delivered to the Medill School of Journalism, Northwestern University, May 13, 1998, and to the Deadline Club, Society of Professional Journalists, New York City Chapter, May 1997.

11. Grove, "The Latter Day Gordon Peterson," p. E7.

12. "An Interview with Jim Kennedy," *Broadcasting & Cable,* June 20, 1994, p. 27.

13. Bill Kirtz, "What Did We Learn?" *The Quill,* October 1997, p. 14.

Chapter 6. The "Ride-Along"

1. Memorandum from Frank Traglia, Acting Executive Director, to Directors, Departments of Social Services, Administrators, Child Support Enforcement Agencies, November 17, 1989 (on file with author).

2. News release from Maryland Department of Human Resources, December 16, 1992 (on file with author).

3. WJZ-TV news broadcast, December 16, 1992 (on file with author).

4. Complaint, *Bond v. Westinghouse Communications,* No. 93279007 CL170904 (Balt. City Cir. Ct., October 6, 1993).

5. John Schmeltzer, "'Tis Always the Time to Take Precautions with Credit Cards," *Chicago Tribune,* December 5, 1992, p. C1.

6. *Ibid.*

7. *Almanac of the Federal Judiciary* (Aspen Law & Business, 1996), Vol. 1, p. 99.

8. Marquis Who's Who, *Who's Who in American Law: 1992–93,* p. 930.

9. Paul D. Rheingold, "Bending the Law: A Story of the Dalkon Shield Bankruptcy," *New York Law Journal,* January 3, 1992, p. 2.

10. *The New York Times,* May 28, 1991, p. B5.

11. *United States v. Sansui,* 813 F. Supp. 149, 159–60 (E.D.N.Y. 1992).

12. *United States v. Sanusi,* 813 F. Supp. 149, 160 (E.D.N.Y. 1992).

13. There was no violation of judicial rules for the judge to hear both cases. Though judges don't generally believe that "regular" people, sitting as jurors, can set aside their predispositions, judges do not usually impose the same limitations on themselves. For federal judges, a statute governs instances when judges should step aside:

    (a) Any justice, judge, or magistrate of the United States shall disqualify himself in any proceeding in which his impartiality might reasonably be questioned.

(b) He shall also disqualify himself in the following circumstances:

(1) Where he has a personal bias or prejudice concerning a party, or personal knowledge of disputed evidentiary facts concerning the proceeding . . .

The provisions, similar to rules championed by the American Bar Association for more than sixty years, are not as troublesome for judges as they might seem to the layperson. For example, courts find there is usually no cause for disqualification where the judge acquired his or her knowledge in a prior court proceeding. See, e.g., In re Corrugated Container Antitrust Litigation, 614 F.2d 958 (5th Cir.), *cert. denied,* 449 U.S. 888 (1980).

14. See, e.g., *Curtis Publishing Co. v. Butts,* 388 U.S. 130 (1967); *Associated Press v. Walker,* 388 U.S. 130 (1967); *New York Times Co. v. Sullivan,* 376 U.S. 254 (1964).

15. *New York Times Co. v. United States,* 403 U.S. 713 (1971) (Pentagon Papers case).

16. See *Florida Star v. B.J.F.,* 491 U.S. 524, 541 (1989) ("where a newspaper publishes truthful information which it has lawfully obtained, punishment may be lawfully imposed, if at all, only when narrowly tailored to a state interest of the highest order"); *Smith v. Daily Mail Publishing Co.,* 443 U.S. 97 (1979) (states may not punish newspapers for publishing truthful information lawfully obtained except under extremely narrow circumstances); *Cox Broadcasting Corp. v. Cohn,* 420 U.S. 469, 495 (1975) (states may not, consistent with the First Amendment, "impose sanctions on the publication of truthful information contained in official court records open to public inspection").

17. *Ayeni v. CBS, Inc.,* 848 F. Supp. 362, 368 (E.D.N.Y.), *aff'd,* 35 F.3d 680 (2d Cir. 1994), *cert. denied,* 115 U.S. 1689 (1995).

18. *Ibid.*

19. Joseph P. Fried, "CBS Reaches a Settlement on Videotaped Search," *The New York Times,* March 20, 1995, p. 44.

20. *Ayeni v. Mottola,* 35 F.3d 680, 686 (2d Cir. 1994), *cert. denied,* 115 U.S. 1689 (1995). *Ayeni* is only the latest indication that even the federal appellate court in New York is redefining its limits on journalists. In 1993, the court retreated from a broad privilege for reporters to quash subpoenas for their testimony, for unbroadcast videotape and for their unpublished notes of interviews with Bruce Cutler, attorney for reputed mobster John Gotti. Cutler claimed he needed the evidence to answer contempt charges for allegedly generating excessive and prejudicial publicity about the Gotti case. However, the court protected reporters

from testifying or producing notes of interviews with federal prosecutors, despite Cutler's argument that he was only answering unfair publicity from the prosecutors. See *United States v. Cutler*, 6 F. 3d 67 (2d Cir. 1993).

21. *Florida Publishing Co. v. Fletcher*, 340 So. 2d 914, 918 (Fla. 1976) (quoting dissenting opinion from Florida District Court of Appeal), *cert. denied*, 431 U.S. 930 (1977). One other aspect of *Fletcher* deserves mention. The fire marshal had asked the newspaper photographer for help in photographing the silhouette. The fire marshal tried unsuccessfully to get a good picture before he ran out of film. The silhouette proved that the teenager's body was on the floor before heat damaged the room. Although the photographer had rendered active assistance to investigators, Florida's highest court did not rely on the newspaper's involvement to find that the newspaper was not liable. Instead, the court ruled, reliance on an official invitation to report on the fire overcame claims of trespass.

22. *United States v. Sanusi*, 813 F. Supp. 149, 156 (E.D.N.Y. 1992).

23. *United States v. Sanusi*, 813 F. Supp. 149, 158 (E.D.N.Y. 1992) (quoting a New York trial court decision, *Anderson v. WROC-TV*, 441 N.Y.S.2d 220, 226 [Sup. Ct. 1981]).

24. *Costlow v. Cusimano*, 34 A.D.2d 196, 311 N.Y.S.2d 92 (1970). Even without trespass as a theory, however, plaintiffs may often claim emotional or reputational damages in actions for invasion of privacy or intentional infliction of emotional distress. Some states permit plaintiffs to seek compensation for these nonproperty damages only if the trespasser's behavior is so unreasonable that a court would permit a claim for punitive damages. Other states, such as California, have effectively dropped all barriers to nonproperty damages in trespass cases. See, e.g., *Miller v. National Broadcasting Co.*, 187 Cal. App. 3d 1463, 1481, 232 Cal. Rptr. 668, 677 (1986). ("Under California law, the 'consequences' flowing from an intentional tort such as a trespass may include emotional distress either accompanied by a physical injury to the person or to the land").

25. For example, the Wisconsin appellate court reinstated a trespass claim against a television reporter who followed a police SWAT team on their search for a suspect who had allegedly shot at four young bicyclists. The shots, police believed, had come from the plaintiff's property. The plaintiff, a biochemist, lived and worked in a combined home, office and laboratory. He admitted that he had warned youngsters to stay away from his property, and that he had fired a .22 caliber rifle that police found in his home. But the plaintiff insisted that he was shooting at gophers, not at the teenagers. Finding that the facts were dissimilar to *Fletcher*, especially where the reporter had shown no "custom and usage," the court agreed that a jury could find that the reporter trespassed. Chipping away at the limitations on damages for trespass, the court reasoned further: "To allow

only nominal damages under the circumstances presented because of lack of physical harm would permit the trespasser to enjoy the benefits of his tort without fully compensating a plaintiff for his loss." *Prahl v. Brosamle,* 295 N.W.2d 768, 781–82 (Wis. Ct. App. 1980).

26. *Wood v. Fort Dodge Messenger,* 13 Media L. Rep. (BNA) 1610 (Iowa Dist. Ct. 1986). A 1996 Montana case comes to the same result when the Montana Fish and Game Service gave CNN permission to accompany them to investigate a report of poison being used to kill eagles on a ranch. Farms and ranches are sometimes apparently regarded more as places of business with less privacy interests than homes. The distinction collapses, however, when a criminal uses his or her home for business—e.g., drug dealing or inventory warehousing.

27. *Anderson v. WROC-TV,* 441 N.Y.S.2d 220 (Sup. Ct. 1981).

28. *Miller v. National Broadcasting Co.,* 187 Cal. App. 3d 1463, 232 Cal. Rptr. 668 (1986).

29. *Baugh v. CBS, Inc.,* 828 F. Supp. 745 (N.D. Cal. 1993). Technically, the court dismissed the trespass count because the plaintiffs had given their apparent consent, despite the plaintiffs' claim that they thought the camera was part of the team. Nonetheless, the court ruled that a jury should decide claims for emotional distress and invasion of privacy.

30. *Carr v. Mobile Video Tapes, Inc.,* 893 S.W.2d 613 (Tex. Ct. App. 1994).

31. Maybe the cases imply a vague limiting principle—courts are less sympathetic to the media when cameras enter an occupied private home, rather than its environs alone. But the implication is far from a rule. The last case described above, involving the videotaping of sick and dying livestock on a ranch—even with the apparent permission of a ranch hand—destroys any attempt to draw a bright line. Similarly, courts have allowed claims by a restaurant against a local television station for filming a tour by a health inspector (*Belluomo v. KAKE-TV,* 596 P.2d 832 [Kan. Ct. App. 1979]), by a New York restaurant surprised by CBS cameras attempting to document reports of health violations (*Le Mistral, Inc. v. Columbia Broadcasting System,* 61 A.D.2d 491 [1978]) and by a prisoner against NBC for videotaping him in a federal prison cell without his permission (*Huskey v. National Broadcasting Co.,* 632 F. Supp. 1282 [N.D. Ill. 1986]). An Oklahoma court even affirmed criminal charges against reporters who entered a public utility's property to cover antinuclear protesters. *Stahl v. State,* 665 P.2d 839 (Okla. Crim. App. 1983), *cert. denied,* 464 U.S. 1069 (1984). But, it's safe to say, successful claims against the media for entry into businesses or other quasi-public places are far less common.

32. Quoted by Larry Neumeister, "Reality TV Could Be Handcuffed by Court

Rulings," Associated Press, September 23, 1994, available in LEXIS, NEWS Library, AP File.

33. "Man Sues Jeffco Law Enforcement," *Rocky Mountain News,* April 5, 1994, p. 13A; Peter G. Chronis, "Robinson Sues Over Media at Search," *Denver Post,* April 6, 1994, p. B5; Ginny McKibben, "Photographer of Nude Girls Gets 8 Years in Prison," *Denver Post,* April 6, 1994, p. B5.

34. True to the signals the Justices gave at oral argument, the Supreme Court ruled unanimously in May 1999 that media "ride-alongs" violate the Fourth Amendment. And true to its trend over the last decade, the Court was virtually silent on the First Amendment issues at stake. Chief Justice Rehnquist, who wrote the opinion for the Court, made a nod toward the press's role in informing the public about the criminal justice system, but he then plowed straight ahead into an analysis that subjugated the First Amendment to the Fourth: "[I]n the present case it is in terms of [the Fourth Amendment] that the media ride-alongs must be judged." The Court failed to make even a reference to the amicus brief filed by over twenty press organizations asserting the First Amendment side of the controversy.

35. *The New York Times,* July 29, 1996, p. A1.

36. Brian Ross, "Money Talks: Grocery Industry Manufacturers' Fees," *20/20* (ABC television broadcast, November 10, 1995).

37. In 1971, *Life* magazine sent reporters, armed with a hidden camera and a radio transmitter, to investigate medical quackery. A trial court awarded A. A. Dietemann $1,000 in damages, even though no one seriously disputed *Life*'s conclusions that Dietemann was a quack. The U.S. Court of Appeals for the Ninth Circuit reasoned:

> Plaintiff's den was a sphere from which he could reasonably expect to exclude eavesdropping newsmen. He invited two of defendant's employees to the den. One who invites another to his home or office takes a risk that the visitor may not be what he seems, and that the visitor may repeat all he hears and observes when he leaves. But he does not and should not be required to take the risk that what is heard and seen will be transmitted by photograph or recording, or in our modern world, in full living color and hi-fi to the public at large or to any segment of it that the visitor may select.

Dietemann v. Time, Inc., 449 F.2d 245, 249 (9th Cir. 1971). *Dietemann* seems to echo another time when front porches were filled with swings and wicker, not burglar alarms. But courts of late have limited *Dietemann* to its unique facts—an office in a home, used by a plaintiff who was not in business, did not advertise his services, and did not charge for them. See, e.g., *Desnick v.*

American Broadcasting Cos., 44 F.3d 1345, 1352–53 (7th Cir. 1995). But a
mystic distinction between home and office has not immunized the undercover
journalist, though the differentiation is frequently effective in defending against
trespasslike claims.

38. *Food Lion, Inc. v. Capital Cities/ABC, Inc.,* 887 F. Supp. 811, 820 (M.D.N.C.
1995).

39. *Kersis v. Capital Cities/ABC, Inc.,* 22 Media L. Rep. (BNA) 2321 (Cal. Super.
Ct. 1994).

40. Joan Biskupic, "Clinton Avoids Activists in Judicial Selections," *The Washington Post,* October 24, 1995, p. A1.

41. John Flynn Rooney, "For Him, It's the Questions That Count," *Chicago Daily
Law Bulletin,* November 3, 1993, p. 3. A recent introduction to an interview of
Judge Posner offers a capsulization of his eminence:

> Richard A. Posner, the Chief Judge of the U.S. Courts [*sic*] of Appeals for the
> Seventh Circuit, has been described as a towering figure in American law, both as
> a judge and as a scholar; 1,250 opinions, 24 books, and almost 200 articles em-
> body his prodigious outpouring of thought. If you want to know about sexuality
> and economics; nuance, narrative, and empathy in critical race theory; Holmes;
> originalism; Greek love and the institutionalization of pederasty; jurisprudence,
> law and literature; economic analysis and the law; Cardozo; radical feminism; eu-
> genics; literary, feminist, and communitarian perspectives on jurisprudence; or
> scores of other abstruse topics, Posner is your man.
>
> But he is not easy. His work, both judicial and extrajudicial, is intricate, often
> labyrinthine—although he describes himself as "a simplifier." But as his hero,
> Justice Holmes, was fond of saying, nothing which is worthwhile comes cheap.
> Judge Posner would no doubt chuckle at the economic implication, for he is
> largely responsible for making systematic economic analysis part of the fabric of
> modern legal analysis.
>
> In this interview he talks about Posnerian pragmatism, his ideal Supreme
> Court, justices Holmes and Frankfurter, judicial opinion writing, radical femi-
> nism, the present state of legal education in America, and more. Whether or not
> you agree with what he has to say, he is always provocative, always penetrating,
> and always worth the price of admission.

> Jeffrey Cole, "Economics of Law: An Interview with Judge Posner," *Litigation:
> The Journal of the Section of Litigation (ABA),* fall 1995, p. 23.

42. Greg Kueterman, "Posner Typifies Aura Surrounding Appellate Jurists," *Indiana Lawyer,* January 11, 1995, p. 26.

43. *Desnick v. American Broadcasting Cos.*, 44 F. 3d 1345, 1351 (7th Cir. 1995).
44. The lower court had been too hasty in dismissing the libel claim against ABC, Posner also found.
45. *Desnick v. American Broadcasting Cos.*, 44 F. 3d 1345, 1354–55 (7th Cir. 1995). For all its promise, *Desnick* will be an isolated victory if courts unduly limit it to situations where reporters pose as customers—a restrictive distinction not justified by Posner's reasoning that would show further hostility to the newsgathering process.

Chapter 7. A Fine Day for the Government

1. Chinua Achebe, *Anthills of the Savannah* (Anchor Press, Doubleday, 1988), p. 93.
2. *New York Times v. Sullivan,* 376 U.S. 254, 270 (1964).
3. The irony of the setting for Sack's pronouncement was lost on the young. Media lawyers had begun to cluster together for an annual ritual when James Goodale, then vice-chairman of the New York Times Company, convened the first Practising Law Institute meeting in the early 1970s, just as Vice President Spiro Agnew was denouncing the media as "nattering nabobs of negativism." In the 1970s, with a string of protective decisions in the libel area and those expanding reporters' rights to shield confidential sources from forced disclosure, the mood at the conference was far more confident than now.
4. David Rudenstine's thorough study *The Day the Presses Stopped: A History of the Pentagon Papers Case* (University of California Press, 1997) argues that there were real threats to the nation in the Pentagon Papers, a conclusion that Adam Clymer of *The New York Times* found highly debatable (see "Classified," *The New York Times Book Review,* April 13, 1997, p. 15). Rudenstine's thesis is based on the government's argument in court that diplomatic efforts to negotiate an end to the war would be discouraged if diplomats feared disclosure of their past efforts; this anxiety could hardly have been feverish given the propensity of all governments to leak (or announce) the details of diplomatic initiatives when it is politically or otherwise expedient to do so. If intelligence sources and methods were really described or compromised in the papers, Rudenstine might have a stronger case, but we won't be able to assess that claim until certain materials that remain classified are declassified by the government.
5. "Rethinking Prior Restraint," 92 *Yale Law Journal* 409 (1983).
6. 403 U.S. 730–731 (1971) (White J., with whom Stewart J. joined, concurring).
7. 403 U.S. 713, 761 (1971).
8. The late Chief Justice Warren E. Burger himself wrote perhaps the two most expansive First Amendment decisions handed down during the era of the Burger

Court: *Nebraska Press Association v. Stuart*, 427 U.S. 539 (1976), containing a broad condemnation of judicially imposed "gag" orders, and *Richmond Newspapers v. Virginia*, 448 U.S. 555 (1980), which created out of whole cloth for the public and its "surrogate," the press, a brand-new First Amendment right of access to attend and observe trials. Later in the two *Riverside (CA) Press Enterprises v. Superior Court of California* cases, 464 U.S. 501 (1984) and 478 U.S. 1 (1986), he extended the right of access to cover voir dire and preliminary hearings. The popular perception that Burger was antipress stemmed from his dislike of aggressive news practices (they offended his sense of decorum). His distaste for the news business tended not to be reflected in his First Amendment decisions. See Bruce Sanford, "The Legacy of Warren E. Burger," *The National Law Journal*, July 17, 1995, p. A22.

9. 403 U.S. 754.

10. *Northern Securities Co. v. U.S.*, 193 U.S. 197, 400–1 (1904).

11. In fact, Grisham's fears were groundless. The *Sunday Times* of London reported "his fans thought he was the greatest thing since Perry Mason. 'Even as a spectator you wanted to cry at times at how he described things,' said Jane Smith, who watched most of the trial." Gina Holland and Nick Peters, "Grisham's law is a thriller in court," *Sunday Times* (London), January 28, 1996.

12. "I Am Not a Camera," *The New York Times Magazine*, October 16, 1994, sec. 6, p. 28.

13. *Ibid.*, and "Out of Focus," *The New York Times Magazine*, November 5, 1995, p. 26.

14. Charles Nesson, "Criminal Trial Reform," *Nieman Reports* 49, no. 3 (fall 1995), p. 26.

15. See *Richmond Newspapers, Inc. v. Virginia*, 448 U.S. 555, 572 (1980).

16. The broadcasting and cable industries, led by the networks and Steve Brill of Court TV, made steady progress throughout the 1970s and 1980s in persuading states to permit cameras to cover what transpires in the courtroom. Federal courts remained unpersuaded. The benefits to the public and judiciary were plentiful. Michigan state courts, for example, no longer use court reporters at all for certain proceedings, instead relying on the videotape of the proceeding. If a litigant wants a transcript, he orders the videotape and hires someone to transcribe it himself. The end result has been widespread access to the workings of the judicial system that previously had not been available to the average citizen.

According to the Radio-Television News Directors Association (RTNDA), as of January 1, 1996, forty-five states had permanent rules in place permitting cameras in at least some courtrooms under certain circumstances, and two additional states were experimenting. Only Indiana, Mississippi and South Dakota, as well as the District of Columbia, have no cameras in any of their state courtrooms. ("News Media Coverage of Judicial Proceedings with Cameras and Microphones: A Survey of the States," Radio-Television News Directors Association [January 1, 1996], at [i]–[iii], B-1, B-2.) The trend now appears to be moving in the other direction, however. Although cameras have now become a fixture in many state courtrooms, in every instance courts have explicitly retained the authority to terminate the coverage, usually at the discretion of the judge, if it proves to be distracting, disruptive or a threat to the fairness of the proceeding. Today, more than ever before, judges are taking advantage of this loophole in the rules permitting cameras, and tossing them out of any case that portends high-profile coverage. "It's not a uniform route," says Jane Kirtley, executive director of the Reporters Committee for Freedom of the Press, 1997. "There are some encouraging signs in some states, but overall the picture is dismal."

The experience of efforts to obtain camera coverage of federal court proceedings is even more telling. Cameras generally have been excluded from all federal courts. In 1991, however, proponents of video cameras in federal courts scored a victory by convincing the Judicial Conference—the governing body for procedures of the federal courts—to experiment with allowing cameras in federal courtrooms during civil cases. In November 1993, the Federal Judicial Center issued an evaluation of the experiment. Among other things, the FJC concluded that "judges and attorneys who had experience with electronic media coverage generally reported observing little or no effect of camera presence on participants in the proceedings, courtroom decorum, or the administration of justice. The FJC also recommended that the Judicial Conference authorize cameras in the courts for civil proceedings." ("News Media Coverage of Judicial Proceedings with Cameras and Microphones: A Survey of the States," Radio-Television News Directors Association [January 1, 1996], at [i]–[iii] 12.) Despite the favorable report and recommendation, the Judicial Conference refused to approve cameras in the courtrooms.

17. Not only do critics of cameras in the courtroom sell short the simple informational value of public access; they also ignore the value to law enforcement that could come with more enterprising and creative use of public trials. Take the problem of tax evasion.

Imagine if the Internal Revenue Service began to take strong steps toward improving tax collections in this country. In 1996, political pressure effectively killed tax enforcement by super-audits, and it generally is now recognized that prosecutions for tax evasion rarely are brought because they rarely succeed (juries not being generally inclined to sympathize with the IRS over a taxpayer unless the taxpayer is someone like Leona Helmsley or Al Capone). But the government could really increase revenue and deter tax evasion by prosecuting and even putting behind bars well-chosen bums. If cameras were allowed in federal court-rooms, a skillful producer could assemble quite a story by jumping from one courtroom to the next, showing the riveting material and skipping the tedium. In the end, the consequences of tax evasion would be known to all, and the trials would have demonstrated that the government was serious about enforcement. None of this is likely to happen without cameras in courtrooms.

18. 408 U.S. 665, 92 S.Ct. 2646 (1972).

19. Laurence H. Tribe, *American Constitutional Law* 972 (2d ed., The Foundation Press, 1988).

20. The reporter's privilege has never been on the firmest ground. Whether journalists have a First Amendment right to refuse to testify in court is not a question the U.S. Supreme Court has definitively answered. In *Branzburg v. Hayes,* the Court rejected a privilege for a reporter who was called to testify in grand jury proceedings about a crime he had witnessed, and in *Herbert v. Lando,* the Court said that reporters cannot decline to answer questions about the editorial process for the purposes of libel litigation. But the *Branzburg* Court splintered 4–1–4 and the decision hinged on a concurring opinion by Justice Lewis Powell. While Powell agreed that a privilege does not apply in a grand jury setting, he said the Court's decision was limited in nature. He wrote:

> The asserted claim to privilege should be judged on its facts by the striking of a proper balance between freedom of the press and the obligation of all citizens to give relevant testimony with respect to criminal conduct. The balance of these vital constitutional and societal interests on a case-by-case basis accords with the tried and traditional way of adjudicating such questions.

Based on this passage, most lower federal courts have held that a reporter's privilege exists, especially in civil cases. These courts frequently have applied a three-part balancing test that asks (1) whether the information sought is relevant to the case, (2) whether there is a compelling interest in the information and (3) whether the information could be obtained from alternative sources. Some lower courts, however, have interpreted *Branzburg* as rejecting the notion of a reporter's privilege. But even then, those courts have generally applied some kind of balancing test when disclosure of a confidential source is at stake.

Since the Supreme Court has left the law somewhat unclear, most states have passed "shield" statutes that outline when a reporter may decline to testify or turn over notes and other documents. Some of the laws grant absolute protection for both confidential and nonconfidential information in all criminal and civil cases, while others provide only a qualified privilege for confidential sources and information. A few states have recognized a privilege embodied within either the state's constitution or common law. Six jurisdictions have neither statutes nor case law on the issue. See Holli Hartman et al., "The Erosion of the Reporter's Privilege," *SPS Reports,* The Society of Professional Journalists, 1997.

21. *El Nuevo Día* and Puerto Rican Cement Co. retained my law firm, Baker & Hostetler, as counsel in the civil rights action.

Chapter 8. "Hello, Houston. We Have a Problem"

1. Susan Beck, "Trial and Errors," *The American Lawyer,* June 1997, p. 43.
2. Five awards of over $2.5 million each were handed down during the twelve months between April 1996 and May 1997, according to the Libel Defense Resource Center in New York.
3. Perhaps the most poignant public figure from the period is retired colonel Anthony Herbert, who slugged it out with CBS for more than a decade of libel litigation over a Mike Wallace documentary on Vietnam. Herbert even established important U.S. Supreme Court precedent along the way, but in the end his claim had been carved away to such a pitiful remaining piece that Judge Irving Kaufman of the Second Circuit decided there was too little left to justify a trial. See *Herbert v. Lando,* 781 F.2d 298 (2d Cir. 1986).

   In another controversial case in the Southern District of New York, plaintiff Nathaniel Davis, who was U.S. ambassador to Chile at the time of the CIA-inspired overthrow of the Allende government, wrote a moving op-ed article for *The Washington Post* after losing his libel lawsuit against the motion picture *Missing* and its producer Costa-Gavras. This "docudrama" purported to depict documented incidents and facts surrounding the murder of Charles Horman, an American citizen who was killed in Chile in 1973, a few days after the military coup. In doing so, it cast Davis as a conspirator to the murder of an American citizen, in the defense of U.S. policies and business interests in Chile, even though no direct evidence of complicity in Horman's death was brought to light in a separate suit against the government which was brought by Horman's family and eventually dropped. At issue in this case was not the film's portrayal of U.S. policies and interests in Chile; rather, as Davis writes, "Killing Americans in order to further improper policy interests strikes so directly at the integrity of public service, including the career U.S. Foreign Service and the professional U.S. military services, that it should cry out for an adjudication of the facts." He explains that in bringing this controversial suit, "we tried to be scrupulous in not assaulting the First Amendment's guarantee of free criticism of public officials for their acts or policies in office." To this end, the complaint was based on the belief that "a person, even a public figure or official, should not be publicly portrayed as a murderer without evidence or support for the charge."

4. Anthony Lewis, *Make No Law: The Sullivan Decision and the First Amendment,* (Random House, 1991), p. 245.
5. *Ibid.,* pp. 234–35.
6. Martin Garbus, "The Media Under Siege," *The Washington Post,* August 4, 1989, p. A23.
7. Floyd Abrams, "Look Who's Trashing the First Amendment," *Columbia Journalism Review,* November–December 1997.
8. *Ollman v. Evans,* 750 F.2d 970, 993 (D.C. Cir. 1984) (Bork, J., concurring).
9. *Ibid.,* p. 997.
10. Cass Sunstein, *Democracy and the Problem of Free Speech* (The Free Press, 1995), p. xviii.
11. *Ibid.*
12. Cass Sunstein, "Even Beef Can Be Libeled," *The New York Times,* January 22, 1998, p. A29.
13. "The communications industry has increasingly become concentrated in a few powerful hands operating very lucrative businesses reaching across the Nation and into almost every home." *Gertz v. Robert Welch, Inc.,* 418 U.S. 323 (1974).
14. Paul Bedard, "White House Counsel to Retire, Cites Workload," *The Washington Times,* September 21, 1995, p. A3.
15. Gerald Eskenazi, "Unsportsmanlike Conduct?" *The New York Times Book Review,* September 3, 1989.
16. See, e.g., Frank Fitzpatrick, "Looking for Ties Between Football, Gambling and the Mob," *Philadelphia Inquirer,* September 3, 1989, p. 4J ("The germ of a compelling story is there, but in Moldea's hands the germ grew into a virus. As a result, Moldea has created little more than a litany of circumstantial evidence, citing countless examples of organized-crime figures' connections with the NFL. Those looking for a smoking gun will be sadly disappointed, perhaps as disappointed as those with an appreciation for good writing"); Sandy Smith, "The NFL and the Mob: Who Calls the Plays?" *The Washington Post,* October 29, 1989, *Book World,* p. 6 ("Moldea dug deep, but sad to say, he came up short. Actual evidence is scant in his book. He does, however, manage to package the fog of suspicions, rumors, allegations and accusations that have enveloped pro football over the years"); Desiree Ward, "Don't Let This Interfere," *Milwaukee Journal,* August 31, 1989 ("Don't buy this book. Don't borrow this book. Don't swap anything for this book. If it's too late and one of the above has already taken place, put the book down and don't read it").

17. *Moldea v. New York Times Co.,* 793 F. Supp. 335, 337 n.3 (D.D.C. 1992).
18. "A Suit Over Sloppy," *The Washington Post,* February 24, 1994, p. A26.
19. 22 F.3d 310 (D.C. Cir. 1994). Citations omitted.
20. A. J. Mikva, "In My Opinion, Those Are Not Facts," *Georgia State University Law Review,* 1995, pp. 291, 296.
21. Lena H. Sun, "Having a Bland Old Time Outside the Starr Jury," *The Washington Post,* April 9, 1998, p. B1.
22. 487 F.2d 986 (1973), 998.
23. *Jones v. Clinton et al.,* 16 F. Supp. 1054 (E.D. Ark. 1998). Judge Wright's decision, typical of judicial rants against the media in the 1990s, overlooked earlier precedents such as *In Re San Juan Star* (in which Justice Stephen Breyer participated when he was a judge on the First Circuit) that identified "significant but limited First Amendment interests" inherent in pretrial discovery materials in a civil case. She instead relied upon a Supreme Court ruling in *Seattle Times v. Rinehart,* a case where a libel defendant was trying to use information about the plaintiff obtained during discovery as a sword to skewer the plaintiff publicly and teach the plaintiff a lesson about suing people who own printing presses. Obviously, the equities were a bit different in *Seattle Times* and unsurprisingly the Supreme Court ruled 9–0 against the newspaper.
24. Quoted by James D. Squires, "Journalism.COM: Press Responsibility in a New Millennium," Roy W. Howard Lecture, Indiana University School of Journalism, October 6, 1997.
25. David Anderson, *The Origins of the Press Clause,* 30, UCLA *Law Review,* 1983, 455, pp. 533–34.

Chapter 9. The Credibility Breakfast

1. Sandra Mims Rowe, "Leading the Way Out of the Credibility Crisis," address to convention of American Society of Newspaper Editors, April 1, 1998, Washington, D.C.
2. Maxwell E. P. King, "Journalism in an Egalitarian Society," lecture given at Washington and Lee University, Lexington, Virginia, 1998.

Bibliography

BOOKS

Achebe, Chinua. *Anthills of the Savannah*. Garden City, N.Y.: Anchor Press, Doubleday, 1988.

Allen, Robert S. *Washington Merry-Go-Round*. New York: Horace Liveright, Inc., 1931.

Anderson, David. *The Origins of the Press Clause, 30*. UCLA *Law Review*, 1983.

The Annals of America. Chicago: Encyclopedia Britannica, Inc., 1968–1987, containing Vol. 14, no. 21, "The Press in Wartime" (1917); Vol. 14, no. 57, "James Bryce: Public Opinion in America" (1921); Vol. 17, no. 45, "George Gallup: Mass Information or Mass Entertainment" (1953); Vol. 17, no. 63, "William Faulkner: On Privacy" (1955).

Arlen, Michael. *The View From Highway 1*. New York: Farrar, Strauss, & Giroux, 1976.

Barnouw, Erik. *The Golden Web: A History of Broadcasting in the United States,* Vol. II, 1933–1953. New York: Oxford University Press, 1968.

———. *Tube of Plenty.* New York: Oxford University Press, 1975.

Bent, Silas. *Newspapers Crusaders: A Neglected Story*. Whittlesey House, 1939.

Bird, George L., ed. *The Press and Society.* Westport, Conn.: Greenwook Press, 1951.

Bogart, Leo. *Press and Public: Who Reads What, When, Where, and Why in American Newspapers,* 2d ed. Hillsdale, N.J.: Lawrence Erlbaum Assocs., Publishers, 1989.

Bollinger, Lee. *Images of a Free Press*. Chicago: University of Chicago Press, 1991.

Bradlee, Benjamin. *A Good Life*. New York: Knopf, 1995.

Broder, David. *Behind the Front Page: A Candid Look at How the News Is Made*. New York: Simon & Schuster, 1987.

Bulman, David, ed. *Molders of Opinion*. Milwaukee: The Bruce Publishing Co., 1945.

Capella, Joseph N., and Kathleen Hall Jamieson. *Spiral of Cynicism: Press and Public Good*. New York: Oxford University Press, 1997.

Chancellor, John, and Walter R. Mears. *The News Business*. New York: Harper & Row, 1993.

Chaney, Lindsay, and Michael Cieply. *The Hearsts: Family and Empire— The Later Years*. New York: Simon & Schuster, 1981.

Childs, Marquis, and James Reston, eds. *Walter Lippmann and His Times*. New York: Harcourt, Brace and Co., 1959.

Cirino, Robert. *Don't Blame the People: How the News Media Use Bias, Distortion and Censorship to Manipulate Public Opinion*. Los Angeles: Diversity Press, 1971.

Cole, Jeffrey. "Economics of Law: An Interview with Judge Posner." *Litigation: The Journal of the Section of Litigation (ABA)*, Fall 1995.

Cronkite, Walter. *A Reporter's Life*. New York: Knopf, 1997.

Dicken-Garcia, Hazel. *Journalistic Standards in Nineteenth-Century America*. Madison: University of Wisconsin Press, 1989.

Dionne, E. J., Jr. *Why Americans Hate Politics*. New York: Simon & Schuster, 1991.

Fallows, James. *Breaking the News: How the Media Undermine American Democracy*. New York: Pantheon, 1996.

Folkerts, Jean. *Voices of a Nation*. New York: Macmillan, 1989.

Francois, William. *Introduction to Mass Communication and Mass Media*. Columbus, Ohio: Grid, Inc., 1977.

Frank, Reuven. *Out of Thin Air: The Brief Wonderful Life of Network News*. New York: Simon & Schuster, 1991.

Friendly, Fred. W. *Minnesota Rag: The Dramatic Story of the Landmark Supreme Court Case That Gave New Meaning to Freedom of the Press.* New York: Random House, 1981.

————. *The Good Guys, the Bad Guys, and the First Amendment: Free Speech v. Fairness in Broadcasting.* New York: Random House, 1975.

Fuller, Jack. *News Values.* Chicago: University of Chicago Press, 1996.

Gallup, George. *Gallup Polls: Public Opinion 1938–1971.* 3 vols. New York: Random House, 1972.

Garment, Suzanne. *Scandal: The Crisis of Mistrust in American Politics.* New York: Times Books, 1991.

Gerald, James Edward. *The Social Responsibility of the Press.* Minneapolis: University of Minnesota, 1963.

Goldstein, Tom, ed. *Killing the Messenger: 100 Years of Press Criticism.* New York: Columbia University Press, 1989.

————. *The News at Any Cost: How Journalists Compromise Their Ethics to Shape the News.* New York: Simon & Schuster, 1985.

Graham, Katharine. *Personal History.* New York: Knopf, 1997.

Grunwald, Henry. *One Man's America: A Journalist's Search for the Heart of His Country.* New York: Doubleday, 1997.

Harris, Louis. *Inside America.* New York: Vintage Books, 1987.

Hearst, William Randolph, Jr., and Jack Casserly. *The Hearsts: Father and Son.* Denver, Colorado: Roberts Rinehart Publishers, 1991.

Hong, Howard V., and Edna H. Hong. *Søren Kierkegaard's Journals and Papers,* Vol. 2, 1970.

Hulteng, John L. *The Fourth Estate.* New York: Harper & Row, 1971.

The Hutchins' Commission on Freedom of the Press. *A Free and Responsible Press.* 1947.

Jamieson, Kathleen Hall. *Dirty Politics: Deception, Distraction, and Democracy.* New York: Oxford University Press, 1992.

Kabler, John. *Luce: His Time, Life, and Fortune.* Garden City, N.Y.: Doubleday & Co., 1968.

Kalven, Harry Jr. *A Worthy Tradition: Freedom of Speech in America.* New York: Harper & Row, 1988.

Kendall, Patricia L. *Radio Listening in America: The People Look at Radio—Again.* New York: Prentice-Hall, 1948.

Kobre, Sidney. *The Yellow Press and the Gilded Age of Journalism.* Florida State University, 1963.

Kurtz, Howard. *Spin Cycle: How the White House and the Media Manipulate the News.* New York: The Free Press/Simon & Schuster, 1998.

———. *Hot Air: All Talk, All the Time.* New York: Times Books, 1996.

———. *Media Circus: The Trouble with America's Newspapers.* New York: Times Books, 1993.

Lazarsfeld, Paul F. *The People Look at Radio.* Chapel Hill: University of North Carolina Press, 1946.

Lee, James Melvin. *History of American Journalism.* New York: Houghton Mifflin, 1923.

Lesher, Stephan. *Media Unbound: The Impact of Television Journalism on the Public.* Boston: Houghton Mifflin, 1982.

Lewis, Anthony. *Make No Law: The Sullivan Decision and the First Amendment.* New York: Random House, 1991.

Lichter, S. Robert, Stanley Rothman, and Linda S. Lichter. *The Media Elite.* Bethesda, Md.: Adler & Adler, 1986.

Liebling, A. J. *The Press.* New York: Pantheon Books, 1961.

Lucas, William A., and Karen B. Possner. *Television News and Local Awareness: A Retrospective Look.* Santa Monica, Calif.: Rand, 1975.

MacDonald, J. Fred. *One Nation Under Television: The Rise and Decline of Network TV.* New York: Pantheon Books, 1990.

MacKinnon, Katherine A. *Only Words.* Cambridge: Harvard University Press, 1993.

Maraniss, David. *First in His Class.* New York: Simon & Schuster, 1995.

Markel, Lester. *What You Don't Know Can Hurt You: A Study of Public Opinion and Public Emotion.* Washington, D.C.: Public Affairs Press, 1972.

Mayer, Martin. *Making News.* Garden City, N.Y.: Doubleday & Co., 1987.

Meeker, Richard H. *Newspaperman: S. I. Newhouse & the Business of News*. New York: Ticknor & Fields, 1983.

Neuharth, Al. *Confessions of an S.O.B.* New York: Doubleday, 1989.

Patterson, Thomas E. *Out of Order*. New York: Knopf, 1993.

Pendergast, Curtis, and Geoffrey Colvin. *The World of Time Inc: The Intimate History of a Changing Enterprise 1960–80*. New York: Atheneum, 1986.

Phillips, Cabell, ed. *Dateline: Washington*. Garden City, N.Y.: Doubleday & Co., 1949.

Pitts, Alice Fox. *Read All About It: 50 Years of ASNE*. Easton, Pa.: American Society of Newspaper Editors, 1974.

Postman, Neil. *Amusing Ourselves to Death*. New York: Elisabeth Sifton Books, 1985.

Povich, Elaine S. *Partners & Adversaries, the Contentious Connection Between Congress & the Media*. Roslyn, Va.: Freedom Forum, 1996.

Powe, Lucas A., Jr. *The Fourth Estate and the Constitution: Freedom of the Press in America*. Berkeley: University of California Press, 1991.

Prichard, Peter. *The Making of McPaper: The Inside Story of USA Today*. Kansas City: Andrews, McMeel & Parker, 1987.

Quayle, Dan. *Standing Firm*. New York: HarperCollins, 1994.

Reston, James. *Deadline: A Memoir*. New York: Random House, 1991.

Rivers, William L. *The Other Government: Power and the Washington Media*. New York: Universe Books, 1982.

Roberts, Chalmers M. *The Washington Post: The First Hundred Years*. Boston: Houghton Mifflin, 1977.

Roper, Burns W. *What People Think of Television and other Mass Media 1959–1972*. New York: Roper Organization, Inc., 1973.

———. *Changing Public Attitudes Toward Television and Other Mass Media 1959–1976*. New York: Roper Organization, Inc., 1977.

Royal Commission on the Press. *Attitudes to the Press*. London, 1977.

Rudenstine, David. *The Day the Presses Stopped: A History of the Pentagon Papers Case*. University of California Press, 1997.

Sabato, Larry J. *Feeding Frenzy: How Attack Journalism Has Transformed American Politics.* New York: The Free Press/Simon & Schuster, 1991.

Salmon, Lucy Maynard. *The Newspaper and Authority.* New York: Oxford University Press, 1923.

Sandman, Peter M., David Rubin, and David B. Sachsman. *Media: An Introductory Analysis of American Mass Communications.* Englewood Cliffs, N.J.: Prentice-Hall, 1976.

Schudson, Michael. *The Power of News.* Cambridge: Harvard University Press, 1995.

Scott-James, Rolfe Arnold. *The Influence of the Press.* London: S. W. Partridge & Co., Ltd., 1913.

Seldes, George. *Iron, Blood, and Profits.* New York: Harper & Brothers, 1934.

————.*Lords of the Press.* New York: Julian Messner, Inc., 1938.

————.*You Can't Do That.* New York: De Capo Press, 1938.

Shaw, David. *Journalism Today: A Changing Press for a Changing America.* New York: Harper's College Press, 1977.

Skornia, Harry J. *Television and Society: An Inquest and Agenda for Improvement.* New York: McGraw-Hill, 1965.

Sloan, William David. *The Media in America.* Worthington, Ohio: Publishing Horizons, 1989.

Small, William J. *To Kill a Messenger: Television News and the Real World.* New York: Hastings House, 1970.

Smith, Anthony. *The Newspaper: An International History.* London: Thames and Hudson, 1979.

Squires, James D. *Read All About It! The Corporate Takeover of America's Newspapers.* New York: Times Books, 1993.

Steffens, Lincoln. *The Autobiography of Lincoln Steffens.* Chautauqua, N.Y.: Chautauqua Press, 1931.

Steiner, Gary. *The People Look at Television.* New York: Knopf, 1963.

Sterling, Christopher. *The Mass Media: Aspen Institute Guide to Communication Industry Trends,* 1978.

Stewart, James. *Blood Sport: The President and His Adversaries.* New York: Simon & Schuster, 1996.

Stoler, Peter. *The War Against the Press: Politics, Pressure and Intimidation in the 80's.* New York: Dodd, Mead & Co., 1986.

Sunstein, Cass. *Democracy and the Problem of Free Speech.* New York: The Free Press/Simon & Schuster, 1993.

Svirsky, Leon, ed. *Your Newspaper.* New York: Macmillan, 1947.

Swanberg, W. A. *Luce and His Empire.* New York: Charles Scribner's Sons, 1972.

Tribe, Laurence H. *American Constitutional Law 972.* 2nd ed., The Foundation Press, 1988.

Trimble, Vance H. *The Astonishing Mr. Scripps: The Turbulent Life of America's Penny Press Lord.* Ames: Iowa State University Press, 1992.

Villard, Oswald Garrison. *The Disappearing Daily: Chapters in American Newspaper Evolution.* New York: Alfred A.Knopf, 1944.

Voss, Frederick S. *Reporting the War: The Journalistic Coverage of World War II.* Washington, D.C.: Smithsonian Institution, 1994.

Weaver, David H., and G. Cleveland Wilhoit. *The American Journalist: A Portrait of U.S. News People and Their Work.* Bloomington, Ind.: Indiana University Press, 1986.

Westin, Av. *Newswatch: How TV Decides the News.* New York: Simon & Schuster, 1982.

Whetmore, Edward J. *Mediamerica: Form, Content and Consequence of Mass Communication.* Belmont, Calif.: Wadsworth Publishing Co., 1987.

Wicker, Tom. *On Press: A Top Reporter's Life in, and Reflections on, American Journalism.* New York: Viking Press, 1978.

ARTICLES

Abbot, Willis J. "The Outlook for Better Papers." *Journalism Quarterly* 2, 1925.

Abrams, Floyd. "Look Who's Trashing the First Amendment." *Columbia Journalism Review,* November/December 1997.

Alter, Jonathan. "New Questions—That's What Media Critics Need." *Media Studies Journal,* Spring 1995.

Anderson, Ross. "What James Fallows Needs Is a Good Local Newspaper." *Seattle Times,* February 14, 1996.

Auletta, Ken. "Peering Over the Edge." *Media Studies Journal,* Winter 1995.

Baker, Peter. "Hillary Clinton Bemoans Influence of 'Right Wing' Media." *The Washington Post,* January 18, 1998.

Beck, Susan. "Trial and Errors." *The American Lawyer,* June 1997.

Bedard, Paul. "White House Counsel to Retire, Cites Workload." *The Washington Times,* September 21, 1995.

Benchley, Robert (Guy Fawkes). "Intermission." *The New Yorker,* March 8, 1930.

———."The Press in Review: A Front Page Crisis." *The New Yorker,* August 13, 1927.

———. "Quiet Please." *The New Yorker,* January 10, 1931.

———. "The Wayward Press: Good Old Days." *The New Yorker,* June 30, 1928.

———."The Wayward Press: The Power of the Press." *The New Yorker,* December 6, 1930.

———. "The Wayward Press: The Public Servant." *The New Yorker,* June 8, 1929.

———. "The Wayward Press: Summer Heat." *The New Yorker,* June 14, 1930.

Bennion, Sherilyn Cox. "Reform Agitation in the American Periodical Press 1920–29." *Journalism Quarterly* 48, 1971.

Bogart, Leo. "Changing News Interests and the News Media." *Public Opinion Quarterly* 32, 1968.

———. "Media and Democracy." *Media Studies Journal,* Summer 1995.

Bollinger, Lee C. "The Hutchins Commission, Half a Century On." *Media Studies Journal,* Spring/Summer 1998.

Bruck, Connie. "Hillary the Pol." *The New Yorker,* May 30, 1994.

———. "Jerry's Deal." *The New Yorker,* February 19, 1996.

Biskupie, Joan. "Clinton Avoids Activists in Judicial Selections." *The Washington Post,* October 24, 1995.

Charen, Mona. "Talk of Adoption Is Hillary Clinton's Latest Version of Femininity." *St. Louis Post-Dispatch,* June 2, 1996.

Cohen, Richard. "Plundered Secrets." *The Washington Post Magazine,* June 14, 1998.

de Sola Pool, Ithiel, and Irwin Shulman. "Newsmen's Fantasies, Audiences, and Newswriting." *Public Opinion Quarterly* 23, 1959–60.

Erskine, Hazel. "The Polls: Opinion of the News Media." *Public Opinion Quarterly,* Winter 1970–71.

Eskenazi, Gerald. "Unsportsmanship Conduct?" *The New York Times Book Revciew,* September 3, 1989.

Fellata, Ken. "Annals of Communication: Awestruck." *The New Republic,* September 11, 1995.

Fibich, Linda. "Under Siege." *American Journalism Review,* September 1995.

Fitzpatrick, Frank. "Looking for Tics Between Football, Gambling and the Mob." *Philadelphia Inquirer,* September 3, 1989.

"The Press and the People—A Survey." *Fortune,* August 1939.

Fried, Joseph P. "CBS Reaches a Settlement on Videotaped Search." *The New York Times,* March 20, 1995.

Gans, Herbert J. "Bystanders as Opinion Makers—A Bottoms-Up Perspective." *Media Studies Journal,* Winter 1995.

Garbus, Martin. "The Media Under Siege." *The Washington Post,* August 4, 1989.

Gartner, Michael. "Public Journalism—Seeing Through the Gimmicks." *Media Studies Journal,* Winter 1997.

Gopnik, Adam. "Read All About It." *The New Yorker,* December 12, 1994.

Grave, Lloyd. "The Latter Day Gordon Peterson." *The Washington Post,* June 16, 1998.

Gunther, Marc. "The Cable Guy." *American Journalism Review,* January/February 1997.

Harris, Huntington, and Paul M. Lewis. "The Press, Public Behavior and Public Opinion." *Public Opinion Quarterly* 12, Summer 1948.

Harrison, Stanley L. "Bibliography of Press Criticism by Robert Benchley (Guy Fawkes) for *The New Yorker*." *Journalism History,* Spring 1993.

Harwood, Richard. "The Cost of Celebrity." *The Washington Post,* January 8, 1996.

————. "Virus in the Newsroom." *The Washington Post,* August 12, 1990.

"How Stands Our Press." *Human Events Pamphlet.* Chicago: Human Events Associates, 1947.

Hughes, Helen MacGill. "Human Interest Stories and Democracy." *Public Opinion Quarterly* 1, April 1937.

Hume, Ellen. "Something's Rotten." *Columbia Journalism Review,* March–April 1996.

Isaacson, Walter. "We're Hoping That We Have Another Child." *Time,* June 3, 1996.

Janowitz, Morris. "The Imagery of the Urban Community Press." *Public Opinion Quarterly* 15, Fall 1951.

Kilpatrick, James J. "In Defense of the Media." *Nation's Business,* February 1984.

King, Maxwell E. P. "Journalism in an Egalitarian Society." Lecture given at Washington and Lee University, 1998.

Kingsbury, Susan M., et al. "Measuring the Ethics of American Newspapers: A Spectrum Analysis of Newspaper Sensationalism." *Journalism Quarterly* 10, June 1933–December 1934.

Kirkhorn, Michael. "This Curious Existence: Journalistic Identity in the Interwar Period." Published in *Mass Media Between the Wars,* edited by Catherine L. Covert and John D. Stevens. Syracuse University Press, 1984.

Kirtz, Bill. "What Did We Learn?" *The Quill,* October 1997.

Kopec, Joseph A. "The Big Chill: A PR Man's Perspective on America's Frosty Attitude Toward Journalists." *Vital Speeches of the Day,* Vol. L, no. 17, June 15, 1984.

Kraft, Joseph. "The Imperial Media." *Commentary* 71, no. 5, May 1981.

Kueterman, Greg. "Posner Typifies Aura Surrounding Appellate Jurists." *Indiana Lawyer,* January 11, 1995.

Lapham, Lewis. "Gilding the News." *Harper's,* July 1981.

————. "Notebook: Trained Seals and Sitting Ducks." *Harper's,* May 1991.

Lazarsfeld, Paul F. "Some Notes on the Relationship Between Radio and the Press." *Journalism Quarterly,* 18, 1941.

————. "The Role of Criticism in the Management of Mass Media." *Journalism Quarterly* 25, June 1948.

Lindstrom, Carl E. "Newspapers Have Failed to Keep Pace with Times in This Critic's Opinion." *The Quill,* December 1956.

MacDougall, Curtis D. "American Press and Public Opinion." *International Journal of Opinion* 3, Summer 1949.

MacNeil, Robert. "Regaining Dignity." *Media Studies Journal,* Summer 1995.

McConnell, Chris, and Paige Albiniak. "Putting a Price on Public Service." *Broadcasting & Cable,* April 6, 1998.

Mikva, Abner. "In My Opinion, Those Are Not Facts." 11 Georgia State University *Law Review* 291, 1995.

"Why Newspapers Mishandle the News." *The New Republic,* April 12, 1943.

"Press-Go-Round." *The New Republic,* June 27, 1981.

"What's Wrong with the Press?" *Newsweek,* November 29, 1965.

Nixon, Raymond. "Changes in Reader Attitudes Toward Daily Newspapers." *Journalism Quarterly* 31, 1954.

Ornstein, Norman J., and Michael J. Robinson. "Why Press Credibility Is Going Down." *Washington Journalism Review,* January/February 1990.

"The Quarter's Polls." *Public Opinion Quarterly,* Summer 1948.

Remnick, David. "Scoop." *The New Yorker,* January 29, 1996.

Roberts, Eugene. "Corporation v. Journalism: Is It Twilight for Press Responsibility?" Press Enterprise Lecture, February 1996.

Robinson, Michael J., and Maura E. Clancey. "Network News, 15 Years After Agnew." *Channels* 4, January–February 1985.

————, and Andrew Kohut. "Believability and the Press." *Public Opinion Quarterly* 52, 1988.

Rooney, John Flynn. "For Him, It's the Questions That Count." *Chicago Daily Law Bulletin,* November 3, 1993.

Ross, Brian. "Money Talks: Grocery Industry Manufacturers' Fees." *20/20* (ABC television broadcast, November 10, 1995).

Rowe, Sandra Mims. "Leading the Way Out of the Credibility Crisis." Address to convention of American Society of Newspaper Editors, April 1, 1998.

Schmeltzer, John. "Tis Always the Time to Take Precautions with Credit Cards." *Chicago Tribune,* December 5, 1992.

Schudson, Michael. "In All Fairness, Media." *Media Studies Journal,* Spring/Summer 1998.

Seymour, Gideon. "The Relationship of the Press to Government and to the People." *Journalism Quarterly* 19, 1942.

Shaw, Eugene F. "The Popular Meaning of Media Credibility." *News Research Bulletin,* no. 3, October 22, 1976.

Sheehy, Gail. "The Road to Bimini." *Vanity Fair,* September 1987.

Sloan, William David. "Historians and the American Press, 1900–1945: Working Profession or Big Business?" *American Journalism* 3, no. 3, 1986.

Smith, Sandy. "The NFL and the Mob: Who Calls the Plays?" *The Washington Post,* October 29, 1989.

Squires, James D. "Journalism.COM: Press Responsibility in a New Millennium." Roy W. Howard Lecture, Indiana University School of Journalism, October 6, 1997.

———. "Newspapers Have Lost Their Zeal to Educate the Public About the Real Issues." *ASNE Bulletin,* November 1992.

Stewart, Raymond. "Surveys of Reader Attitudes Toward Newspaper Combinations." *Journalism Quarterly* 30, 1953.

Sun, Lena H. "Having a Bland Old Time Outside the Starr Jury." *The Washington Post,* April 9, 1998.

Sunstein, Cass. "Even Beef Can Be Libeled." *The New York Times,* January 22, 1998.

Swanson, Charles E. "The Midcity Daily." *Journalism Quarterly* 26, 1949.

———. "What They Read in 130 Daily Newspapers." *Journalism Quarterly* 32, Fall 1955.

Sweeney, John. "Media Arrogance Spoils Fun." *The News-Journal,* January 7, 1990.

Thalheimer, J. A., and J. R. Gerberich. "Reader Attitudes Toward Questions of Newspaper Policy and Practice." *Journalism Quarterly* 12, 1935.

"Journalism Under Fire: A Growing Perception of Arrogance Threatens the American Press." *Time,* December 12, 1983.

"Uneasy Press Sets Out to Refurbish Its Image." *U.S. News & World Report,* June 29, 1981.

Vinyard, Dale, and Roberta S. Sigel. "Newspapers and Urban Voters." *Journalism Quarterly* 48, 1971.

Ward, Desiree. "Don't Let This Interfere." *Milwaukee Journal,* August 31, 1989.

Weigle, Clifford F. "Two Techniques for Surveying Newspaper Readership Compared." *Journalism Quarterly* 18, 1941.

White, Lee A. "The Press and the Public." *Journalism Quarterly* 17, 1940.

Wilson, Elmo C. "The Press and Public Opinion in Erie County, Ohio." *Journalism Quarterly* 18, 1941.

Wisehart, Bob. "NBC Pays Price for 'Bottom-Line' News." *Sacramento Bee,* February 15, 1993.

Young, Consuelo C. "A Study of Reader Attitudes Toward the Negro Press." *Journalism Quarterly* 21, 1944.

Acknowledgments

The research, organizing and writing of this book took ten years. My interest in the subject of public attitudes toward the media grew out of my experience as a lawyer working with jury consultants in selecting jurors for libel trials. The idea of a book germinated at a breakfast conversation I had in 1987 with Charles E. Scripps, then chairman of the E. W. Scripps Co. and grandson of the founder.

"Why don't you write a book reminding people of the value of an aggressive press," Charles suggested. "A sort of *Profiles in Courage* about how various news stories have made a difference in communities across the nation."

"There's such hostility toward the press out there," I replied. "I don't think anyone wants to read a book about the good things that the press does."

"Well, then, explain where the hostility comes from and how it can damage us," said this gentle patriarch. He is a man whose life teaches us all about our responsibilities to one another.

And so, properly inspired, over the last decade I sifted through polling data, media criticism, autobiographies and academic works and interviewed more than a thousand reporters, editors, producers, correspondents, executives and owners. I am grateful for their insights, anecdotes and introspection. This work also benefits from the conversations I had with news subjects and the candor they generously offered. Most, but by no means all, of these people in and out of the media are mentioned in the foregoing pages. To single out a few, or even a hundred, would fail to recognize the contributions to this work of the rest. For their time and thoughts, I owe them all vast appreciation.

Some people deserve special recognition. Bob Barnett believed in this book and took it to a legendary editor, the late Erwin Glikes, who helped me shape a sprawling subject—public attitudes toward the media—into a book, just as he had helped Allan Bloom with *The Closing of the American Mind,* Robert Bork with *The Tempting of America* and innumerable other authors. After Erwin's death, The Free Press's Bruce Nichols inherited the manuscript and gave me many years of his encouragement, ideas, incisive editing and patience. For his constant support and enthusiasm and that of Paula Duffy, publisher of The Free Press, I am enormously indebted. No author could have found a better editor or publisher.

Stephanie Abrutyn, Bruce Brown, James Houpt, Robert Lystad and David Schram provided research, creativity and thoughtful assistance. My gifted assistant, Marsha Zamperini, kept me organized and as much on schedule as one could expect from a lawyer with a demanding practice. Andy Kohut and Lawrence McGill helped me comprehend the maze of polling data in the area. Four leaders of the Freedom Forum—Robert Giles of the Forum's Media Studies Center in New York, Peter Prichard and Paul McMasters at the Forum's headquarters in Washington and John Seigenthaler of the Forum's First Amendment Center at Vanderbilt University— were always there when I needed them for help. Friends like Dan Thomasson, Rosalie and Mike Maloney, Robert Hawley, George Freeman, Peter White, Judith Roales, Don Baer, Ellis Levine, Bill Ketter, Henry Hoberman and Lucy Dalglish were tolerant enough to let me bore them for hours with my meanderings about this book and always offered me valuable nuggets as well as the occasional whack in the head when I got carried away.

My family bore the brunt of this book. It robbed them of time together. For the constancy, love and hopefulness of my wife, Marilou, and the support and good humor of my children, Lisa, Ashley and Barrett, I shall always be grateful.

Washington, D.C.
August 1999

Index

First Amendment
  conservative defense of,
    181–82
  Food Lion case as attack on,
    145–46
  media's rights under, 8–9, 103
  origins and justification of,
    193–94
  Pentagon Papers case and, 154
  predicted backlash vs., 190–92,
    203
  Quayle's fight for, 63–64
  recent erosion of, 151–52,
    179–85
  "shield laws" and, 128
  Sullivan case and, 176–79
  Supreme Court and, 13, 130,
    176–81
Fisher, Kelly, 111–12
*Florida Publishing Company v.
    Fletcher,* 133–34, 216n21
Food Channel, 197
Food Lion, 144–46
Ford, Gerald, 63
Ford Foundation, 199
Fortune, 15, 40, 51
Foster, Vincent, 185
Frankel, Max, 159–60
Frankfurter, Felix, 189
Frantz, Douglas, 2
Freedom Forum, 23, 40, 69, 85,
    199, 202–3, 205n5

Freedom of Information Act
    (FOIA), 63
Freedom Speaks, 113
Freeman, George, 153, 167
Free Press/Fair Press, 85, 202
Free TV for Straight Talk, 203n41
Frey, Glenn, 73
Friday, Elmer, 162–63
Fritts, Eddie, 89
Fuhrman, Mark, 111
Fusté, José A., 172–73

Gag orders, 158, 162–63, 167,
    220n8
Gailey, Philip, 90
Galella, Ron, 191–92
Gallagher, Mike, 2, 5–6
Gallagher, Tim, 76
Gallup polls, 14–16, 40, 209n47
Gannett Co., 1–6, 8, 97–98
Garbus, Martin, 181
Gartner, Michael, 93–96, 117
Gates, Bill, 108
General Motors, 3, 93, 132–33
Gephardt, Richard A., 5
Gibbs, Wolcott, 52
Giles, Robert H., 85, 203
Gingrich, Newt, 5, 71–72, 85
Ginsburg, Douglas, 159
Ginsburg, Ruth Bader, 155
Ginsburg, William, 112, 118
Goldberg, Lucianne, 118